Messick
Individuality in
learning

DATE DUE

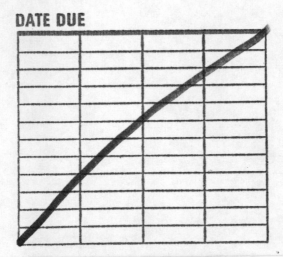

Samuel Messick
& Associates

Individuality in Learning

 Jossey-Bass Publishers

San Francisco · Washington · London · 1976

INDIVIDUALITY IN LEARNING
Implications of Cognitive Styles and Creativity for Human Development
by Samuel Messick and Associates

JACKET DESIGN BY WILLI BAUM

FIRST EDITION

Code 7609

Preface

This book seeks to accelerate the application of psychological research to learning and educational practice—in particular to explore the practical implications of recent research on cognitive styles and creativity for higher education. It is designed for both college educators and behavioral scientists, two groups that must collaborate effectively if we are to create new instructional options on a sound conceptual basis for the improvement of higher learning. The book is thus aimed at two primary audiences: college and university faculty members, administrators, and other policy makers in postsecondary education who are concerned that our educational institutions take into account basic human differences in learning, thinking, and creative expression and who seek better means of individualizing instruction for more effective learning; and behavioral scientists who are concerned with problems of learning and adaptation, personality and cognition, and social and environmental influence.

Behavioral scientists and educators have long known that teaching is more effective when individual differences in students' prior knowledge and level of development are taken into account. Evidence for the importance of these individual differences is so widely known that this book assumes no one needs to be reminded of it. What is only now beginning to be recognized, however, is that differences in *style* of learning and thinking also require the attention of educators and researchers. Concern about differences in prior learning and achievement and in level of social and cognitive development is not enough. We must move beyond these differences in *content* and *level* of learning to more subtle differences in the *processes* of cognition and creative thinking to find effective bases for individualizing education. This book is therefore not concerned with what a student already knows, with his current range and level of academic accomplishment, but rather with the manner in which he acquires knowledge and with his characteristic modes of processing information and experience.

Because recommendations for educational practice involve value judgments that should be well grounded in conceptual understanding, the major chapters of the book have been prepared by research specialists in personality and socioeducational development. They explore the theoretical and empirical foundations of individual differences in cognitive styles and creativity, sex-related and culturally related differences among students in their approach to learning and thinking, and the impact of institutional environments and teaching techniques or "treatments" on these differences. Each of these research-oriented chapters is followed by commentaries written by scientist/educators who combine the perspectives of psychological research and educational practice and who examine and develop the pedagogical implications of the longer chapters.

The ensuing interactions between research and application make it clear that many of the key controversies about individualization of instruction concern social values and not pedagogy and that the transition from research into practice must be mediated by resolutions of ideological differences. The basic issues are whether and how to match educational treatments to individuals and who should decide among the alternatives. In the concluding chapter, I attempt to resolve some of these problems of prescription and choice by illuminating a variety of options for both and by arguing that in higher education the ideal of self-matching of individuals to treatments is a viable possibility.

The production of this volume was facilitated by a number of individuals and groups. To begin with, the book is an outgrowth of an invitational conference on cognitive styles and creativity in higher education held in Montreal, Canada, under the sponsorship of the Graduate Record Examination Board. I wish to thank the GRE Board for their intellectual and financial support of this enterprise and Maryann Lear, the Secretary to the Board, for her attentive efforts in supervising the conference arrangements. Further, I wish to thank several individuals who agreed to serve as chairpersons and moderators of the conference sessions, for their role in guiding the conference interactions: Benjamin DeMott of Amherst College, Bernard Harleston of Tufts University, Lyle Jones of the University of North Carolina, Michael Pelczar, Jr. of the University of Maryland, Mina Rees of the City University of New York, and Donald Taylor of Yale University. Their pointed comments and skillful efforts to pace the discussion and keep it on target were instrumental in stimulating lively and provocative interchanges.

I also wish to thank William Ward of the Educational Testing Service, whose careful summaries of the conference discussions contributed much to the introductory statements preceding each part of the book. And very special thanks go to Ann Jungeblut, who assisted in all phases of the editorial work. She reviewed the entire manuscript in detail, reworking many passages in the process, and her suggestions were especially helpful in improving the substance and phrasing of the sections I wrote.

This book is dedicated to the memory of Donald W. Taylor, late Eugene Higgins Professor of Psychology and Dean of the Yale University Graduate School. Dr. Taylor, a former Chairman of the Graduate Record Examination Board, served as a session moderator at the conference on which this book is based and contributed both critical acumen and practical wisdom to the enterprise. Through his scientific and scholarly studies of creativity and problem solving, he made seminal contributions to this developing field that mark him as one of the important intellectual forebears of the current work.

Princeton, New Jersey   Samuel Messick
August 1976

Contents

Contents   xi

In memory of
Donald W. Taylor

Contributors

ARTHUR W. CHICKERING, vice president for policy analysis and evaluation, Empire State College

MICHAEL COLE, director, Laboratory of Comparative Human Cognition, and professor of ethnographic psychology and experimental anthropology, Rockefeller University

NORMAN FREDERIKSEN, director, Division of Psychological Studies, Educational Testing Service

EDMUND W. GORDON, executive director, Institute for Urban and Minority Education, Educational Testing Service and Teachers College, Columbia University, and professor of education and pediatric psychology, Columbia University

RAVENNA HELSON, associate research psychologist, Institute of Personality Assessment and Research, University of California, Berkeley

WAYNE H. HOLTZMAN, president, Hogg Foundation for Mental Health, and Hogg professor of psychology and education, University of Texas

LIAM HUDSON, director, Research Unit on Intellectual Development, and professor of educational sciences, University of Edinburgh

DAVID JENNESS, executive associate, Social Science Research Council

NATHAN KOGAN, professor of psychology, graduate faculty, New School for Social Research

GERALD S. LESSER, director, Laboratory of Human Development, and Charles Bigelow professor of education and developmental psychology, Harvard University

BRIAN N. LEWIS, deputy director, Institute of Educational Technology, and professor of applied educational sciences, Open University, United Kingdom

WINTON H. MANNING, vice president for development, Educational Testing Service

JACQUELYN A. MATTFELD, president, Barnard College

SAMUEL MESSICK, vice president for research, Educational Testing Service

DONALD C. PELZ, director, Center for Research on Utilization of Scientific Knowledge, Institute for Social Research, and professor of psychology, University of Michigan

HAROLD M. PROSHANSKY, president, Graduate School and University Center, City University of New York

ELEANOR BERNERT SHELDON, president, Social Science Research Council

RICHARD E. SNOW, associate professor of education, Stanford University

MICHAEL A. WALLACH, professor of psychology, Duke University

SEYMOUR WAPNER, chairman, department of psychology, and G. Stanley Hall professor of genetic psychology, Clark University

HERMAN A. WITKIN, chairman, Personality and Social Behavior Research Group, Educational Testing Service

Individuality in Learning

IMPLICATIONS OF COGNITIVE STYLES AND CREATIVITY FOR HUMAN DEVELOPMENT

Part One

Introduction: Individual Differences and Individualized Education

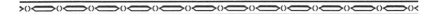

Two major themes run contrapuntally through this book. One is the empirical generalization that individuals differ substantially in their styles of thinking and modes of creative expression. The other is the value position that education, especially higher education, should actively foster individual fulfillment and hence should adapt to, and perhaps even capitalize on and extend, these essential human differences to promote greater learning and creativity. The first of these themes is introduced in Chapter One by Samuel Messick and the second in Chapter Two by Wayne Holtzman. The counterpoint then continues with increasing tension throughout the volume, with the first theme being dominant in discussions of sex differences and group differences and the second theme predominating in discussions of talents and treatments. The tension ultimately becomes embodied in a unifying motif: the problem of the match between individ-

1

uality and instruction. This problem requires further resolution, and its ramifications are explored in the concluding
chapter.

Chapter One examines some of the major individual
differences affecting learning and creativity. Messick describes a number of cognitive styles, paying special attention
to the critical ways in which these stylistic dimensions of personality differ from intellectual abilities and noting their
pervasive effects on behavior. He also focuses on stylistic
consistencies in cognition and personality predictive of creative performance and considers the possibility of designing
environmental conditions and instructional treatments to
foster learning and creativity.

Since these stable individual differences in cognition
and personality influence the ways in which individuals learn
and perform, one might expect that differential instructional treatments would be adopted to take them into account.
But, as pointed out in Chapter Two, traditional methods
have tremendous inertia. Until recently, only crude attempts
at accommodation have been mounted, and these usually
have been based on grouping by curriculum tracks or ability
levels rather than on matching methods to the individual
functional characteristics of learners. During the past decade, however, new social and economic forces have magnified the need for individualized education. New kinds of
students in higher education have amplified the range and
diversity of student needs and concerns, while increased
costs of education have underscored the urgency of improving productivity. Chapter Two delineates these pressures
for change. Individualized instruction, Holtzman argues,
might serve both the social and economic needs, the former
need by expanding and diversifying program options to better match the diversity and pluralism of the student population, the latter by improving the quality of educational
outcomes without corresponding increase in cost. Further,
since technological advances promise to make individualized instruction feasible on a large scale, the cost effectiveness of education could be even more dramatically improved

by using audiovisual and computer-based technology. Holtz-man reviews in detail two major computer-based systems of individualized instruction, demonstrating that the issue is no longer feasibility but commitment.

1

Personality Consistencies in Cognition and Creativity

SAMUEL MESSICK

One of the central themes of this book is that individual differences make a difference—that characteristic differences in cognition and creativity cast the form of individual learning and performance and hence have profound implications for teaching and training. This chapter examines the nature of some of these key individual differences, mainly those core personality dimensions that underlie our typical modes of cognitive and creative functioning. These personality dimensions are revealed in the individual's stylistic consistencies in behavior across diverse areas.

Cognitive Manifestations of Personality

Characteristic Modes of Mental Functioning. Each individual has preferred ways of organizing all that he sees and remembers and thinks about. Consistent individual differences in

4

these ways of organizing and processing information and experience have come to be called cognitive styles. These styles represent consistencies in the manner or form of cognition, as distinct from the content of cognition or the level of skill displayed in the cognitive performance. They are conceptualized as stable attitudes, preferences, or habitual strategies determining a person's typical modes of perceiving, remembering, thinking, and problem solving. As such, their influence extends to almost all human activities that implicate cognition, including social and interpersonal functioning.

An example might help clarify the nature of these stylistic dimensions and their pervasive involvement in learning, thinking, and social interaction. One of the most widely studied of these styles, *field independence versus field dependence*, refers to a consistent mode of approaching the environment in analytical, as opposed to global, terms. The field independent person tends to articulate figures as discrete from their backgrounds and to easily differentiate objects from embedding contexts, whereas the field dependent person tends to experience events globally in an undifferentiated fashion. Field independent (or analytical) individuals have more facility with tasks requiring differentiation and analysis, whether in identifying more easily the presence of logical errors or in understanding more quickly the point of a joke, and this analytical penchant leads as well to a high degree of differentiation of the self from its context. Field dependent (or global) individuals, on the other hand, tend to identify with a group, exhibiting a social orientation in which they are more perceptive and sensitive to social characteristics such as names and faces than are field independent persons; but they are also more susceptible to external influence and more markedly affected by isolation from other people (Witkin, Dyk, Faterson, Goodenough, and Karp, 1962). Field independence versus field dependence is discussed in much more detail by Herman Witkin in Chapter Three, along with a consideration of its role in learning, teaching, and academic development. To give some indication of the variety of stylistic dimensions uncovered so far, several cognitive styles are briefly described in the glossary at the end of this chapter.

Although cognitive styles are viewed as habitual modes of information processing, they are not simple habits in the technical sense of learning theory for they are not directly responsive to principles of acquisition and extinction. They develop slowly and experientially and do not appear to be easily modified by specific tuition or training (Kagan and Kogan, 1970; Kogan, 1971). In this regard, it is important to distinguish cognitive styles, which are high level heuristics that organize and control behavior across a wide variety of situations, from cognitive strategies, which are decision-making regularities in information processing that at least in part are a function of the conditions of particular situations (Bruner, Goodnow, and Austin, 1956; Shouksmith, 1970). Examples of cognitive strategies include the use of organizing mediators (such as meaningful grouping) in serial learning and the use of wholist and partist hypothesis-testing strategies in concept attainment (C. H. Frederiksen, 1969; Goodenough, 1976). Cognitive strategies are selected, organized, and controlled in part as a function of larger-scale, more general cognitive styles and ability patterns, but they are also determined in part as a function of task requirements, problem content, and situational constraints; hence in comparison to styles, strategies are likely to be more amenable to change through training under varied conditions of learning. It may thus be possible for individuals to learn to use optimal problem-solving and learning strategies consonant with their cognitive styles and even to learn to shift to less congenial strategies that are more effective for a particular task than are their preferred ones.

The stability and pervasiveness of cognitive styles across diverse spheres of behavior suggest deeper roots in personality structure than might at first glance be implied by the concept of characteristic modes of cognition. Cognitive styles may entail generalized habits of information processing, to be sure, but they develop in congenial ways around underlying personality trends. Cognitive styles are thus intimately interwoven with affective, temperamental, and motivational structures as part of the total personality; they provide one aspect of the matrix, as it were, that determines the nature or form of adaptive traits, defense mechanisms, and pathological symptoms (Shapiro, 1965). In this view, a core personality structure is manifested in the various levels and domains of psychological functioning—intellectual, affective, motivational, defensive—and its manifestation in cognition is cognitive style. Consider, for instance, the authoritarian personality (Adorno, Frenkel-Brunswik, Levinson, and Sanford, 1950). Deriving from a core impulse structure of aggressiveness combined with ambivalence, the content of the authoritarian's belief system is ethnocentric prejudice. His typical mode of cognition has been called dogmatism or closed-mindedness (Rokeach, 1960). The authoritarian thinks in terms of rigid categories and stereotypes. He believes in oversimplified explanations for phenomena and applies these beliefs dogmatically in ambiguous circumstances, thus exhibiting a marked intolerance of ambiguity. As another instance, field independence is viewed as the manifestation in perception of a more general articulated versus global cognitive style, which itself is reflective of a still broader dimension of psychological differentiation (Witkin and others, 1962).

Distinctions Between Styles and Abilities. Cognitive styles differ from intellectual abilities in a number of ways, and contrasting them with abilities serves to illuminate their distinctive features. Ability dimensions essentially refer to the content of cognition or the question of *what*—what kind of information is being processed by what operation in what form? Indeed, one of the major theories of intellect classifies abilities in terms of which of *five* operations is used to process which of *four* kinds of informational content in which of *six* forms (Guilford, 1967). Cognitive styles, in contrast, bear on the questions of *how*—on the manner in which the behavior occurs. The concept of ability implies the measurement of capacities in terms of maximal performance, with the emphasis upon level of accomplishment; the concept of style implies the measurement of characteristic modes of operation in terms of typical performance, with the emphasis upon process.

Abilities, furthermore, are generally thought of as uni-polar, while cognitive styles are typically considered to be bipolar in the sense of pitting one syndrome or complex of interacting characteristics—what Vernon (1973) has called a "dynamic gestalt"—against a contrasting complex at the op-posite pole of the distribution. Abilities vary, then, from zero or very little to a great deal, with increasing levels implying more and more of the same facility. High spatial ability, for example, predisposes a person to achieve in certain areas, but its absence implies only that he very likely will not succeed in those areas. Cognitive styles, on the other hand, range from one extreme to an opposite extreme, with each end of the dimension having different implications for cognitive func-tioning. The field independent person, for example, is more analytic than his field dependent counterpart and the field dependent person is more socially sensitive than the field independent one. Conceptualizing cognitive styles as con-trasts between dynamic gestalts has a certain typological fla-vor, and styles are often described as if they were types, or even stereotypes, when in reality individuals are distributed continuously between the extremes with considerable varia-tion in the cluster and degree of components comprising the style. As long as these continuities and complexities are appropriately accommodated in our methodology and the-orizing, however, such shorthand stereotypic characteriza-tions are not necessarily dysfunctional. As Vernon (1973) has pointed out: "We expect the typical athlete or aesthete, the mother-in-law, the Jew, the hippie, and so on, to show certain combinations of characteristics, certain traits and attitudes. . . . They help us to pigeonhole people we meet, to anticipate their reactions and understand them. Yet at the same time we are quite aware that any one mother-in-law or Jew whom we get to know well may show few of the attributes of the stereotype. The social psychologist usually condemns stereotypes as sources of prejudice. I would say rather that they typify the way we normally think, by helping us to classify and respond to the infinite diversities of people we meet" (p. 131).

Another major way in which cognitive styles differ from abilities is in the values usually conferred upon them. Abilities are value directional: having more of an ability is better than having less. Cognitive styles are value differentiated: each pole has adaptive value in different circumstances. The high end of ability dimensions is consistently more adaptive, whereas neither end of cognitive style dimensions is uniformly more adaptive; in the latter case adaptiveness depends upon the nature of the situation and upon the cognitive requirements of the task at hand. Witkin (1974) has emphasized that the differentiated character of their value implications makes cognitive styles a less threatening concept to people than are abilities or intelligence, and hence information about an individual's cognitive style is more easily communicated directly to him. The utility of this information in guidance is also enhanced by the positive aspects of the message, regardless of which end of the cognitive style the individual leans toward.

Cognitive styles also differ from abilities in their breadth of coverage and pervasiveness of application. An ability usually delineates a basic dimension underlying a fairly limited area. In Guilford's (1967) case, for example, an ability is restricted to a particular operation-content-form combination, such as memory for figural units. In the case of Thurstone's (1938) primary mental abilities, somewhat broader dimensions cover such areas as reasoning, verbal, numerical, and spatial abilities. By and large, then, abilities are specific to a particular domain of content or function. Cognitive styles, in contrast, cut across domains. They appear to serve as high-level heuristics that organize lower-level strategies, operations, and propensities—often including abilities—in such complex sequential processes as problem solving and learning (Messick, 1972, 1973). They function in part as controlling mechanisms determining an individual's characteristic regulation and control of impulse, thought, and behavioral expression in diverse areas (Gardner, Holzman, Klein, Linton, and Spence, 1959; Gardner, Jackson, and Messick, 1960; Klein, 1958, 1970). In factor-analytic terms, if abilities and temperament traits and affective consistencies are first- or second-order factors, then cognitive styles are higher-order factors linking those domains (Royce, 1973).

One other difference between cognitive styles and abilities is worth noting, but it is historical and not essential. Cognitive styles and abilities differ in the methods by which they are ordinarily measured. Abilities have their roots in mental test theory and have had close ties since the beginning of the century with education. Psychologists concerned with the identification and utilization of abilities have tended to develop measuring instruments suitable for administration in school settings and usually to large groups; these instruments have typically taken the form of paper-and-pencil tests. One natural consequence of this is that ability measures emphasize correctness or accuracy of response and level of overall achievement. Cognitive styles, in contrast, have their roots in the study of perception and personality and thus have had close ties since their inception with the laboratory and the clinic. Psychologists concerned with the identification and understanding of cognitive styles have tended to utilize measures derived from laboratory apparatus or clinical tools, such as the Rorschach or word-association procedures; these measures typically have required individual administration. One natural consequence of this is that cognitive style measures, at least at the level of interpretation, emphasize process of responding as revealed through multiple part scores which frequently include indexes of speed and latency. These differences in measurement are not intrinsic to the variables measured, however, and attempts have been made to develop paper-and-pencil cognitive style measures suitable for group administration that would still be amenable to process interpretation (Messick and Fritzky, 1963; Messick and Kogan, 1966).

These several differences between cognitive styles and abilities have been stated in somewhat stereotypic terms, representing distinctions between pure forms, as it were, of the two constructs. In actuality, however, these distinctions are not so sharply etched; there are varying degrees of difference and overlap between particular cognitive styles and abilities in terms of both conception and measurement. As examples, some cognitive styles, such as field independence versus field dependence, are assessed in terms of accuracy or correctness of performance, as in an ability test (Wachtel, 1968). For some other styles, such as complexity versus simplicity, accuracy is not a critical issue in assessment, but greater value is usually attached to one end of the dimension than to the other (Kogan, 1973; see also Chapter Six of this volume). Some stylistic dimensions ordinarily considered to fall within the purview of intellect, such as flexibility and fluency, appear to be of this latter type, part way between abilities and cognitive styles.

Cognitive Styles and Creative Performance

Several stylistic dimensions of the type just described are central to that aspect of human endeavor called creativity. In the realm of creativity, there is an intimate intertwining of abilities and cognitive styles and other stylistic dimensions that share some of the features of both, suggesting that distinctions in this area are labile and boundaries permeable.

Standards of Goodness. Although many dimensions relevant to creativity are not assessed in terms of correctness or accuracy of response, they are nevertheless subject to standards of adequacy which entail value distinctions favoring one end of the dimension over the other. Such dimensions involve what might be called creative responses, in contrast to ability dimensions which involve intelligent ones. Intelligent responses are judged in terms of correctness or rightness, evaluations dealing with the degree to which certain objective and logical criteria have been satisfied. The criteria of correctness tend to be categorical: they usually admit only one answer, or a relatively restricted set of solutions, with all other responses regarded as incorrect or in error. Creative responses are judged in terms of goodness or worth, evaluations dealing with the degree to which certain subjective and psychological criteria have been satisfied. The criteria of goodness tend to be continuous: they admit a wide range of responses that vary in the degree of their acceptability. In the simplest terms, then, the labels "correct" and "good" apply respectively to intelligent and creative performances; and judgmental standards of adequacy, though different, apply to both, thereby accruing directional value judgments for both kinds of dimensions. Judgmental standards for creative responses are described in detail by Jackson and Messick (1965).

Approaches to the Study of Creativity. Several stylistic dimensions of this type—such as fluency, flexibility, originality, and elaboration—contribute in critical ways to the creative process and, hence, presumably represent important features of the creative personality. But this raises the issue of when the accolade of creativity ought to be bestowed. Is a person creative because he displays certain characteristics important in the creative process, such as fluency or flexibility, or possesses other personal qualities shared with known creative people, such as openness or independence (Nicholls, 1972)? Or is a person creative because he exhibits a product deemed to be worthy when judged in terms of acceptable standards of goodness? Many writers on creativity plunk for the latter case, feeling that the former at best represents precursors of creativity—predisposing characteristics that increase the likelihood of creativity but do not guarantee it (C. W. Taylor, 1958, 1959, 1964).

Three of the terms just mentioned—the *creative process,* the *creative person,* and the *creative product*—represent three of four major foci of creativity research; the fourth is *creative press,* those environmental factors tending to initiate and foster creativity (Dellas and Gaier, 1970; Golann, 1963; Jackson and Messick, 1968). As previously indicated, many writers hold that the touchstone of creativity is the creative product and that a person should be deemed creative on the basis not of qualities but of talented accomplishments. To do this requires some consensus in human judgment according to accepted criteria about the excellence of the product or accomplishment. Products might be evaluated in terms of their relative novelty, for example, or their degree of appropriateness or fit, both internally among the parts and externally with the context. They might be judged for the extent to which they embody transformations that transcend immediate constraints or the extent to which they summarize the essence of the matter in sufficiently condensed form to warrant repeated examination (Jackson and Messick, 1965). The application of such criteria conjointly would make it possible to distinguish degrees of quality within the class of creative products, once the requirements have been met for considering a product to be nominally creative in the first place. In this connection, it is generally agreed that the minimal properties required for a product to be called "creative" are unusualness and appropriateness, with the latter being included primarily to rule out the bizarre and absurd (Barron, 1963; Jackson and Messick, 1965; Wallach and Kogan, 1965). In Chapter Twelve, Michael Wallach underscores the centrality of products in appraising creativity and in particular highlights the role of past talented accomplishments as predictors of future accomplishments in the same field (compare to Albert, 1975).

Nathan Kogan, in Chapter Six, focuses on aspects of person and process, especially as they relate to sex differences in creative performance. He examines the crucial role of cognitive styles in the creative process, particularly the role of such stylistic dimensions as ideational fluency, and considers their power in predicting "real-world" creative accomplishments. The moderate level of these predictions cautions us that cognitive styles, important as they may be as contributors to the creative process and as precursors of creative performance, are only part of the total picture (Golann, 1963; McNemar, 1964; Vernon, 1967). Many other factors weigh in the balance.

Some of these other factors are motivational (Dellas and Gaier, 1970; Maddi, 1965) and some are environmental, two features of the enterprise that are likely to interact in com-

plex ways. Donald Pelz, in Chapter Fifteen, focuses upon
environmental characteristics that are apt to stimulate and
foster creative productivity, especially as these combine with
personal characteristics, such as curiosity and self-confidence,
to recruit personal involvement in challenging problems.
Another aspect of environmental press, highlighted by Richard Snow in Chapter Eighteen, is pedagogical—those instructional procedures and conditions designed to stimulate
and foster learning and creativity, particularly as these are
tailored to interact with personal characteristics, such as abilities and styles, to optimize achievement and growth. Subsequent chapters will deal with this topic more fully.

Glossary of Cognitive Style Dimensions

Field independence versus field dependence refers to a consistent
mode of approaching the environment in analytical, as opposed to global, terms. It denotes a tendency to articulate
figures as discrete from their backgrounds and a facility in
differentiating objects from embedding contexts, as opposed
to a countertendency to experience events globally in an undifferentiated fashion. The field-independent pole includes
competence in analytical functioning combined with an impersonal orientation, while the field-dependent pole reflects
correspondingly less competence in analytical functioning
combined with greater social orientation and social skills (Witkin, and others, 1954; Witkin, Dyk, and others, 1962; Witkin,
Oltman, and others, 1973).

   Field articulation embraces two relatively independent
modes of perceiving complex stimulus arrays: *element articulation* involves the articulation of discrete elements from
a background pattern; *form articulation* highlights large figural forms against the patterned background (Messick and
Fritzky, 1963; Mos, Wardell, and Royce, 1974; Wachtel,
1968).

   Conceptualizing styles are individual consistencies in the
utilization of particular kinds of stimulus properties and relationships as bases for forming concepts, such as the routine

use of thematic or functional relations among stimuli (*relational conceptualizing*) as opposed to the analysis of descriptive attributes (*analytic-descriptive conceptualizing*) or the inference of class membership (*categorical-inferential conceptualizing*). These three formal bases for conceptualizing appear to be developmentally ordered, with relational being more characteristic of young children, analytic-descriptive being more characteristic of older children and widely used by adults, and categorical-inferential being more characteristic of adults. To view relational categorizing as primitive because of its early emergence is an oversimplification, however, because it seems to be complexly related to creativity as well (Kagan, Moss, and Sigel, 1960, 1963; Wallach, 1962; Wallach and Kogan, 1965).

Breadth of categorization entails consistent preferences for broad inclusiveness as opposed to narrow exclusiveness in establishing the acceptable range for specified categories. Also referred to as *category width* or *equivalence range* or *band width,* this dimension reflects differential tolerances for different types of errors, with broad categorizers tolerating (or preferring) errors of inclusion and narrow categorizers tolerating errors of exclusion. The narrow categorizer is thought to be conceptually conservative, whereas the broad categorizer is thought to be more tolerant of deviant instances (Bruner and Tajfel, 1961; Fillenbaum, 1959; Messick and Kogan, 1965; Pettigrew, 1958; Wallach and Caron, 1959).

Conceptual differentiation refers to individual differences in the tendency to categorize perceived similarities and differences among stimuli in terms of many differentiated concepts or dimensions. It is usually assessed using free-sorting tasks which require the spontaneous classification of heterogeneous stimuli (objects, persons, behaviors, and so forth) into an unrestricted number of groups, each containing an unrestricted number of more or less related items. This task differs in fundamental ways from the ostensibly similar category-width tests, in which each item assesses the perceived limits of one conceptual realm. Thus this style refers to the relative multiplicity of distinctions between or among concepts, while category width or equivalence range refers to the extent of a single concept's range of reference (Clayton and Jackson, 1961; Gardner, 1953; Gardner, Lohrenz, and Schoen, 1968; Gardner and Moriarty, 1968; Gardner and Schoen, 1962; Glixman, 1965; Sloane, Gorlow, and Jackson, 1963).

Compartmentalization refers to consistent tendencies to isolate ideas and objects into discrete, relatively rigid categories. This discreteness and rigidity entail a certain inertia in thinking and a possible limitation in the production of diverse ideas (Messick and Kogan, 1963; Wallach and Kogan, 1965).

Conceptual articulation (Bieri), or conceptual discrimination (Schroder), refers to individual differences in the extent to which stimuli or items of information are treated in dimensional rather than class terms, that is, the extent to which instances of a concept are discriminated from each other in a number of intervals or ordered categories within a concept's range of reference. This notion is related to category width (which refers to the perceived or judged extent of the concept's range of reference, within which either fine or coarse discriminations might be made among instances). Constructs evolved through experiential or naturalistic learning, such as those used in construing other persons, change developmentally primarily through progressively more refined articulation and discriminating use of dimensions already in the repertoire; whereas constructs (or, more pointedly, "instructs") established through didactic learning or instruction, such as those used in construing other nations, change developmentally primarily through the acquisition of differentiated dimensions for making new and more varied distinctions within the domain (Bieri, Atkins, and others, 1966; Schroder, Driver, and Streufert, 1967; Signell, 1966).

Conceptual integration, or integrative complexity, refers to individual consistencies in the extent to which categories or dimensions of information are perceived to be interrelated in multiple and different ways. Higher levels of integration involve the extent to which various combinations of interrelations can be generated to form alternative perspectives about a domain, which themselves can then be further compared, synthesized, and hierarchically interrelated (Harvey, Hunt, and Schroder, 1961; Schroder, Driver, and Streufert, 1967).

Cognitive complexity versus simplicity refers to individual differences in the tendency to construe the world, and particularly the world of social behavior, in a multidimensional and discriminating way. A complex individual's conceptual system is highly *differentiated* (consisting of a large number of distinct dimensions or concepts), finely *articulated* (each dimension capable of discriminating the strength or magnitude of varied instances or stimuli), and flexibly *integrated* (the dimensions being multiply interrelated and amenable to the formation of alternative perspectives or schemata of organization). This contrast of complexity versus simplicity of conceptual systems is sometimes referred to as the *abstract versus concrete* dimension of system variation (Harvey and others, 1961). It is not sufficient to view cognitive complexity as the extent to which conceptual differences are emphasized (as in sorting into many distinct groups or using many dimensions of judgment). Complex individuals may use many dimensions, to be sure, but the use of many discrete dimensions, each of which represents a fixed category or pigeonhole wherein stimuli are clumped rather than discriminated, may instead reflect compartmentalization, which is a relatively simple and concrete form of conceptualization. Likewise, an emphasis upon conceptual similarities (as in rating stimuli as relatively more similar than different or using few broad groups in object sorting) may reflect cognitive simplicity if it results from a failure to perceive differences, but it might instead stem from a tolerance of perceived differences or from the use of a hierarchically superordinate concept that provides an integrated summary of subsumed differences. Thus, the judging of two things to be similar might reflect the identification of commonalities in terms of multiple criterial attributes (an active and complex achievement), or it might reflect a failure to perceive differences (a lack of differentiation more indicative of primitive, concrete, and simple conceptualizaton). Therefore, to distinguish cognitive complexity from cognitive simplicity requires some combination of the criteria of dimensionality, articulation, and hierarchic integration. Cognitively complex individuals, being attuned to diversity, conflict, and inconsistency, are more certain and effective in processing dissonant information; while cognitively simple individuals, being primed for consistencies and regularities in the environment, are more confident and discerning in processing consonant information (Allard and Carlson, 1963; Bieri and others, 1966; Harvey and others, 1961; Kelly, 1955; Langley, 1971; Messick and Kogan, 1966; Schroder and others, 1967; Scott, 1962, 1963, 1974; Signell, 1966; Tripodi and Bieri, 1964, 1966; Vannoy, 1965; Wyer, 1964; Zimring, 1971).

Leveling versus sharpening concerns reliable individual variations in assimilation in memory. Persons at the leveling extreme tend to blur similar memories and to merge perceived objects or events with similar but not identical events recalled from previous experience; differences in remembered objects tend to be lost or attenuated. Sharpeners, at the other extreme, are less prone to confuse similar objects and may even magnify small differences between similar memory traces, thereby exaggerating change and heightening the difference between the present and the past (Gardner and others, 1959; Holzman, 1954; Holzman and Gardner, 1959, 1960; Holzman and Klein, 1954; Holzman and Rousey, 1971; Israel, 1969; Santostefano, 1964).

Scanning refers to individual differences in the extensiveness and intensity of attention deployment, leading to individual variations in vividness of experience and the span of awareness. The propensity of extensive scanning is associated with meticulousness, concern with detail, and sharp yet wide-ranging focus of attention; tasks are attended to intensely yet with extensive coverage of relatively incidental aspects of the field. Extreme scanning is related to defense mechanisms of both isolation and projection, suggesting that extensive scanning may serve different purposes under different circumstances or, perhaps, that there may be two distinct types of scanning. The association with isolation, a preferred defense of obsessives, suggests that scanning may occur in the service of information seeking, as reflected in the obsessive's concern with exactness to offset doubt and uncertainty. The association with projection, a preferred defense of paranoids, suggests that scanning may occur in the service of signal detection, particularly danger-signal detection, as reflected in the paranoid's concern with accuracy to offset suspicion and distrust. In the former case, scanning may occur with a broad beam or wide focus and in the latter with a narrow focus (Benfari, 1966; Gardner and Long, 1962a, 1962b; Holzman, 1966, 1971; Schlesinger, 1954; Silverman, 1964; Wachtel, 1967).

Reflection versus impulsivity involves individual consistencies in the speed and adequacy with which alternative hypotheses are formulated and information processed, with impulsive individuals tending to offer the first answer that occurs to them, even though it is frequently incorrect, and reflective individuals tending to ponder various possibilities before deciding. This dimension is thus mainly concerned with the degree to which an individual reflects on the validity of his hypotheses for solution in problems that contain response uncertainty (Block, Block, and Harrington, 1974; Kagan and Kogan, 1970; Kagan and Messer, 1975; Kagan, Rosman, and others, 1964; Yando and Kagan, 1968).

Risk taking versus cautiousness refers to consistent individual differences in a person's willingness to take chances to achieve desired goals as opposed to a tendency to seek certainty and to avoid exposure to risky situations. Risk takers are more likely, for example, to guess on difficult multiple-choice items, to speculate or gamble, to express confidence of judgment, and to rate the self in extreme terms, while more cautious persons show opposite tendencies. Risk taking implies that low probability-high payoff alternatives are generally preferred over high probability-low payoff alternatives, whereas cautiousness implies the reverse. Such generalized propensities are not uniformly displayed, however, because

marked moderator effects occur as a function of anxiety and
defensiveness. Highly anxious and defensive individuals are
most disposed toward generalized risk taking or caution,
whereas individuals low in such motivational disturbance are
more task-centered in their strategies, being consistently
risky or cautious on similar but not on dissimilar tasks (Kogan
and Morgan, 1969; Kogan and Wallach, 1964, 1967; Slovic,
1962).

   Tolerance for unrealistic experiences is a dimension of differential readiness to accept perceptions and ideas at variance
with conventional experience. The tolerant pole of the dimension reflects a predisposition to accept and report events
and ideas which are markedly different from the ordinary,
while the intolerant extreme implies a tendency to remain
closely oriented to reality and to prefer conventional ideas.
Persons tolerant of unrealistic experiences, for example, tend
more than their intolerant peers to report wider ranges of apparent movement when exposed to flashing lights, more rapid
reversals when viewing reversible figures, more form-labile
responses on the Rorschach, and more and longer associa-
tions on word-association tests (Gardner and others, 1959;
Klein, Gardner, and Schlesinger, 1962; Klein and Schlesinger, 1951).

   Constricted versus flexible control is a dimension of individual differences in susceptibility to distraction and cognitive interference. It involves the extent to which an individual
restricts attention to relevant cues and actively inhibits competing learned responses (Gardner and others, 1959; Jensen
and Rohwer, 1966; Klein, 1954; Santostefano and Paley,
1964).

   Strong versus weak automatization refers to an individual's
relative ability to perform simple repetitive tasks compared
to what would be expected of him in this regard from his general level of ability. This dimension is closely related to constricted versus flexible control in that the same measurement
indexes are often used to tap both constructs, but automatization is conceptualized differently—in ipsative rather than
normative terms. In the ipsative view, cognitive styles are

revealed in relationships between abilities within individuals and thus represent dimensions of intraindividual personality organization. Empirically, in ipsative analyses, relative facility in performing simple automatized tasks has been found to be in opposition to relative skill in perceptual analysis and disembedding, thereby generating an intraindividual bipolarity of *automatization versus restructuring.* Evidently the automatized tendency to respond to the obvious stimulus properties in simple repetitive tasks is dysfunctional on tasks where the obvious stimulus attributes must be set aside or restructured to reach solution. Differences between strong and weak automatizers have been noted in regard to occupational level (with strong automatizers having higher status occupations than did weak automatizers who did not differ in normative intelligence or educational level) as well as physical attributes, the latter presumably being mediated by hormone functioning (Broverman, 1960a, 1960b, 1964; Broverman and others, 1964; Broverman and others, 1968).

Conceptual versus perceptual-motor dominance is another intraindividual dimension, but this time having reference to novel or difficult tasks rather than simple repetitive ones. On novel or difficult tasks, conceptually dominant individuals show relative specialization of conceptual behaviors and relative deficiency in perceptual-motor behaviors, while perceptual-motor dominant individuals exhibit the opposite pattern (Broverman, 1960a, 1960b, 1964; Broverman and Lazarus, 1958).

Sensory modality preferences refer to individual consistencies in relative reliance upon the different sensory modalities available for experiencing the world. The three major sensory modes for interacting with the environment and organizing information are the kinesthetic (leading to what has sometimes been called physical or motoric thinking), the visual (leading to figural or spatial thinking), and the auditory (leading to verbal thinking). These three sensory modes of understanding experience—through the mind's hand, as it were, or the mind's eye or the mind's ear—have also been referred to respectively as *enactive, ikonic,* and *symbolic* modes

of representation (Bruner, Olver, and Greenfield, 1966).
Two important developmental shifts occur with respect to
these sensory modes. One involves a progression from a preference for the kinesthetic modality in the early years to a
later preference for the visual modality and ultimately for
the auditory or verbal modality. The other involves a progressive increase in the capability to coordinate and integrate
information obtained through one sensory modality with
information obtained through the others. Although in adults
all three modalities can function in parallel, with information from one clarifying and supplementing information
from the other two, individuals differ markedly in their preferred reliance upon one or another of these three sensory
modes of representation, resulting in characteristic differences in learning and thinking styles (Bartlett, 1932; Birch
and Lefford, 1963, 1967; Bissell, White, and Zivin, 1971;
Bruner and others, 1966; De Hirsch, Jansky, and Langford,
1966; Roe, 1951, 1952; Smith, 1964; Sperry, 1973).

Converging versus diverging represents the degree of
an individual's relative reliance upon convergent thinking
(pointed toward logical conclusions and uniquely correct or
conventionally best outcomes) as contrasted to divergent
thinking (pointed toward variety and quantity of relevant
output). Convergence versus divergence has been studied as
a manifestation of an intelligence versus creativity distinction, with special emphasis upon ideational fluency in the
production of unique, original, or novel responses as the
hallmark of creativity. The two poles of the dimension have
also been viewed as reflecting rival systems of defenses which
are related to a science versus arts bias (Cronbach, 1968;
Getzels and Jackson, 1962; Hudson, 1966, 1968; Kinsbourne,
1968; Wallach and Kogan, 1965).

2

Education for Creative Problem Solving

WAYNE H. HOLTZMAN

For generations, academicians have debated the purposes of higher education, the content of college curricula, and the nature of good teaching. Traditions have evolved that characterize the various disciplines of postsecondary education and that rather rigidly shape our thinking about students, classrooms, and course work. Chemistry professors only reluctantly abandon required laboratory work. It would be almost unthinkable for a history instructor to teach large numbers of sophomores in any format but regular fifty-minute lectures. Small discussion sections in English, recitation in French, and quizzes in mathematics—all with ample amounts of reading for homework—are traditional methods of instruction dominating our campus life. We expect every student to keep essentially the same pace or drop out. (For remediation we sometimes slow down that pace or repeat

23

material, but rarely have we shifted in any substantive way from the traditional approach.)

These time-honored traditions, instructional methods that have served us well in the past, are currently being questioned in many quarters, even among faculty members themselves. There is a call for education that is less routinized and more personalized, for education that not only imparts adopted knowledge but implants adaptive thinking, for education that does not just master belatedly the solutions of the past but that solves creatively the problems of the present and foresees realistically the issues of the future. In the light of this new call, our purpose here is threefold: first, to examine some recent trends in higher education that have led to new demands, then to review some promising developments in emerging technologies that may help to overcome the rigid patterns of traditional instruction, and, finally, to define some specific issues requiring expanded theory and research if education for creative problem solving is to become a reality.

New Students: New Concerns

The growth in higher education during the past decade has been the greatest that we shall probably ever see. For nearly a century, postsecondary enrollments have doubled every fifteen years. The explosive spurt of the 1960s represented a doubling of enrollment in less than ten years. Almost half of this rise reflects the high birthrate during the 1940s. In addition, there has been a sharp rise in enrollment rate. Sons and daughters of blue-collar workers are entering postsecondary institutions in large numbers, and the new students include ethnic minorities and women who in the past have stopped their formal education during the high school years.

The fastest growing section of higher education is that of the community colleges and the urban branches of state universities. With deep commitment to egalitarian concepts of education, community colleges open their doors to anyone interested in continuing his education who has the equivalent of a high school diploma. New community colleges have been springing up across the country at the rate of one a week. The Carnegie Commission on Higher Education (1971) estimates that with only about two hundred more schools constructed in the right places, 95 percent of our population will be within commuting distance of a college. Universality of access to some form of higher education should be a reality by the early 1980s, thereby expanding even further the number and variety of students to be served.

Expenditure for higher education has increased at an even faster rate than has enrollment. But as many of us reluctantly have come to realize, this is a trend that cannot continue. During the 1960s, costs for a full-time student rose at an average rate that exceeded the rate of increase of the consumer price index by 3.3 percent (Carnegie Commission on Higher Education, 1972b). Yet during the past thirty years, unlike most sectors of our economy, the productivity of education in terms of credit hours granted for each constant unit of input has failed to rise (O'Neill, 1971). Might not the cost effectiveness of education be markedly increased through the large-scale introduction of new forms of individualized instruction, especially if based on rapidly evolving technology?

One great difficulty is that many new university and community college students have mediocre school records, histories of academic failure, and low scholastic aptitude as measured by traditional standardized tests. Why are these young people going on to higher education in such large numbers? Primarily because they believe that a college education will be the key to future success in life. And, at least to some degree, they are right. But their progress through standard postsecondary programs is hampered by the lack of fit between traditional instruction and the variety of ability patterns, motivational dispositions, and cultural preferences they bring with them. Might not the effectiveness of education be improved, then, by increasing the variety of program options to provide a better match to student needs and preferences?

Another major force that is helping to reshape higher education is the cultural revolution. While campus unrest and demand for academic reform are hardly new, the voices we hear today are more strident than those of the past. Led by the restless, articulate activists on our campuses, a general shift in values and life styles continues to take place. Longing for personalization and self-enhancement, emphasis on sensory experiences, spiritual hunger, disrespect for authority, concern for the environment, community involvement, personal freedom, and cultural pluralism—all are typical of the concerns expressed. The Carnegie Commission's (1972c) large-scale survey of campus attitudes revealed both specific areas of strong dissatisfaction and general approval of academic life. Among the changes most strongly endorsed were better teaching, more relevant courses, abolition of grades and required courses, more personal contacts with faculty, and more outlets for creative interests.

Unlike the decade of the 1960s, the next ten years will see a leveling off of enrollment and expenditures. If our estimates are correct (Carnegie Commission on Higher Education, 1971), growth will come to a halt during the 1980s and increase slowly again in the last decade of the century. Consequently, the next ten years are likely to be the most favorable for reform. As we shall see in subsequent chapters, fresh knowledge and insights about cognitive style, learning, motivation, and creative problem solving point toward new directions in education, among which are increased individualization of instruction and enriched flexibility of choice among varied program options. These may well provide a basis for timely responsiveness to student needs and desires.

Educational Technology

Open admissions in higher education has created a crisis in traditional instruction that can only be resolved by major reform. The most dramatic example of this challenge to traditional methods is the situation at the City University of New York. After several years experience with a special admissions program for randomly selected high school graduates from low income neighborhoods—mostly Black and Puerto Rican—City University opened its doors in the fall of 1971 to any student in the top half of his graduating class. One half of the freshmen in City College alone were placed in two or more remedial courses dealing with mathematics, reading, speech, or writing. Many of these new students had been alienated from learning by traditional instruction. With the aid of federal funds and foundation grants supplementing their own funds, City College is developing a new instructional system involving tutorial laboratories, modular courses, audiovisual media, self-paced learning, programed texts, and other technologies as they become available. Whether City University succeeds or fails in this noble effort to reach thousands of poorly prepared students with an effective form of instruction is a matter of concern to all of us. A fresh mix of electronic technology, more personal faculty-student contacts, and instructional design based on the best available information concerning motivation, cognitive processes, and learning could make the difference.

Numerous forms of technology in education are making their mark. Multimedia classrooms, self-instructional units in language laboratories, individual learning laboratories, audiolistening centers, instructional television, and videotapes are already commonplace. A study by Jarrod Wilcox at the Massachusetts Institute of Technology (Carnegie Commission on Higher Education, 1972a) defined nine basic technologies for instruction which exist in some form today: routine audiovisual techniques, programed instruction, routine computer-assisted instruction, computer simulation, advanced computer-assisted instruction, computer-managed instruction, remote classroom broadcasting and response, student-initiated access to audiovisual recordings, and computer-aided course design. Usually these technologies are employed for only a fraction of a given college course, leaving intact the traditional structure of the curriculum and the faculty-student relationship. In some instances, however, the impact of these technologies on instructional

organization and practices is already apparent. Even the
large state universities, overcoming some of their tremendous inertia, are evidencing major changes in faculty-student
roles, organization, and concepts of instruction as a result
of new technologies.

My own institution, the University of Texas, is a good
example. Computers are now used to a significant extent for
instructional purposes in forty-eight of fifty-nine departments. With support from the National Science Foundation,
a major program of computer-based education is now under way. In some content areas the computer terminal is the
primary resource for problem solving, simulation, and instruction, while in other fields it is only an occasional acces-
sory. Through a network of exchange and special services,
a large number of faculty and students are using computers
for the first time. For example, a second-semester course for
chemistry majors has been reorganized to include one hour
of lecture, one hour of small-group discussion, and one hour
of computer-based interactive lessons each week. Individualized instruction by computer ranges from drill and tutorial
materials to simulated laboratory experiments. As compared
with a control group, those in the computer-assisted chemistry class covered more material and obtained higher grades
on departmental examinations.

Another flexible option growing rapidly at the University of Texas involves Keller's Personalized System of Instruction (Keller, 1968). A given course is broken down into
small units or modules that contain explicit objectives, reading
assignments, study questions, references, and, where appropriate, a combination of computer-based tutorials, audio-
tapes, television, and self-assessment examinations. The
student moves through the entire course at his own pace,
demonstrating mastery of one unit before proceeding to the
next. Proctors are always available, offering a good deal of
personal-social interaction. The Keller plan has been widely
adopted in the College of Engineering. Similar self-paced,
individualized courses are available in chemistry, psychology,
and education. Keller's Personalized System of Instruction

provides a flexible framework within which the new technologies can be easily accommodated. The student becomes more responsible for his own learning at a time, place, and rate that is compatible with his personal style and objectives.

Use of the new technologies in self-paced tutorial programs is a particularly attractive way to provide for individual differences. Student progress is assessed on the basis of the rate at which they learn rather than on how well they have mastered a skill or subject matter in a fixed period of time. This feature is especially important for the student who has been poorly prepared for college because of his past academic failures. Successful completion of small units of learning produces a sense of accomplishment that might even lead a student to like a subject and to want to learn more about it. At the same time, frequent assessment and branching are essential if capable students are to move through the curriculum as efficiently as possible.

The Evolving Electronics. Many observers believe that education faces the first great technological revolution in five centuries with the advent of novel electronic means of storing, transmitting, and displaying information by computers and television. Our national inventory of computers now exceeds 88,000, one computer for every 730 families.

Two major demonstrations of computer-assisted instruction in higher education have been launched with multimillion-dollar support from the National Science Foundation: the PLATO (Programed Logic for Automatic Teaching Operations) IV project, directed by Donald Bitzer at the University of Illinois and the TICCIT (Time-shared Interactive Computer-Controlled Information Television) system being developed by Kenneth Stetten of Mitre Corporation and Victor Bunderson of Brigham Young University (Bitzer and Skaperdas, 1970; Bunderson, 1970; Hammond, 1972). The heart of the PLATO system is a new student terminal. The basic terminal consists of a plasma display panel on which graphic information can be presented, a keyboard, a random-access slide projector, and associated electronics. Additional accessories include a random-access audio device that can both record and play and an infrared sensor system that responds to the touch of a finger on any part of the display. The thin glass display panel contains fine wires in a 512 by 512 grid. Voltage applied to selected points of the grid ionizes a gas between the thin glass sheets, producing very sharp images and virtually any type of characters. The pneumatically operated slide projector superimposes colored images on the computer-generated graphics, providing a highly versatile display. Since the image does not have to be constantly refreshed, interaction with a remote computer is possible over ordinary telephone lines. One large computer can handle hundreds of these terminals.

It is anticipated that relatively inexperienced teachers can develop courses for PLATO using TUTOR, a programing language based on English grammar and syntax. A Latin course at the University of Illinois is typical of the successes already achieved on an earlier version of PLATO. It was determined that four times as many students could be handled with PLATO as with traditional methods. Nearly all of the students reached the desired level of mastery and covered 30 percent more material than in the traditional course. Student response was so enthusiastic that enrollment doubled the next year.

The TICCIT system is built around small computers with multimedia terminals composed of a standard color television set, a small integrated circuit memory to refresh the television screen, a keyboard, headphones, and computer-controlled audio messages. The use of cable television permits sharp images with up to seventeen lines, each of which contains forty-three characters as specified by the programer. Over a hundred students can be served simultaneously by two interconnected minicomputers; one handles the terminals while the other processes the individual student's responses.

A unique feature of TICCIT is the extent to which instructional technology based on learning research will be employed in the design of courses. Together with programers, media specialists, and subject matter experts, educational psychologists have written, pretested, and revised the elements of the curriculum modules under Bunderson's direction in order to produce turnkey products that are then field tested on a large scale. The resulting courses are viewed as mainline college-level instruction that may radically change the role of the classroom teacher.

Both PLATO and TICCIT are expected to be more cost-effective in the long run than is traditional instruction at the college level, particularly with mass production. Bitzer has estimated that a fully implemented PLATO system could cost less than a dollar per student-hour of individualized instruction, direct costs running as low as fifty cents (an estimate that has proven to be overly optimistic). The Mitre Corporation predicted that a 128-terminal TICCIT system could be built for about four hundred thousand dollars, yielding direct-cost estimates as low as thirty-five cents per student-hour of junior college instruction (again, an overly optimistic estimate). But, even if these estimates are off by a factor of ten, the cost of PLATO and TICCIT will be competitive with current costs of junior college instruction.

The main focus of these two major projects is the junior college curriculum in mathematics, computer science, and English, which account for about 20 percent of the total instruction. Remedial as well as standard courses are being developed because of the urgent need for more effective instruction of disadvantaged and lower-ability students. In addition, for PLATO, plans are under way to develop and test courses in chemistry, biology, physics, psychology, and political science. Both systems are being subjected to field tests and full-scale evaluations.

Issues and Priorities

Properly developed, the new technologies can accelerate educational reform for the betterment of mankind. Pressures to manufacture and market computer hardware are mounting rapidly. Efforts to develop software for harnessing the electronics are also under way. But the use of the hardware and software to develop instructional modules lags far behind, largely because of the embryonic state of the art in the design of instructional materials and the lack of hardware-software standardization. The most critical issue of all, however, is the absence of powerful theoretical and empirical bases for describing, predicting, and controlling learning and achievement.

Research concerning the conditions of learning, retention, and transfer as they interact with individual differences must be stepped up greatly (as will become increasingly apparent later in this volume, especially in Parts Seven and Eight). Computer-assisted instruction offers an unparalleled opportunity to conduct such research very efficiently on a large scale. A multiplicity of cognitive, motivational, and instructional variables influences learning, and computers permit the simultaneous treatment of large numbers of interacting variables. Work in the field of motivation and personality, for example, leads us to emphasize the interplay of such motives as achievement, affiliation, and power; to examine the interaction of anxiety with type of learning; and to stress the effects of culture, earlier development, and individual differences in abilities as they affect learning. Cognitive theorists emphasize the organization of knowledge, the formative influence of perceptual features, the need for learning with understanding, and the importance of cognitive feedback and goal setting as motivation for learning. Stimulus-response theories of learning stress the importance of learning by doing, of overlearning for retention, of immediate reinforcement, and of practice in varied contexts to encourage appropriate generalization and discrimination. Can a challenging contemporary theory of instruction be developed and applied in time to harness effectively the new electronic technologies? Or are we heading for a fuzzy-minded period of trial and error with potentially disastrous results? While I am uncertain of the final answer to these important questions, I am not at all optimistic concerning our ability to muddle through on an ad hoc basis. Although there is no certainty that we can develop a powerful, flexible theory of instruction, we know that we most certainly shall fail unless major efforts to do so are launched immediately.

The discipline of detailed instructional design forces us to make explicit our specific objectives. If we follow the line of least resistance, there is a danger of overemphasizing skill training while neglecting broader educational objectives that cannot yet be specified behaviorally. Strenuous efforts and ingenuity are badly needed to specify objectives concerning personality development—the social, moral, and humanistic values that we all cherish in personal terms as a part of liberal education. To be understood and preserved, they need not be specified behaviorally in the narrow sense at all. The apparent threat of technology is in the hand and mind of the user and can serve as either a pitfall or a promise. Properly applied, technology will not drive these liberal objectives and values out of existence, but rather will force these issues into the open so that they will have to be dealt with pedagogically.

Built upon the concepts of individualized, self-paced learning with immediate reinforcement of student behavior, the new technologies show great promise for the immediate future. As these different instructional programs expand, new roles will be defined for students, teachers, counselors, administrators, engineers, programers, developers, publishers, and manufacturers. As is true of any genuine revolution, one can only dimly perceive the ultimate consequences of such radical reform.

Creative problem solving for education must precede education for creative problem solving. It requires some imagination, but little effort to visualize plausible alternative futures for higher education. It requires a great deal of effort and creativity to influence the course of the future. The issues addressed in this volume on cognitive styles and creativity in higher education are only a beginning. But, in the scholarly discourses and debates that follow, may we all reach a higher level of understanding of what must be done and how it can be achieved.

Part Two

Cognitive Styles in Learning and Teaching

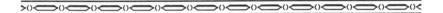

The pervasive role of cognitive style in intellectual and inter-personal functioning has been pointed to previously. A concrete sense of this pervasiveness is now provided in Chapter Three, in which Herman Witkin documents in detail the varied influences of the most widely studied of the cognitive styles, field dependence versus field independence. Among these influences are several of consequence to higher education. Cognitive styles are related to vocational preferences and choice of major field, for example, as well as to choice of specialization and relative performance within fields. In contrast to intellectual abilities, then, which are predictive of general levels of achievement, cognitive styles predict the direction of achievement and hence provide a potentially powerful basis for career guidance.

Cognitive styles also influence the ways in which teachers teach, especially their choice of preferred teaching meth-

ods, as well as the ways in which students learn, as revealed
in their differential use of mediating strategies, for example,
or their differential responsiveness to social reinforcement.
Possibly even more important, cognitive styles influence the
ways in which teachers and students interact. Teachers and
students who are similar in cognitive style, for instance, tend
to view each other with greater mutual esteem than do those
who are dissimilar; they also tend to communicate more effectively with one another, as if they were on the same wavelength. Such findings lead naturally to the notion of matching
teachers and students in terms of cognitive style and of choosing instructional methods that are mutually congenial.

Seymour Wapner, in Chapter Four, disputes this notion, however, and initiates what proves to be a continuing
tension throughout this volume, namely, a conflict over the
relative value of matching educational treatments to learner
characteristics as opposed to mismatching them. Although
matching may be appropriate when the aim is to improve
subject-matter achievement, mismatching, Wapner contends,
is needed when the aim is to promote flexible and creative
thinking; obstacles, opposition, and conflict are necessary to
stimulate individual development and creativity. Wapner
also proposes a reconceptualization of cognitive styles as
properties of organism-environment systems, wherein shifts
in style might occur as a function of the context. The amount
of shift would be an individual differences variable, and persons would be characterized by a range of stylistic behaviors
rather than by a type or degree of stylistic behavior. Since
the emphasis upon stability of cognitive style may be one
factor predisposing educators toward the matching strategy,
this reconceptualization—highlighting as it does intraindividual variability and the potential flexibility of cognitive style—
serves to reinforce mismatching as a viable alternative.

The problem however, is not only to choose between
matching and mismatching as a preferred strategy, as Arthur
Chickering points out in Chapter Five, but to create alternative treatments that permit a clear match or mismatch to
learner attributes (or that entail a mix of matching and mis-

matching deliberately constructed to exploit the merits of both; see Chapter Twenty-One). Typically we are faced with program alternatives that neither match nor mismatch learner attributes; available programs are generally misaligned with functional characteristics of the learners, some features facilitating and others debilitating performance. In Chapter Five, Chickering illustrates this type of double bind by examining the fate of field dependent and field independent students in each of two major new alternatives in higher education—contract learning and programed learning.

3

Cognitive Style in Academic Performance and in Teacher-Student Relations

HERMAN A. WITKIN

The past two and a half decades have seen a vast amount of research on cognitive styles, and it is a tribute to the value and vigor of this effort that, increasingly, the concepts and methods derived from cognitive style research can be fruitfully applied to a very wide array of psychological issues. Perhaps the most promising and exciting prospects for a cognitive style approach lie in the field of education. While

The preparation of this report was supported by a grant (MH-21989) from the United States Public Health Service, National Institutes of Health and a grant from the Graduate Record Examination Board. The period following the conference for which this paper was originally written has produced a burgeoning of research on field independence which would be impossible to review exhaustively in a single chapter. Accordingly, for specialized reviews of work on the field-dependence-independence cognitive style beyond those studies from our own laboratory cited here, see Goodenough (1976); Witkin and Goodenough, 1976; Witkin, Moore, Goodenough, and Cox (in press).

relatively little research has been done, compared to what is possible and needed, it is already clear that cognitive style is a potent variable affecting a number of areas: the student's academic choices and vocational preferences, the student's continuing academic development, how students learn and teachers teach, and how students and teachers interact in the classroom. These are the issues that will be of primary concern in this chapter, but first let me say something of the nature of cognitive styles as revealed by research.

The Nature of Cognitive Styles

From evidence accumulated in the course of more than twenty years of research in many different centers, we now know that all of us have characteristic modes of functioning that we reveal throughout our perceptual and intellectual activities in a highly consistent and pervasive way. We call these modes of functioning cognitive styles.

One such cognitive style may illustrate the family of cognitive styles now on record. This particular style—field dependence versus field independence—has been of special interest to us over the years (Witkin, Dyk, Faterson, Goodenough, and Karp, 1962; Witkin, Lewis, Hertzman, Machover, Meissner, and Wapner, 1954). The best way to begin an account of field dependence versus field independence is to describe the actual situations used to identify individual differences along this dimension.

Tests of Cognitive Style. One kind of test is conducted in a completely darkened room. The apparatus consists of a square frame coated with luminous paint and a rod, pivoted at the same center as the frame, also coated with luminous paint. This is all the subject is able to see. Rod and frame can be tilted clockwise or counterclockwise, together or separately. In a typical trial the subject, on opening his eyes, finds rod and frame in tilted positions. If he reports that the rod is tilted, he is asked to adjust it to a position where it appears upright, while the frame remains in its initial position of tilt.

People in various age groups differ markedly from each other in how they perform this task. At one extreme of the performance range are people who, in order to perceive the rod as upright, require it to be aligned with the surrounding frame. If the frame is tilted 30 degrees to the left, they will tilt the rod 30 degrees to the left; and when the rod is in that position, they will say it is perfectly upright. If the frame is tilted 30 degrees to the right, they will then tilt the rod 30 degrees to the right and say the rod is perfectly upright in that position. At the other extreme of the performance range are people who are able to bring the rod close to the upright more or less independently of the position of the surrounding frame.

In another test we use the object of perception is not a stick but the subject's body. The apparatus for this test consists of a small room containing a chair. Room and chair can be tilted clockwise or counterclockwise, together or independently of each other. At the outset of each trial, the subject's chair and the room are brought to prepared tilted positions, and the subject's task is to adjust his body to an upright position. Here again we find very marked individual differences in performance. There are people who, in order to perceive the body itself as upright, align it with the surrounding tilted room. Astonishing as it may seem, some people actually can be tilted as much as 30 degrees and in that position report that they are perfectly straight, stating, "this is the way I sit when I eat my dinner," or "this is the way I sit in class." At the other extreme of the performance range are people who are able to bring the body more or less to the upright position, regardless of the position of the surrounding room.

A third test, although quite different in construction from the first two, is very similar in essence. The subject is first shown a simple figure. It is then removed, and he must locate it in a complex design of which it is a part. While this situation does not involve space orientation, as did the first two, the structure of the task is essentially the same. Here, too, the subject is presented with an item—now a simple figure rather than the rod or the body—which is contained in a complex, organized field. Once again, we attempt to ascertain the extent to which the surrounding visual frame-work dominates perception of an item within it. We incor-porate the lines of the simple figure in various subwholes of the complex design, so that, perceptually, the simple figure no longer seems to be there. Here again, individual differ-ences in performance are very marked and similar in nature to the ones described for the first two tasks. For some people, the sought-after simple figure more or less pops out of the complex design; others are not able to find it in the three minutes allowed for search.

In the first two tests, the subject's score is the number of degrees of tilt of rod or body when the subject reports them as straight. In the Embedded Figures test, the subject's score is the time taken to locate the simple figure in the com-plex design. In all three situations, we come out with a quanti-tative indicator of the extent to which the subject's perception of an item has been influenced by the organized field sur-rounding it. In these three tests of field dependence versus independence, a more field independent style is associated with greater accuracy. Situations also have been devised where adherence to the prevailing visual field results in more accurate performance so that the person who is relatively field dependent turns out to be accurate and the more field independent person inaccurate (Witkin, 1950, 1952). Impor-tant for the concept of cognitive style is the evidence that people tend to be self-consistent in performance across these three tasks. If the same subjects are tested in these three situ-ations, we find that the person who tilts the rod far toward the tilted frame is likely to be the person who tilts his body far toward the tilted room, and he is also likely to be the per-son who takes a long time to find the simple figure in the complex design.

As must be evident from the descriptions above, the common denominator underlying individual differences in performance in all these tasks is the extent to which a person is able to deal with a part of a field separately from the field as a whole, or the extent to which he is able to disembed items from organized context—to put it in everyday language, the extent to which he is analytical. At one extreme of the performance range, perception is strongly dominated by the prevailing field; we speak of this mode of perception as field dependent. At the other extreme, the perception of an item is relatively independent of the surrounding field, and we refer to this mode of perception as field independent.

We should note that people are strikingly stable, even over many years, in their characteristic mode of perceiving (Bauman, 1951; Witkin and others, 1954; Witkin, Goodenough, and Karp, 1967). We should also note that there are sex differences in field dependence. Test results revealed, for instance, that girls and women are likely to tilt the rod farther toward the tilted frame and their bodies farther toward the tilted room than do boys and men, and they take significantly longer to find the simple figure in the complex design.

Thus far we have been considering the ways in which people function when dealing with an immediately present stimulus configuration—how they perceive. Extensive accumulated evidence shows that the style we first identified in perception appears in problem-solving behavior and in thinking as well. The individual who cannot keep an item separate from the surrounding field is also likely to have difficulty with the kind of problem that requires taking some critical element out of the context in which it is presented and restructuring the problem material so that the element is now used in a different way. This is often the requirement in problems of mathematical reasoning, for example. Please note, however, that it is only with problems that require disembedding of a salient element from context that field dependent persons experience difficulty. Field dependent and field independent persons are not particularly different in their performance of other sorts of problem-solving tasks, for example, tasks involving verbal skills of the kind so heavily featured in the usual standard test of intelligence.

Of the three main factor components of the commonly used Wechsler scales (Cohen, 1957, 1959; Goodenough and

Karp, 1961; Karp, 1963), one happens to be essentially identical with the field-dependence-independence dimension,
based as it is on three particular Wechsler subtests assessing
competence in disembedding. It is therefore not surprising
that measures of field dependence relate very highly to scores
for this factor but minimally to scores for the other two factors. In view of the important cognitive domains constituting
an individual's intellect to which field dependence versus
field independence does not relate, we clearly cannot equate
the field dependence versus field independence dimension
with general cognitive competence, or intelligence, even
though that dimension must be considered an ingredient of
intellect.

Cognitive Style and Social Interaction. The concept of cognitive style does not imply that there are two types of people—field dependent or field independent. Scores on any
test of this dimension form a continuous distribution, and
as with a characteristic such as height, a person's standing on
the dimension is defined relative to the mean. But there is
now a good deal of evidence that this style extends into psychological domains beyond cognition. Persons who tend to
be field dependent also differ from relatively field independent persons in important personal characteristics. For
example, the person who, in the laboratory, is strongly influenced by the surrounding visual framework in his perception of an item within it is also likely, in social situations, to
use the prevailing social frame of reference to define his attitudes, his beliefs, his feelings, and even his self-view from
moment to moment. Thus, if you substitute for the square
wooden frame a social frame of reference, and for the rod,
an attribute of the self, such as an attitude or a sentiment,
there is indeed continuity in what a person is likely to do in
both laboratory perceptual situations and social situations.

Many studies have explored the relation of this cognitive style to social interaction, and it is of value to cite some
of the results. In forming their attitudes on an issue, field
dependent persons are especially prone to be guided by the
positions attributed to an authority figure or peer group

(Bell, 1964; Deever, 1968; Linton and Graham, 1959). Reflecting their use of external sources of information for self-definition, field dependent persons are selectively attentive to the human content of the environment. Thus, they literally spend more time looking at the faces of those with whom they are interacting than do field independent persons (Konstadt and Forman, 1965; Nevill, 1971; Ruble and Nakamura, 1972). The face is, of course, a major source of information about what others are feeling and thinking. To the extent that they look at faces more, it is not surprising that field dependent persons also tend to be better at remembering faces (Crutchfield, Woodworth, and Albrecht, 1958; Messick and Damarin, 1964). Their special attention to the social environment is not limited to faces of others; it is reflected also in their superiority over field independent persons in attending to, and hence remembering, verbal messages that are more social in content (Eagle, Fitzgibbons, and Goldberger, 1966; Eagle, Goldberger, and Breitman, 1969; Fitzgibbons and Goldberger, 1971; Fitzgibbons, Goldberger and Eagle, 1965; Goldberger and Bendich, 1972). Later, when we discuss the role of cognitive style in teacher-student interaction, we will see further evidence that field dependent persons are particularly sensitive and attuned to the social environment. They present an overall picture of highly developed social skills.

The evidence cited above clearly indicates that field independence is a manifestation in the perceptual sphere of a broad dimension of personal functioning which extends into the sphere of social behavior and into the sphere of personality as well (see Witkin and others, 1954; Witkin, 1965; Witkin and others, 1962). It is important to bear in mind that cognitive style refers to personal as well as cognitive characteristics, for, as we shall see, both must be considered in making predictions and interpreting findings on how cognitive style figures in various aspects of the educational process. It is also worth noting that because these styles show themselves in perception, where they are readily accessible to observation and assessment by controlled laboratory techniques, they offer an objective route to the study of individual differences in personal functioning. How do these individual differences arise? This problem has been pursued in two directions. One has been to examine the effects of child rearing and socialization and the other has been to examine the role of genetic factors.

Determinants of Cognitive Style. Studies of the family experiences of children who turn out to be relatively field dependent or field independent have indeed demonstrated that the kind of relations the growing child has with his mother is very influential in determining his cognitive style (Dyk, 1969; Dyk and Witkin, 1965; Seder, 1957; Witkin and others, 1962). The characteristic of child rearing that seems most closely associated with the development of a more field independent style of functioning, for example, is the early encouragement of autonomous functioning. In a further effort to identify the socialization experiences contributing to the development of a more field dependent or field independent style, cross-cultural studies have been undertaken. The strategy in these studies has been to examine the wide variation existing naturally in the world to locate more extreme variations in child-rearing practices than are available in our ordinary work settings. Recently, Witkin, Price-Williams, Bertini, Christiansen, Oltman, Ramirez, and van Meel (1974) have completed a study of children from two small and relatively self-contained villages in each of three countries—Italy, Holland, and Mexico. The two villages in each pair were chosen because of the marked difference between them in the child-rearing practices earlier found relevant to the development of field dependence versus independence. Other investigators, following a similar strategy, have selected for assessment of cognitive style other cultural settings as radically different from our own as, for example, the Temne of Sierra Leone, Africa; the Eskimo of Baffin Bay, the Arunta of Australia, and the Boat People and Hakka of Hong Kong (Berry, 1966; Dawson, 1967a,b, 1969, 1971). The evidence accumulated from these many cross-cultural studies demonstrates impressively that development of a more field dependent or more field independent cognitive style is indeed related to socialization and, moreover, that the socialization procedures associated with one trend or the other in development are essentially those we identified in the earlier Western studies.

As previously mentioned, the possibility that genetic factors enter into the development of this rather basic cognitive style is also being pursued. There has been a persistent finding, now demonstrated in hundreds of studies performed in many different parts of the world, of sex differences in field dependence. If genetic factors are involved in field dependence, the sex chromosomes are especially likely to be implicated, although not necessarily to the exclusion of autosomal chromosomes. Three kinds of studies pursuing this possibility are now under way. One, conducted by Goodenough, Pizzamiglia, Ancona, and Witkin, is a study of family-correlation patterns in measures of field dependence. In this study, a check is being made of predictions about the extent of resemblance of son and daughter to each parent; the predictions derive from the hypothesis that a recessive gene on the X chromosome plays a role in the development of individual differences in field dependence. The second study, conducted by Goodenough, Hirschhorn, Mednick, Schulzinger, Schiavi, Phillip, and Witkin, examines cognitive style in men who have an extra Y chromosome (XYYs) or an extra X chromosome (XXYs) in addition to the usual XY sex-chromosome complement. The case-finding part of the study, now well under way, is being done in Denmark because of the excellent social records maintained there. In the third study, by Goodenough, Pizzamiglia, Ancona, and Witkin, the linkage method is being used. For this study, three-son families have been identified in which two sons share one of the mother's two X chromosomes and the third son has received her other X chromosome. To make these chromosomal determinations, such X-linked somatic characteristics as color blindness and blood features were used as markers. If there is indeed a gene on the X chromosome contributing to the development of individual differences in field dependence versus field independence, the two brothers with the same X chromosomes should be significantly more similar on this dimension than either is to the third brother.

In overview, it seems fair to say from the evidence now on hand that socialization factors are undoubtedly of overwhelming importance in the development of individual differences in field dependence versus field independence. At the same time, it may be that genetic factors are implicated as well, although probably to a much smaller degree. If they are implicated, we should know about the role they play in interaction with social factors.

We have examined here in some detail one well-studied cognitive style to give you some impression of the nature of these styles. As mentioned previously, a number of other cognitive styles have been described in the literature (see Chapter One). Among these are the styles of leveling versus sharpening, constricted versus flexible control, reflection versus impulsivity, tolerance versus intolerance for unrealistic experience, analytical versus relational versus inferential categorizing, and strong versus weak automatization (Broverman, 1960; Gardner, Holzman, and others, 1959; Gardner, Jackson, and Messick, 1960; Kagan, Moss, and Sigel, 1963; Kagan, Rosman, Day, Albert, and Phillips, 1964). These styles have not been investigated as extensively as the field dependence versus field independence dimension, and most have not yet been examined in terms of their implications for educational problems. Accordingly, in the discussion that follows, the evidence considered comes particularly from studies in which field dependence versus field independence was the cognitive style variable considered.

Cognitive Style in Academic Evolution

The evidence is now clear that cognitive style is an important variable in the preferences students express and in the choices they actually make at the various points in their academic development when options are available to them. Thus, the extent to which a student is field dependent or field independent plays an identifiable role in his selection of electives and majors, in the vocational preferences he expresses early in his academic career, and in the vocational choice he makes later on. Field dependence versus field independence has also been related to performance in different subject matter areas in school and in vocation chosen. It is especially impressive that a linkage between cognitive style and academic choice and achievement is already clearly evident as early in a student's academic career as the elementary and high school levels.

The connection between field dependence versus field independence and academic and vocational choices is, first of all, based on the degree to which a given academic or vocational area calls for the particular cognitive skills involved in either a more field dependent or more field independent style. Contributing to the connection as well are the personal characteristics associated with these cognitive styles. The frequently found sex differences in field dependence also seem to enter into the differences that have been observed between men and women in academic choices and vocational preferences. Finally, cognitive style has been implicated in the important phenomenon of shifts in major during the college years.

A Longitudinal Study. The evidence reviewed, as we consider each of these issues in more detail, comes from extensive work by others as well as from a large-scale longitudinal study that Witkin, Moore, Oltman, Goodenough, Freedman, and Raskin are now doing on the role of cognitive style in academic evolution at the higher education level. In that study the entire entering class of sixteen hundred men and women in a large municipal college was assessed at admission on tests of field dependence and also on tests of verbal comprehension, another salient cognitive dimension. This class was graduated in 1970. For each student we have transcripts of his or her complete college record. Included in the record is information about courses taken, grades received, majors chosen, changes in major, academic difficulty, special achievements, and, finally, graduate school choices, when made. For a subsample of students we also have the results of an extensive battery of tests we administered over their four years in college. Included in the battery was a wide array of cognitive tests as well as interest inventories, personality tests, and an interview. The extensive and varied data on these students make it possible to examine the relation between cognitive style and a number of features of academic performance.

The availability of data on the verbal comprehension dimension has now also allowed us to take the important step of examining the way in which particular cognitive *patterns* figure in students' academic development. The patterns being examined are given combinations of field dependence versus field independence and verbal comprehension ability. To this end, we identified for special study five groups of students, consisting of both men and women, each presenting a different pattern in terms of performance level in the two domains. The first group was field independent and high in verbal-comprehension ability; the second was field dependent and also high in verbal comprehension ability; the third, relatively field dependent and relatively low in verbal comprehension ability; the fourth, relatively field independent and again relatively low in verbal comprehension ability; and the fifth, intermediate on both dimensions. Of particular interest to us are the groups showing a marked discrepancy in the level of functioning between these two cognitive domains—in other words, cognitive splits. Among the groups with such cognitive splits, the fourth group listed shows a pattern likely to be characteristic of those from culturally deprived backgrounds and therefore deserves particular attention in this period of concern with education of the underprivileged. While analyses of data from this study are still under way, there are already some results that are relevant to the issues we are considering. These will be cited along with the results of studies by others.

Student Interest, Preferences, and Achievement. Students' scores on interest inventories and vocational preference inventories have been examined in relation to field dependence in a multitude of studies, using a variety of inventory forms and considering students at different educational levels (see, for example, Chung, 1967; Clar, 1971; DeRussy and Futch, 1971; Glatt, 1970; Krienke, 1970; Linton, 1952; Pierson, 1965; Zytowski, Mills, and Paepe, 1969). Not surprisingly, a consistent finding of most of these studies is that more field independent students favor domains in which analytical skills are called for, whereas more field dependent students avoid such domains. Examples of analytical areas are the physical and biological sciences, mathematics, engineering, and technical and mechanical activities.

Equally clear is the strong preference of the more field dependent students for domains that feature interpersonal relations and in which day-to-day work requires involvement with people. Examples are the social sciences, rehabilitation counseling, elementary school teaching, social science teaching, persuasive activities (that is, those requiring dealing and meeting with people and promoting projects or things to sell), the humanities, office managing, selling real estate. The orientation toward the social environment reflected in these choices by field dependent persons also shows itself in their tendency to prefer occupations favored by their peer group (Karp, personal communication, 1957; Linton, 1952). Karp's finding was obtained with ten-year-old boys, suggesting, as noted earlier, that the cognitive-style variable begins to affect career pathways quite early in life. Also reflecting an early start was the finding of Glatt (1970) that engineering was favored by eighth-grade boys who were field independent. In addition, examination of the high school records of the students in our longitudinal four-year college study showed that those who tested as field independent at college admission had taken more advanced optional mathematics and science courses in high school than had those who were field dependent.

A highly similar picture to the one found when interests and preferences are examined emerges when actual choices of majors in college are studied. This was shown, for example, in the study by Clar (1971). It was evident as well in the data from our own longitudinal study. It is worth noting, however, that in our study, choice of major showed no relation to standing on the verbal comprehension dimensions.

Cognitive style has also been examined in students showing high achievement in particular subject matter areas, in students committed to a given profession, and in persons already working within a profession (Arbuthnot and Gruenfeld, 1969; Barrett and Thornton, 1967; Bieri, Bradburn, and Galinsky, 1958; Frehner, 1971; Holtzman, Swartz, and Thorpe, 1971; MacKinnon, 1962; Rosenfeld, 1958; Rosett, Nackerson, Robbins, and Sapirstein, 1966; Sieben, 1971; Stein, 1968). In most of these studies the anticipated relation to field dependence versus field independence was found.

There is also evidence connecting cognitive style to choices and performance within a given domain. Thus, first-year graduate students entering a program in clinical psychology—the "human" end of the psychological spectrum, if you will—were significantly more field dependent than were students in the same school entering an experimental psychology program—the "abstract" end of the spectrum (Nagle, 1968). This outcome is undoubtedly a product of both self-selection by students and selection by program staff. Another study (Quinlan and Blatt, 1973) found that high-achieving students in psychiatric nursing were significantly more field dependent than were high-achieving students in surgical nursing, who tended to be field independent. And in still another study (Nussbaum, 1965), systems engineers were found to be more field independent than were engineers in other categories. Relevant here is the observation by Rosett and others (1966) that engineering students whose interests were mainly restricted to the physical sciences were more field independent than were those whose interests extended into other domains as well.

An important contribution to broad-spectrum assessment of cognitive style in relation to interests, preferences, and achievement was made by Chung (1967). Her study, already cited, examined Kuder Preference Scale performance in relation to the cognitive styles of leveling versus sharpening, constricted versus flexible control, and equivalence range, in addition to field dependence versus field independence. Whereas field dependence versus field independence related to interests, the other three styles showed little relation when considered individually. The patterns of the four styles taken together, however, showed interesting relations to expressed preferences. As one example, those who favored elementary school teaching tended to be field dependent, flexible, and intermediate both in leveling versus sharpening and equivalence range. Those favoring the natural sciences tended to be field independent, broad in equivalence range, and intermediate in constricted versus flexible control and leveling versus sharpening.

We have thus far examined the role of cognitive style in interests, preferences, choice, and achievement. There is also evidence that relatively field dependent and field independent students differ in their conceptualizing of occupations and in the ease with which they make educational and vocational choices. Some of the evidence comes from studies with children, again indicating the rather early influence of cognitive style in this domain.

Tyler and Sundberg (1964) examined the ways in which ninth-grade Dutch children classified occupational concepts. One kind of classification was characterized as concrete, immature, and primitive, with subjects using association rather than similarity as a basis for grouping. Tyler and Sundberg found that children who never employed this variety of occupational classification almost all achieved scores on the field independent side in our tests, although the converse was not true. Glatt (1970) found that field independent eighth-grade boys showed relatively greater readiness for occupational planning, as judged from interviews with them. To assess readiness Glatt used such criteria as awareness of factors relevant to curriculum choice and to occupational choice, ability to verbalize strengths and weaknesses, and accuracy of self-appraisal of cognitive abilities. And in still another study (Clar, 1971), this time with college students attending a university counseling center, the more field independent students were rated by counselors as more realistic in their vocational choices and more articulated in vocational interests; they also showed more specialized choices and more primary interests. The field dependent counselees, in contrast, were more often quite undecided about vocations at the termination of counseling. Osipow (1969) has reported results consistent with this last finding: a group of college women uncommitted to a course of study and admitting difficulty in making career choices were significantly more field dependent than were each of four other groups of women who were enrolled in specific programs and who made career choices with relative ease. From these first few studies of the processes by which career choices develop as a function of cognitive style, a pattern emerges: regardless of age, relatively field-dependent students have more difficulty in defining and articulating their career choices.

In view of the well-documented case for sex differences in field dependence, it is interesting to examine the domain of interests, preferences, and choices for men and women separately. The relations described between this domain and field dependence versus field independence have been found to hold within each sex. Men tend to exhibit interests in areas requiring analytic skills (technical and mechanical activities, for example). Women tend to prefer activities that involve dealing with people. As a parallel to the tendency for men to be more field independent than women and for field-independent persons to favor mathematics and science, we found in our longitudinal college study that more than twice as many men as women ended up majoring in these areas. Similarly, an overwhelmingly larger number of women than men majored in education, an area generally favored by more field dependent persons. Of the women in the college class we studied, 27 percent majored in education; only 2 percent of the men did so. We may add to this network of facts the observation that relatively field independent women strongly favor an "intellectual role" for themselves, whereas relatively field dependent women favor with equal strength a "women's role" (Greenwald, 1968). This observation is consistent with the repeated finding that among women (as among men) those who are more field independent tend to score at the masculine end of masculinity-femininity scales (Crutchfield, Woodworth, and Albrecht, 1958; Fink, 1959; Miller, 1953).

We can hardly assume that the marked sex differences found in occupational preference and choice are to be fully explained on the basis of field dependence versus field independence. Sex differences in this cognitive style, which appear to be established before the time in life when occupational choices are made, may indeed be a factor in these choices. More important, it seems likely that the sex role assignments within our society which contribute to development of sex differences in field dependence versus field independence also play an overriding role in the sex differences found in occupational choices.

In documenting the existence of sex differences, whether in cognitive style or in educational and occupational interests, preferences, and choices, we are simply describing the situation as we now find it. There is no assumption, of course, that this is the way it must be. Should it be considered desirable to do so, whether by the individual or by society, the sex-differences patterns in the linked characteristics of cognitive style and of interests, preferences, and choices can undoubtedly be altered. We will, however, be in a better position to bring about such changes if we become more fully aware of the sex differences that do exist and if we better understand the forces responsible for their development. We should also note that sex is likely to be an important moderator variable, influencing the relation between cognitive style and performance in the educational setting (Mebane and Johnson, 1970; Perney, 1971). This is an important area for further investigation.

Shifts in Majors. A final aspect of academic evolution should be considered in relation to cognitive style: the important phenomenon of shift in majors. The previously mentioned longitudinal study provides the relevant data. We determined for each student whether or not a shift took place from the major specified on college admission and the nature of the change when it occurred. First, we found that shifts tended to be more common among our relatively field dependent students.

Examination of the subject matter areas involved in switches in major gives more specific meaning to the role of cognitive style in affecting change. Taking a lead from the observation that field independent students tend to favor the mathematics-science domain and field dependent students the social sciences-humanities domain, we looked specifically at shifts between these two domains as a function of cognitive style. A first finding was that shifts out of mathematics and science were frequent, whereas shifts out of the social sciences and humanities were quite rare. We found that shifts out of mathematics and science were particularly common among the more field dependent students. A related finding revealed that among students who initially designated themselves as premedical, a science domain, the more field dependent ones more often abandoned this goal without ever applying to medical school. These shifts reflect movement toward a better fit between ability and career choice. Undoubtedly they resulted from the experiences these students must have had in their mathematics and science courses, experiences that indicated to them their lack of the analytical skills necessary for adequate performance in these areas. Just as impressive as their ability to read the signs and to change major, however, was the great frequency with which the more field dependent students made inappropriate initial choices.

In contrast to the frequent shifts out of the mathematics and science categories, we found, as noted above, strikingly few shifts when the social sciences and the humanities were the initial choices, with no difference between the more field dependent and the more field independent students in frequency of shifts. We may speculate that the pattern of few shifts out of the social sciences-humanities domain and frequent shifts out of the mathematics-science domain reflects the difference in relative specificity of the cognitive skills required by each domain. Clearly, in the mathematics-science domain, analytical ability is a specific requirement; without that ability it is difficult to make a comfortable home for oneself in this domain. Social sciences and humanities, on the other hand, are broad—gauged in their requirements. Though field dependent persons more often favor these disciplines, field independent persons may also find a congenial existence there. Psychology, with its clinical and experimental ends, provides an example. As we saw, relatively field dependent graduate students who entered this discipline gravitated toward the clinical end and the more field independent ones toward the experimental end. In view of these considerations, it should not be surprising that narrow-gauged areas like mathematics and science should show more of an exodus than broad-gauged areas. Nor should it be surprising that more field dependent students should be the main participants in the movement out of mathematics and science.

The basic four-year college longitudinal study is now being extended in two directions. We are retrospectively examining the high school records of our students and are also beginning a follow-up study of these same students into graduate school. In taking the latter step, we can examine the role of cognitive style in the decision to go on to graduate school, in the kind of graduate school favored, in eligibility for graduate school, in specialty selected, and in performance in different graduate subject matter areas. The downward extension of our longitudinal study into the high school period in conjunction with this follow-up into postgraduate study provides us with a twelve-year period over which we may pursue the implications of an individual's cognitive style for various facets of his academic development. In another study, the academic development of a group of children was followed from ages ten to twenty-four. The study showed that an individual's standing on the field dependence versus field independence dimension remains relatively stable over this fourteen-year period (Witkin and others, 1967). It is thus reasonable to predict that for students in the longitudinal study the cognitive assessments we made at the time of their admission into college are likely to reflect the students' cognitive makeup both in the earlier high school period and in the later graduate school period.

Teaching, Learning, and Teacher-Student Interaction

From all that has been said about the cognitive characteristics involved in field dependence or field independence and about the personal characteristics associated with these contrasting styles, it is easy to see that a teacher's cognitive style may influence his way of teaching, that a student's cognitive style may influence his way of learning, and that a match or mismatch in cognitive style between teacher and student may determine how well they get along, with important consequences for the learning process. Interestingly enough, the evidence available on these issues comes almost entirely from studies in which the students were of elementary or high school age. Essentially no work has been done with students on the college or graduate school levels.

While this neglect of the higher education period has many bases, one undoubtedly is the frequently made assumption that at the college level such issues no longer matter. The advanced scholarship of the instructor and his devotion to his subject matter, on the one hand, and the strong motivation of students who have made the voluntary choice to seek advanced training, on the other, are assumed to insure good teaching and good learning. I would seriously challenge this assumption. As will be seen later in this chapter, the role of cognitive style in other social interactions (for example, patient-therapist and interviewer-interviewee contexts) is similar to its role in teacher-student interaction. This similarity, even with variations in ground rules from one social context to another, suggests that the results of studies with younger students on the importance of cognitive style in teaching, learning, and teacher-student interaction are probably applicable to older students as well. Thus we could make a compelling case for extending these lines of work to the higher education level.

I will consider first the role of cognitive style in teacher behavior, then in student behavior, and finally in teacher-student interaction. As you will see, most potent in its effect on the classroom situation is the particular combination of teachers' and students' styles, the critical issue being whether they are matched or mismatched.

Teachers' Choices of Specialty Areas. As we have already noted, those who favor teaching as a profession are, as a group, likely to be relatively field dependent. This observation fits the well-documented finding that field dependent persons tend to favor occupations in which they spend their work time with others rather than alone. Though teachers tend to be field dependent as a group, there are obviously differences among them in regard to field dependence versus field independence. A good illustration of these differences lies in the choice of specialty area among teachers, which is directly related to the extent of field dependence or field independence (DiStefano, 1969). Teachers who select mathematics or science, for example, are likely to be relatively field independent; those who select social sciences are likely to be more field dependent. For reasons considered in the discussion of narrow-gauge and broad-gauge disciplines, it seems reasonable to expect that one would find a heavy concentration of more field independent teachers in the mathematics-science domain and a wider range of individual differences in cognitive style in the social sciences-humanities domain.

Teachers at the higher education level must pass through a longer period of self-selection and selection by others than teachers at other levels. Moreover, the advanced material they teach is more demanding. These facts lead to an interesting question: Are teachers within a specialty at the higher education level likely to show less diversity in cognitive style as compared to teachers at lower educational levels? Are teachers of college mathematics, for example, more homogeneously field independent than high school teachers of this subject? Only further research can provide answers.

Teaching Strategy. Relatively field dependent teachers have been found to prefer a discussion method of teaching to the lecturing or discovery methods preferred by relatively field independent teachers (Wu, 1968). Here again, the tendency of field dependent persons to seek interpersonal engagement, clearly more involved in a discussion approach than in lecturing, shows itself. The lecturing and discovery methods are more directive, giving greater responsibility for organizing the learning situation to the teacher. It is therefore not surprising that field independent teachers should favor such teaching methods. Confirming this observation, Ohnmacht (1967a) found that relatively field independent teachers are more direct in their attempt to influence students. Undoubtedly reflecting a similar difference, Ohnmacht also found that relatively field dependent teachers have a more favorable attitude toward the use of democratic classroom procedures than do field independent teachers (1967b, 1968).

It is impressive that the cognitive style of therapists has been found to have an effect on the conduct of therapy congruent with what has just been described for the teaching situation. Like the field dependent teachers who favor approaches that involve them with their students, field dependent therapists have been found to favor modes of therapy that make use of interpersonal relations with the patient as a vehicle for therapy. Field independent therapists, on the other hand, favor either directive or noninvolving approaches, both essentially noninterpersonal (Pollack and Kiev, 1963). Results from another study (Witkin, Lewis, and Weil, 1968) had a similar meaning: field dependent therapists interacted more with their patients than did the field independent therapists.

Studies by Ohnmacht (1967b, 1968) and Wu (1968) emphasize the important fact that patterns of teacher characteristics may relate to teacher behavior even when the characteristics taken singly do not. The Ohnmacht study showed

that teachers who were field dependent and high in dogmatism were less likely to be imaginative and stimulating in
the classroom than were those who were field independent
and low in dogmatism. Yet neither field dependence alone
nor dogmatism alone, dimensions which are orthogonal,
showed a relation to these characteristics of classroom behavior. In Wu's study the same combination of field dependence
and high dogmatism was associated with greater effectiveness in handling student questions involving logical fallacies;
the teacher had to detect these fallacies and then guide pupils toward finding the answers themselves.

Related to these studies of teachers' cognitive styles and
their impact on teaching is a study by Rennels (1970) which
evaluated the effect of teaching styles conceived to follow
either a field dependent or a field independent approach.
Using disadvantaged urban black children selected from
the two extremes of the field dependence versus field independence dimension, Rennels attempted to train them in
perception of spatial relations by either an analytic method,
which he attempted to pattern in accord with a field independent approach, or a synthetic method, supposedly
patterned after a field dependent approach. Contrary to
expectations, both field dependent and field independent
children did better with training by the analytic method than
they did with training by the synthetic method. An important question raised by these results is whether or not the
learning of a particular kind of material (in this case spatial
relations) may be favored by a particular kind of teaching
method (in this case analytical), overriding the effects of
teacher or student cognitive style. The role of such situational
factors as material to be learned is important to consider in
examining the effects of teachers' and students' cognitive
styles.

How Students Learn. Having examined the way in which
teaching may be influenced by the teacher's cognitive style,
let us turn now to the other side of the coin and consider how
cognitive style may influence the way a student learns.

First, it has been shown that the amount of knowledge students acquire by different teaching methods tends to be related to their cognitive styles (Grieve and Davis, 1971). In this study, a comparison was made of the amount of geography learned with either an expository or discovering method of teaching by extremely field dependent and extremely field independent ninth-grade children. In the discovery method "verbalization of generalizations being taught was delayed until the end of the instructional sequence," whereas in the expository method "verbalization of the required generalizations was the initial step of the instructional sequence" (page 139). One interesting finding was that the more field dependent the boy, the more likely was he to benefit from discovery instruction. This outcome makes sense when we consider that in the discovery method, as compared to the expository method, learning takes place through interaction with the teacher, a context congenial to the social orientation of the more field dependent student.

Research on cognitive style as a factor in another kind of social interaction—patient-therapist relations—has produced a finding that may have implications for the teacher-student interaction. Greene (1972) recently reported that therapists significantly more often chose supportive therapy for their field-dependent patients than for their field-independent patients, for whom modifying therapy was favored. Karp, Kissin, and Hustmyer (1970) obtained a similar result in a study of alcoholic patients. In light of the field dependent person's need for structure from external social sources, it indeed makes sense that supportive therapy should be recommended for them. It seems reasonable to predict from such evidence that field dependent students would find the learning situation more congenial and, hence, would learn more in a supportive setting.

We have already noted how strongly a student's cognitive style affects his choice of major and educational preferences. Ordinarily, students may be expected to do better in subject matter areas that fit their cognitive styles. However, such a generalization should by no means lead us to give up on field dependent students who are in areas which do not fit their styles. For example, while field dependent students may be limited in how far they are able to progress in advanced mathematics, it is likely that by teaching methods specifically attuned to their cognitive style, such students may do better than we now imagine. Spitler (1971), for example, has spelled out alternative methods of teaching mathematics to field dependent and field independent students, each method exploiting the cognitive style of the student for whom it is intended. It is also worth noting here the repeated observation that children with learning difficulties, especially in the area of reading, tend to be field dependent (Bruininks, 1969; Keogh and Donlon, 1972; Robbins, 1962; Severson, 1963; Stuart, 1967). Though there is not sufficient space to consider what I believe to be the underlying basis of this connection, I merely cite it to show that cognitive style may provide a useful approach to the investigation of specific learning problems.

On still another front is a connection suggested between cognitive style and learning. Social reinforcement, usually taking the form of praise for good deeds and criticism for bad ones, is, of course, a common technique used by teachers as a stimulus to learning. The idea that there may be a relation between field dependence versus field independence and social reinforcement arises very naturally in view of the social characteristics of children with contrasting cognitive styles. This relation has been examined in many studies (Busch, 1971; Ferrel, 1971; Fitz, 1971; Konstadt and Forman, 1965; Paclisanu, 1970; Randolph, 1971; Ruble and Nakamura, 1972; Shapson, 1969; Stark, Parker, and Iverson, 1959; Wade, 1972). As may be expected, the evidence suggests that field independent people are likely to learn more than field dependent people under conditions of intrinsic motivation. No differences in learning are found under conditions of external rewards, but criticism has a greater impact on the learning of field dependent people. It is not difficult to imagine the important consequences of such differences in response to social reinforcement for learning and teaching.

Teacher-Student Interaction. The results of a study by DiStefano (1969) provide evidence on the consequences of match or mismatch in cognitive style between teacher and students. DiStefano had extremely field dependent and extremely field independent teachers describe their students, all of whom had been assessed for field independence. Similarly, these students were asked to describe their teachers (teachers and students were all males). The results were very striking. Teachers and students matched for cognitive style described each other in highly positive terms, whereas teachers and students who were mismatched showed a strong tendency to describe each other negatively. Especially important in its implications for how teachers evaluate their students' abilities was the finding that teachers valued more highly the intellects of students similar to themselves in cognitive style and not only the personal characteristics of these students. Similarly, students viewed more favorably the cognitive competence and personal characteristics of teachers similar to themselves in cognitive style. Findings such as these raise an important question: Is it not too simplistic to speak just of good teachers and bad teachers, even though by some criteria of competence such designations may be justified? It would seem more appropriate to think of teachers as good or bad for a particular kind of student and, similarly, to consider students good or bad for a specific kind of teacher.

Effects of match or mismatch in cognitive style similar to those just described have been found in other kinds of interaction situations, pointing to the generality of these effects. Greene (1972), in the study cited earlier, found that patients from patient-therapist dyads in which patient and therapist both were field dependent or in which both were field independent tended to rate the therapist's relation toward them more positively than did patients from dyads incongruent in cognitive style. It is noteworthy that neither patient's style or therapist's style had a significant effect on interpersonal attraction when considered alone.

The powerful influence of the particular combination of cognitive styles in a social interaction, beyond the contribution made by the style of each participant considered separately, was also evident in the patient-therapist interaction study cited earlier (Witkin and others, 1968). Field dependent patients and field dependent therapists each participated more in the interaction than their field-independent counterparts, as judged by the number of interactions during the therapeutic hour. When therapist and patient were matched in terms of cognitive style, the combined effect of these tendencies was particularly striking. For example, the combination of the most field dependent therapist with his field dependent patient produced 5.1 interactions per minute or 268 interactions in the course of the therapeutic hour. In contrast, the combination of the most field independent therapist and his field independent patient produced only .8 interactions per minute, or 38 interactions during the hour. Another indication of the interacting effect of dyad members' cognitive styles is found in the way in which the therapist's behavior is affected by the style of the patient. Though field dependent therapists tended to intervene more than field independent ones, the therapists, regardless of cognitive style, showed a higher rate of intervention with their field dependent patients than with their field independent ones. We may also recall here that in the studies by Greene (1972) and by Karp and others (1970) therapists adapted their therapeutic approach to the cognitive style of their patients, favoring a more supportive kind of therapy for field dependent patients and a modifying form of therapy for their field independent patients.

It appears that the contribution of cognitive style to mutual attraction or dislike is evident even after a very short period of interaction. In the study by Witkin and others (1968) the effects noted were obtained in the very first hour of therapy. In a recently completed study by Oltman, Goodenough, Witkin, Freedman, and Friedman (1975), evidence of cognitive style effects was obtained after twenty-five minutes of interaction. Quite clearly the processes by which these effects are achieved work very quickly. Might this mean that the consequences of cognitive style for the classroom situation are already established in the very first session teacher and student spend together? If so, are they strengthened with time or can they be modified? These are questions in need of research.

Still to be considered in its implication for the classroom is the effect of the subject matter being studied on teacher-student interaction as a function of their cognitive styles. Take mathematics, for example. In view of the clear linkage between field independence and competence in mathematics, would match or mismatch have different effects if mathematics is the subject matter area rather than, for example, the social sciences? The importance of taking situational factors into account in assessing the effects of match or mismatch in cognitive style was shown in the dyadic interaction study (Witkin and others, 1968) by the finding that characteristics of the task around which the subjects had to interact could modify cognitive style effects.

The finding that people matched in cognitive style are likely to get along better in such social contexts as teacher-student, patient-therapist, and interviewer-interviewee interactions provides still another demonstration that similarity makes for mutual attraction. Of special interest here, however, are the cues associated with cognitive style that people pick up about each other in the course of their interaction, even after a brief period of time together. They do not know each other's rod and frame test scores, and even if they did, I am sure they would not know what to make of them without the lengthy explanation given here. Compared with the high visibility of similarity in attitude on the Vietnam war, for example, the cues reflecting on cognitive style are surely less tangible; yet they must be there and usable for the effects described to occur at all.

The question of cues leads to the larger question of the processes involved in the interactions between people which have liking or disliking as their end-product. The answer to this complex question obviously has important implications for human relations in general. My colleagues and I are in the midst of studies which we hope may help answer this question, at least in the context of teacher-student interaction.

The evidence on hand at the time we planned this study suggested that persons matched in cognitive style tend to get along better for three possible reasons: first, because of shared foci of interest; second, because of shared personal characteristics; and, third, because of similarity in communication modes, making for easier and more effective communication. Let me comment on each of these factors.

Bases for Interpersonal Attraction with Matched Cognitive Styles. With regard to shared foci of interest, the evidence clearly shows that relatively field dependent persons are especially sensitive to the social surround. Their shared tendency to attend selectively to the social content of the environment is likely to help two people of this kind to get along better when they interact. Similarly, when two field independent persons interact, their shared interest in the more impersonal, abstract aspects of their surround should again make for a positive outcome in feelings toward each other.

One further piece of evidence should be added to the extensive evidence in the preceding sections showing the strong social orientation of field dependent persons. Concerning what may be considered a "visible" aspect of social orientation, meaning that it shows itself in overt behavior directly manifest to others, this evidence comes from a recent study by Justice (1970) which investigated the use of interpersonal space as a function of field dependence. The method used for this investigation was really very simple. The subject was asked to prepare a brief talk on an assigned topic and then to go into an adjacent room to present this talk to the experimenter sitting there. On the whole this request tended to be rather anxiety-provoking. The distance between the subject and the experimenter was then measured. A chalk mark and ruler were the only props needed in this procedure. The findings revealed that relatively field dependent subjects ended up significantly closer to the experimenter than did the more field independent subjects. This behavior reflects in a very concrete way the field dependent person's need for closeness to others, especially under conditions of discomfort. It could well be that this difference in need for physical proximity between relatively field dependent and field independent persons has a jarring effect when two such people come together, and it may produce in them negative feelings toward each other. In contrast, persons similar in cognitive style may be more likely to assume positions in the physical space they share which are more congenial to each of them, again with more positive consequences for getting along.

Another item of evidence having to do with visibility will serve to illustrate the second possible basis for greater mutual attraction between persons of like cognitive style, which is similarity in personal characteristics. In their study, White and Kernaleguen (1971) found that the more field dependent female students were likely to wear their clothes at a length commonplace for their peer group, whereas the more field independent students tended to wear clothes that were relatively unusual in length. The clothing a person wears is plain for all to see. Could differences in manner of dress between persons differing in cognitive style possibly contribute to irritation, perhaps even immediately on encountering each other?

There is also significant evidence suggesting that persons of the same cognitive style use similar modes of communication and that this, in turn, facilitates understanding, again with positive consequences for their ability to get along with each other. Here too I want to focus on characteristics that tend to be visible. First, from studies of psycholinguistic differences as a function of cognitive style, there is evidence that in their ongoing speech field dependent and field independent persons differ in the frequency with which they use particular word categories. One difference is in the extent of reference to themselves versus reference to the external field, particularly to other persons. Thus, it has been found (Jennings, 1968) that field dependent persons make fewer self-references in their speech. Confirming this, Luborsky (personal communication, 1969) found that the ratio of other-people references to self-references was significantly higher in the speech of field dependent persons; that is, proportionately, they referred more to other people than to themselves. As still another example, Doob (1958) found that field independent persons use the personal pronoun and active verbs more often than do their field dependent counterparts. Findings such as these indicate that people with contrasting cognitive styles reflect in their linguistic modes the differences in their overall personal orientations. If when nominally discussing the same topic, two people are in effect talking about different things—not speaking the same language—it is not likely that they will get along very well. That people of similar cognitive style do better at reading each other's verbal messages is suggested by a finding of Shows (1967). In this study Shows had field dependent and field independent persons prepare verbal descriptions of a series of pictures. Subjects of a given cognitive style did significantly better in matching verbal descriptions to pictures when they were given descriptions prepared by subjects who had the same cognitive style as they had.

There is another communication mode in which field dependent and field independent persons are different. Building on an earlier observation that in the course of interaction persons differing in characteristic rate of speech are likely to adapt their speech rates to each other, Marcus (1970) examined this congruence phenomenon as a function of field dependence. She found that movement toward congruence in an interaction between people was the particular contribution of the relatively more field dependent partner. In this evidence of the field dependent person's greater sensitivity in tracking the speech of others, we have still another demonstration of their attentiveness to other people.

Finally, in still another communication modality—hand gestures accompanying speech—field-dependent and field-independent persons again are different (Freedman, O'Hanlon, Oltman, and Witkin, 1972).

These observations suggest that specific features of communication are associated with cognitive style. It seems that persons of the same cognitive style emit similar signs. To the extent that this puts them on the same wavelength, it is reasonable that they should relate better to each other. It seems equally reasonable that communication should be less effective between persons of contrasting cognitive style, making for greater difficulty in getting along.

As I mentioned above, studies of the effect on social interaction of match or mismatch in cognitive style are well under way. In one study (Oltman, Goodenough, Witkin, Freedman, and Friedman, 1975) now completed, we examined dyadic interactions under conditions of initial conflict. In another study we are examining teacher-student interactions. The main purpose of this study is to identify the specific interaction processes through which match in cognitive style leads to mutual positive evaluation and mismatch to mutual negative evaluation.

In concluding this discussion of teacher-student interaction, I should stress that I have focused on the positive features of match between teachers and students in cognitive style only because that is what the evidence currently available has shown. There may be negative features as well. Moreover, we do not yet know whether teacher-student match in cognitive style makes for better student learning in addition to greater interpersonal attraction. A decision on which teacher-student combination achieves the best learning results obviously requires consideration of many other cognitive styles, as well as of variables of other sorts. To make appropriate decisions about teacher-student mixes, we need to build up a fund of knowledge, gained through systematic research, on the many other variables that influence teaching and learning effectiveness. I hope the studies we are currently involved in will enrich this fund of knowledge.

Applications

Application of the concepts, techniques, and findings from cognitive style research to problems of education is just in its beginning phase. Sparse as the evidence I have been able to muster is therefore, I trust it has been sufficient to demonstrate the potential value of a cognitive style approach to a wide range of educational problems.

Perhaps the best way to summarize the value of this approach is to note some of the ways in which it is particularly suited to the kind of assessment of students and teachers needed in the educational setting and to identify some of its advantages for this task over standard intelligence tests.

First, cognitive style research is leading to the identification of a number of salient cognitive dimensions beyond those now represented on typical intelligence tests. Together with the fact that cognitive style encompasses perceptual as well as intellectual functioning, this means that the cognitive style approach gives promise of more comprehensive coverage of the cognitive domain than do our usual intelligence tests. Moreover, because cognitive styles are dimensions of individual functioning which extend beyond the cognitive domain, they reveal much about personality and social behavior. Characterization of an individual in terms of cognitive style thus covers a great deal of psychological territory.

As I have noted elsewhere (Witkin, 1969b), it is not far-fetched to imagine that test batteries emerging from cognitive style research may in time replace intelligence tests. Historically, the development of intelligence tests outran the development of a theory of intelligence. This is understandable, for with the compelling need to classify children in the schools, test development could not await adequate theory. Thus the tests that have emerged have more of an empirical basis than a theoretical basis. Essentially they consist of groups of tasks which, by experience, have been found to discriminate between slow-learning and fast-learning children. But we do not know as much as we should about the psychological processes involved in carrying out these tasks. Nor do we always have an adequate rationale for using the particular tasks we do. In fact, there is the paradox that much work has gone into finding a conceptual rationale for these tasks *after* they have long been in use. The work on cognitive style is following a more rational course toward test development: a progression from theory, to specific test rationale, to test construction.

It is worth noting here that the tests now used to assess individual differences in field dependence versus independence emerged after half a dozen years of intensive research on the perceptual processes underlying performance in the kinds of tasks these tests feature. Test standardization, which was undertaken only after our interest in individual differences developed, was enormously aided by knowledge gained through the basic perceptual research which preceded it. This kind of history of test development makes it possible to infer underlying process from scores achieved on such tests to a far greater extent than is possible with the usual intelligence tests, with their quite different developmental histories.

Another important contrast between a cognitive style approach and the abilities approach emphasized in intelligence tests lies in their implications for placement in the broadest sense. With abilities, virtue lies in their possession; to lack them is to be deficient. The value emphasis is thus unipolar. With cognitive styles the cognitive and personal characteristics involved allow persons at either pole a proper share in the world's work. As we saw, relatively field dependent and field independent persons gravitate, appropriately, toward different subject matter areas in school and toward different occupations afterward. We also saw that each style is likely to contribute to high achievement in the area to which it is suited. Recall, for example, that field independent student nurses did particularly well in surgery; field dependent student nurses did particularly well in psychiatry.

With growing knowledge about salient cognitive styles, I am confident that in time we will be able to identify each person's cognitive pattern, composed of his particular cognitive styles. A major factor-analytic study of cognitive styles, in progress for a number of years under the leadership of Samuel Messick, is now nearing completion. Represented in this work have been all the cognitive styles on record at the time the study was undertaken. Those of us who have been close to this research expect, with good reason, that it will lead to a major advance in the definition and codification of cognitive styles and in the identification of reliable tests for a number of cognitive styles which have not yet been examined to the same degree as the field dependence versus independence dimension.

Cognitive maps offer promise of a rich, complex, and comprehensive way of characterizing individuals both in their cognitive functioning and in their broader psychological functioning. An individual's cognitive pattern represents his unique cognitive makeup, including areas of strength and weakness. An outcome of the cognitive pattern approach is to emphasize the multiplicity of ways in which people may be different from each other. The cognitive pattern concept emphasizes individuality and deemphasizes placement along a single better-or-worse continuum. For us, as educators, individuality is surely a quality to be cherished in our appreciation of students and teachers.

4

Commentary:
Process and Context
in the Conception of
Cognitive Style

SEYMOUR WAPNER

The program of research conducted under Herman Witkin's leadership for more than a quarter of a century has produced an integrated pattern of knowledge about cognitive style and is as vigorous today as it was in its inception. Because of space limitations, let me simply assume that you too are convinced that Witkin and his associates have taken a giant step in their creative, novel approach to some central problems of education: a cognitive style approach to academic development of the student, to the processes of learning and teaching, and to the interactions of students and teachers. Having accepted this conclusion that the approach has enormous potential, I will turn abruptly to the problems and issues of next steps. My formulations here, as might be expected, are

Supported, in part, by Research Grant MH 00348 from the National Institute of Mental Health.

grounded in the assumptions underlying my own perspective, which is organismic, holistic, systemic, and developmental in emphasis (Wapner, Kaplan, and Cohen, 1973). My comments are largely restricted to four issues: achievement-oriented versus process-oriented studies, conceptualization of cognitive style, the nature of the social context, and the ideal dyadic relation for learning and teaching.

Process versus Achievement

It seems to me crucial that cognitive style research be shifted from achievement-oriented to process-oriented studies (Werner, 1937). Witkin clearly recognizes this need in his discussion of studies on occupational planning and on interpersonal interactions having liking or disliking as the end-product. Here, I want to emphasize that correlational studies of end-products—expressions of interests, preferences, choices, feelings—are necessarily limited. Since the relationship between achievement and underlying process is not one-to-one, a given behavioral outcome may result from a variety of underlying processes, and a given process may be manifest in many outcomes. The expressed choice to be a social science teacher may have multiple processes underlying it—peer influence, the influence of a social science teacher, a personal assessment of one's own capacity, and so forth. Conversely, the single process of being responsive to an authority figure, a teacher or father, for example, may underlie multiple end-achievements, such as becoming an engineer, a social science teacher, or a bricklayer.

It is my conviction that achievement-oriented approaches using a restricted number of dependent measures in a circumscribed situation will fail in providing the precision of prediction we desire in identifying potential graduate students. I am convinced, moreover, that this holds true regardless of whether such approaches focus on intellectual accomplishment and ability, as does the Graduate Record Examination, or on cognitive style. We may already be successful with achievement-oriented instruments in weeding out those who are clearly the poorest risks; but, only from a basic understanding of the processes which underlie and link the end-products will we be able to approach the ideal of predicting accurately throughout the entire range of potential performance. While a shift to process-oriented studies is one condition necessary for accomplishing such a goal, it would be an error to think that it is the only necessary condition.

Conceptualization of Cognitive Style

Another direction for future development of the cognitive style approach to problems of education relates to a possible variation in its conceptualization. Convenience of presentation sometimes erroneously makes it sound as if field independence and field dependence were personality types. In fact, Witkin rejects a typology and treats field independence versus field dependence as a personality dimension, with individuals differing in the degree to which they are located toward the independence or dependence poles; further, their position on this continuum is idealized as restricted to a narrow band and as stable. Test-retest correlations are relatively high, as are correlations among different test situations presumed to measure the same dimension. But since these correlations do in fact fall far short of unity, they do not account for a large proportion of the variance. I maintain that personality dimensions are not independent of the context in which they operate and should not be defined as such; even cognitive styles, which speak to personal characteristics, must be conceptualized as properties of organism-environment systems.

This approach suggests an avenue for capturing the basis of the variance unaccounted for by the correlations reported by Witkin. First, the approach assumes that there are crucial aspects of the environmental context other than those embodied in the rod and frame test and the embedded figures test, the classical measures of field dependence versus independence. Second, these aspects of the environmental context are assumed to interact with intrapsychic and intrasomatic factors, including those underlying field dependence versus independence. Third, it is expected that, within ranges differing from one person to another, shifts in style may occur in response to these special features of the environmental context (social and physical) in which the person is operating on the given occasion. Thus, for example, there may be students who are more field dependent in the presence of an aggressive teacher and relatively less field dependent in the presence of a submissive teacher. To characterize people as occupying a *range* on the field dependence versus field independence dimension, with their manifest behavior depending on the particular environmental context, involves a significant reconceptualization. In this view cognitive style does not deal with surface structure but rather with deeper aspects of microstructure. The reconceptualization represents a shift from a concept that is based on similarities of behavior to a concept of cognitive style that can subsume seeming polarities and contrarieties of manifest performance. This reformulation avoids making cognitive style into an ideal typology; it permits a closer-to-life characterization of the person that incorporates surface contradictions. Accordingly, it may add significant power to the cognitive style approach and thereby provide the precision necessary for more accurate prediction.

The Social Context

In order to put this conceptualization to work, it is not only necessary to sample a variety of environmental contexts, but to treat a specific context in a more general way. Though the teacher is a very significant part of the classroom situation, the social context of learning goes beyond the teacher and must be treated broadly. The social context encompasses the spirit of a place, the rules and norms which govern the actions of its inhabitants, the expectations about how things are to be done, the modes of interaction of people, the general atmosphere of the classroom, laboratory, hallways, and the coffee shop. Even within a given discipline, there are striking differences in the ethos and spirit of graduate departments; these differences are linked to the goals, philosophy, rules, and methods, as well as to the particular group of teachers comprising the department. Consider two extremes: On the one hand, we have a large graduate department with a rigidly fixed curriculum, requiring a strict sequence in completing the "rites of passage," with graded tests and papers as part of the ever present bit-by-bit feedback to the student. On the other hand, we have a small department with a flexible curriculum, with deemphasis of more formal piecemeal evaluation, with little day-to-day feedback, with students left to monitor themselves and to find their own way of learning by doing and by contagion in an atmosphere of productive scholarship (Taylor, Garner, and Hunt, 1959). The first department is highly structured and outer-directed in form, whereas the latter department is relatively unstructured and inner-directed. Which is more optimal for the field independent or field dependent student and teacher? Even if assessing cognitive style yielded stable characteristics, it is not an easy question to answer.

The Dyadic Relation Between Student and Teacher

Witkin, of course, touched on this general question of optimal relationships when he dealt with the dyadic relation between teacher and student in terms of match or mismatch in cognitive style. He suggested, on the basis of a number of studies, that with a match in cognitive style there is greater mutual attraction of student and teacher, greater communication through use of similar communication modes, and greater understanding and creation of a good atmosphere for learning. But is this the kind of environment that is optimal for learning? Clearly, such a question raises the more general issue of what constitutes an environment that will maximize individual development and individual creativity. Is an environment optimal if it conforms to the student's expectations? Is an environment optimal if the student and teacher have understanding because they share similarity of viewpoint? A powerful argument can be made that opposition, contradiction, and obstacles are necessary conditions for individual development and creativity. Perhaps placing the field-dependent person in the unstructured, inner-directed environment advances his creativity. Surely, optimal conditions for this dyadic relation must vary according to the goals of the educational situation in question—nursery school, elementary school, high school, college, graduate or professional school, or a particular discipline within a graduate school. Optimal conditions differ according to the goals a given graduate department defines: education for research, education for undergraduate teaching, or education for application in industry and private practice. There are differences that depend on whether the goal of the department is for the student to learn a subject matter or to become a creative scholar. And, surely, whether or not a dyadic match or a mismatch is optimal depends on the goals of the particular student. The analysis which will yield answers to the questions of optimal conditions for training of individuals of a given cognitive style, as well as answers to the questions of selecting and placing graduate students in environments which can maximize individual development, must take into account the student; it must consider his goals and instrumentalities; it must also consider the general features of the environmental context—the ethos, rules, goals, and philosophy of the training setting—as experienced, viewed, and construed by the participants.

In sum, the main directions I have described for next steps include several shifts: to process-oriented studies, to a notion of cognitive style that allows for individual variability, to a broadening of the notion of social context, and to a search for optimal conditions for learning and development that involve contrariety and opposition as well as conformity. Hopefully, these are directions which will lead us to uncover effective methods of selection and of training and will thereby help us to create a synergistic relationship of people in educational environments that will actualize the goals of higher education.

5

Commentary: The Double Bind of Field Dependence/Independence in Program Alternatives for Educational Development

ARTHUR W. CHICKERING

Witkin's studies of field dependence and field independence are important to higher education for two reasons: first, because his work has major implications for researchers and theoreticians interested in understanding how varied institutional environments and educational practices influence the cognitive and affective development of college students; second, because it has major implications for college administrators and faculty members who must make decisions about those environments and practices. This latter group is especially significant now when so many new alternatives are being considered, created, and examined. Let me start, however, by considering some of the implications of Witkin's work for research.

Stability and Development of Cognitive Style

Although cognitive styles are apparently quite stable, a question remains as to whether this stability necessarily implies fixity or whether cognitive styles are modifiable through education or training. Witkin, Goodenough, and Karp (1967) studied the same group of persons over an age range of ten to twenty-four years and found that an individual's relative standing on field dependence versus field independence within the group was highly stable. At the same time, the group as a whole displayed a progressive increase in extent of field independence up to age seventeen, with little further change up to age twenty-four.

This period of negligible average change from age seventeen to twenty-four is of particular importance because it corresponds roughly to the college years. Why the cessation of the trend toward increasing field independence? Was an asymptote reached that limited further individual change? Was there a change in socialization experiences? Were some individuals placed in environments that continued to facilitate positive changes for them while others confronted environments inducing negative changes, thereby cancelling each other's trends when individuals were pooled to form group averages? In my own research on college impacts, there were in some cases no mean changes occurring on measures of autonomy, complexity, and intellectual interests, and in some institutions these findings really reflected minimal college impact and little change. But at other institutions, even though there were no mean changes, there were substantial individual changes in contrary directions, changes that reflected differential impact depending upon the fit between the characteristics of the students and the characteristics of the institution.

The change data which emerge from the current longitudinal study by Witkin and his colleagues should be very interesting. It is difficult for me to believe that change does not occur on the field-dependence dimension during the college years and that such changes are not related to differences in college experiences and activities. Witkin himself suggests that this dimension is heavily related to socialization experiences and, despite sex differences, only minimally to genetic factors. In addition, the Yando and Kagan (1968) study reports changes toward greater reflectiveness on the part of students taught by reflective teachers. Higher education research has documented changes in other areas very closely associated with the reflection versus impulsivity dimension, such as impulse expression, authoritarianism, autonomy, complexity, liberalism, and intellectual disposition. The research of Witkin and his associates already has established relationships between field dependence and some of these variables. If no change occurred in field dependence and if no relationships to educational experiences and activities were found, it would mean that the field dependence versus independence characteristic has a stability among young adults that is not shared by several other similar variables.

There is one other research issue that is simple to state and critical for educational planning. What is the distribution of field dependence and field independence in the normal population? I understand that it is continuous. Is it normal? skewed? bimodal? Is it possible to identify proportions of the population above and below particular criteria? These questions lead directly into the issues faced by educational administrators, and such information would help administrators make more sound decisions about their own programs.

Differentiation and Integration in Educational Development

In *Education and Identity* (Chickering, 1969) I urged educational decision makers to recognize two simple and self-evident developmental principles. The work of Witkin and his associates has powerful implications for these principles. The first principle is that much significant human development occurs through cycles of differentiation and integration. (John Dewey had a simpler term; he called it "the reconstruction of experience.") Increased differentiation occurs when one comes to see the interacting parts of something formerly seen as unitary, when one distinguishes among concepts formerly seen as similar, when one's actions are more finely responsive to individual purposes or to outside conditions, when one's interests become more varied, tastes more diverse, reactions more subtle—in short, as one becomes a more complex human being. It is to foster increased differentiation that a liberal arts college aims to free an individual from the limitations of outlook brought from his own locale, his family, his social class, his national heritage—a freeing that opens him to all the possibilities and impossibilities of the world around him, a freeing that can lead to heightened sensitivity and awareness and that can also lead to coldness and insensitivity as the monstrous inconsistencies in the ways of the world are more clearly seen and more sharply experienced. Increasing differentiation, however, must be accompanied by increasing integration. Relationships among parts must be perceived or constructed so more complex wholes result. Concepts from different disciplines must be brought to bear on one another and connected in ways appropriate to varied tasks and problems. Effective education essentially is the amplification of those two basic developmental processes, and when it works it makes persons different, different from what they were before and different from each other.

Such education must be distinguished from training. Training, when it works, makes persons more alike. It aims to develop a shared language, shared skills, shared information, shared objectives, and, in time, shared values. Training starts with the task and conforms the learner to it; education starts with the learner and uses tasks in the service of increased differentiation and integration.

The second simple principle, also rather universally ignored, is that the impact of an experience depends upon the characteristics of the person who encounters it. When individuals differ, a single experience can have diverse developmental outcomes. The impact of a class, course, or curriculum, of a teacher, peer, or college subculture varies with the background, ability level, and personality characteristics of the student.

The work of Witkin and his associates, I repeat, has obvious implications for these two basic principles. A fundamental difference between field-dependent and field-independent students lies in their analytic ability: in their perceptual and cognitive ability to distinguish figure from ground, to separate a construct from its surrounding context, and to restructure problem situations so that a construct can be used in a different way. This amounts to a continuum of individual differences in the capacities required for those basic developmental cycles of differentiation and integration.

The field-dependent student, in comparison to her independent peer, needs stronger triggers if differentiation is to occur; the faculty member, fellow student, book, lecture, film, field experience—all must present a greater degree of discontinuity and must reveal it more obviously and powerfully if it is to be perceived and acted on. Differentiation for the field-independent student, however, will be triggered much more readily. She may be blasted wide open by an experience that has little impact on her field-dependent classmate. Consequently, she may need to move much more quickly toward activities through which a higher level of integration may be achieved—quiet reflection, writing, long conversations with friends who are coping with similar issues. To be required to face a more extended and extensive barrage of stimuli may at the least be a waste of time, and at worst it may create serious problems. She may be faced with such a wide array of complex realizations that she is unable to organize and digest them before important decisions are required, or she may grasp too quickly and totalistically a new alternative which reduces anxiety and uncertainty, but which itself creates a new array of problems. We have seen both kinds of outcomes in our colleges and universities: students who have been untouched and students who have been bowled over.

As Witkin's findings make clear, effective education depends upon a sound match between the characteristics of the

student and the characteristics of the programs and persons
the student encounters, and the field dependence versus
field independence continuum represents a dimension of
difference to take into account. It must also be taken into
account for effective training, and all students need both
training and education. The training program which is effective for the field-dependent student may not be for the
field-independent one. Training usually involves an authoritarian dynamic and often a working relationship with
a supervising authority. This dynamic is much more likely
to interfere with the successful achievement of the field-
independent student than with his more dependent counterpart and more often will need to be explicitly recognized
and dealt with. It will probably also be the case that the field-
independent student will more frequently be distracted by
questions of value and will more frequently want to know
the whys and wherefores of various training requirements
and procedures.

The situation, however, is more complicated than the
above generalizations suggest. And it is at this point, as one
who is trying to think through and help develop a new institution, that I wish Witkin and his colleagues would quietly
scuttle their research and burn their papers. The problem
is that they move me far beyond my own capacity to create
an effective integration at the level of complexity required
by the rich differentiations made possible by their research.

The Misalignment of Program Alternatives

Higher education in this country and abroad is testing two
major new alternatives which, for the sake of parsimony, can
be called contract learning and programed learning. The
varied approaches to contract learning usually share the
following major characteristics. Programs are individually
designed and implemented through conferences with a faculty
member who is variously termed a mentor, adviser, precep-
tor, counselor, and so forth. The emphasis is on building individualized educational programs which take each student's

interests and purposes seriously and which respond flexibly to those needs when they change. Often the programs can include field experiences as well as the more typical academic activities, such as readings, writing, courses, and the like. The varied approaches to programed learning reveal a range of complexity and organization. There are highly articulated and systematized computer-assisted instructional programs that provide for complex branching on the basis of frequent examinations administered and corrected by the computer; there are systematically organized printed materials that include periodic papers and examinations that are sent to correspondence tutors for correction as well as assigned readings; and there are other more loosely organized study guides and reading lists, these last making little provision for systematic examination or feedback.

Now a bit of thought about the characteristics of field-dependent and field-independent students, and also about the characteristics of field-dependent and field-independent teachers, will suggest that neither of these new approaches is really on target. Both create double binds for students and problems for administrators and teachers.

Take the field-dependent student first. The contract approach offers rich opportunities for human interaction. A student can actually sit down alone with a faculty member periodically and discuss her education at some length. Furthermore, she can build into her educational program working relationships with other students and apprentice relationships with other adults in ways that were not open to her before. The teaching approach is nonexpository, much closer to the discussion method than to the lecturing method. In these aspects it appears ideal for the field-dependent student. It may be especially comfortable when she is working with a field-dependent teacher who is drawn to the contract approach primarily because of the opportunities for close human relationships with students and who lacks the tough analytic capacities of the field-independent teacher. But at the same time, the contract approach is highly self-referent. Students are asked to identify and clarify their own purposes and plans. They are asked to think about why they are going to college and what they want to accomplish by doing so. They are asked to take initiative for their own education, to say over and over, "I do," rather than "I am done to." But as is made clear by the Jennings (1968), Luborsky (personal communication), and Doob (1958) studies of communication patterns and by much of the other research reported, the capacity of the field-dependent student to be self-referent is limited. She finds it difficult to take herself, her own ideas, values, attitudes, plans, and impulses as the starting point for thinking and action. Given this double bind, it is not surprising that few field-dependent students, if I may now use the term loosely, have been found in the student-centered institutions and programs of the past and that few are flocking in that direction today.

Programed learning presents a different set of problems for the field-dependent student. In programed learning the root assumption is that the student wants to learn what the program has to teach. Few programs really test that assumption beyond spelling out the objectives so that the student can make his choice on a reasonably informed basis. Then they simply start helping the student go to it. Programed learning, therefore, does not raise the self-referent questions posed by contract learning. The difficulties for the field-dependent student are that it is expository, it usually puts a premium on analytic skills, and it offers little or no opportunity for human interaction.

The field-independent student faces a different combination of problems. Contract learning suits very well her self-referent orientation and her capacity to operate effectively without strong guidelines from authorities. She can tailor her level of study to her shifting levels of complexity and intensity and to her changing interests and purposes. But she may find it very difficult to obtain the challenges to her analytic skills that she needs to move through more complex and rapid cycles of differentiation and integration; and if she is not careful, her relative lack of social sensitivity may alienate her field-dependent faculty member. Programed learning is no answer for this student because its authoritarian dynamic, its lack of flexibility, and its unresponsiveness to her strong desires to pursue particular interests and ideas to more complex and comprehensive levels make it difficult for her to work at any single program very long. So there are still problems to be solved, despite the promise of these new alternatives.

I would predict that carefully implemented studies of college dropouts and transfers would document these dynamics. I would hypothesize that the major reasons for the very high attrition rates for varied new alternatives that emphasize approaches analogous to programed learning—from the traditional correspondence courses to the brand new British Open University—are essentially the same as those which account for the migration of students out of the biological and physical sciences into the humanities and social sciences. High proportions of field-dependent students leave the hard sciences because those studies place a heavy emphasis on specific analytic skills and on independently derived conclusions based on those skills. Human exchange and interaction is seldom a major concern. Field-dependent students move toward the social sciences and humanities because their strengths in social sensitivity and their orientation toward human interaction are more appropriate to those studies and to the occupations which follow. Studies of dropouts and transfers from traditional institutions already document the case for the field-independent student. She has consistently been found to be more autonomous, more complex, more impulsive, and less oriented toward practical achievement and traditional standards of success than the field-dependent student.

It would be unfair to teachers and administrators who are interested in either contract learning or programed learning if I did not close with some solutions to these problems. Before you move to the edge of your chair, however, let me reassure you that like most solutions, they are utopian. That is to say, they are easy to describe and impossible to implement. The solution to contract learning lies simply in em-

ploying teachers who can distinguish the field-dependent
student from the independent one and vary their teaching
behavior accordingly. They can provide sufficient warmth
and sufficient structure so that the field-dependent student
can experience the human relationships that are so important
to her and can also have the benefit of authoritative suggestions geared to her tentative, vague, superficial, or other-
directed statements of purpose and interest. When they meet
a field-independent student, these teachers can temper their
authoritative guidelines, cool off the interpersonal dimension, and pose tough questions which challenge the analytic
interests and skills the student brings. Such teachers can be
found, but they are rare. If contract learning is going to serve
more than a narrow spectrum, we will have to pursue con-
tinual in-service training to develop that very complex combination of characteristics required for effective teaching by
this method.

The problems presented by programed learning are
equally simple to solve. The answer lies in the direction of
small modules at varying levels of complexity and compre-
hensiveness. And the answer also lies in a reconception of the
typical program format. Most learning programs aim toward
a relatively singular outcome. It may be relatively broad in
scope, but everyone who begins is supposed to get there.
There may be many diverse branches and routes which are
acceptable, but eventually all students are supposed to end
up in about the same place. A fat diamond is perhaps one
way to present the typical approach visually. It is narrow at
the beginning and narrow at the end, even though there may
be multitudinous interlocking networks along the way. The
new approach to programed learning must create materials
that look much more like a forest of elms. Each trunk leads
to sets of branches that become farther and farther apart as
one moves higher and higher. In our metaphorical forest
the trees must be close enough together so that the monkeys,
by swinging from branch to branch, can travel from tree to
tree and range widely around the forest. Then the field-
dependent monkey who wants to go straight up can do so,

and the field-independent one can move around more freely through a wide range of interlaced alternatives.

Through such utopian solutions as these, we may reach the level of complexity required to respond in part to the insights generated by Witkin and his associates, even as he shudders at our oversimplifications. Witkin rightly urges educators to recognize the need for cognitive maps, and we may be able to do so some time in the future. Right now, however, we would do well simply to give serious attention to the basic directional signals he has supplied.

Part Three

Masculine and Feminine Modes of Functioning

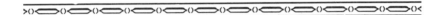

The nature and educational import of sex differences in cognition and creativity are examined in this section, and the following section focuses in similar fashion upon cultural group differences. In weighing the implications of individual differences for education, it is important to determine whether there are also any associated group differences as a function of sex, ethnicity, or sociocultural background. There are two major reasons for this. One is that if sizable group differences do exist, group membership might offer a convenient means of classifying students for differential instruction. However, since group differences on cognitive and personality dimensions are almost always dwarfed by enormous individual variability within each group, resulting in considerable overlap in the score distributions for contrasted groups, such a procedure would at best be a crude first approximation. The other reason is that if individual differences do happen to have consistent group correlates, then differential treatment on the basis of individual characteristics may produce outcomes differentiated by group. That is, if regularities exist between individual differences and group differences, any clustering of students in terms of individual characteristics will to some degree also lead to clustering by correlated group characteristics. Such a segregation of effects by group, especially if by sex or ethnic group, raises serious ethical and political questions relating to equality of opportunity and outcome.

In Chapter Six, Nathan Kogan maintains that to the extent that assorted sex differences operate in cognition and personality, they cannot be explained in a single comprehensive framework. There is evidence for a biological basis for some sex differences (a genetic contribution to spatial ability, for instance), but the abundance of interactions between sex and other demographic variables argues against any exclusive biological explanation. A social learning interpretation also accounts for many sex differences—and is especially attractive because it promises an easy equalization of the sexes through the manipulation of environmental contingencies—but cognitive functioning appears to be largely unresponsive to social learning principles. Kogan's review of research on sex differences reveals a field riddled with equivocal and inconsistent findings. What little order he does perceive is questioned in Chapter Seven by Eleanor Sheldon and David Jenness, who emphasize additional ambiguities and complexities in male-female comparisons. Overall, then, the sexes apparently do not differ in sizable and systematic ways in their cognitive functioning or ability levels, at least not enough to make any practical difference educationally.

In marked contrast to the negligible sex differences in cognitive processes and abilities emphasized by Kogan are the enormous sex differences in social behavior, motivation, and interests underscored by Ravenna Helson in Chapter Eight. Intimately bound up with sex-role functioning, these differences have massive educational consequences; they affect career choices, orientations to higher education and scholarship, styles of work, and the ways in which men and women go about getting educated in real-life circumstances.

6

Sex Differences
in Creativity and
Cognitive Styles

NATHAN KOGAN

>0⟨⟩0⟨⟩0⟨⟩0⟨⟩0⟨⟩0⟨⟩0⟨⟩0⟨⟩0⟨⟩0⟨⟩0⟨⟩0⟨

I should like to begin by noting that none of the research in which I have been involved set out deliberately to discover sex differences in psychological characteristics. Rather, in the course of studying creativity, cognitive styles, or any other psychological dimension, sex differences more often than not have intruded upon us. For years, I have been inclined to regard the presence of such sex differences as something of a nuisance. Explaining sex differences between males and females in mean level of performance on some cognitive task is troublesome enough. The difficulties are compounded when the pattern of the relationships between various psychological dimensions is not the same for the two sexes. Such correlational differences place a great strain on the interpretive ingenuity of researchers, compelling them to generate two sets of explanations instead of a single one of a more general character. We would be spared countless book and journal pages in the literature of psychology if these

intrusive sex differences did not exist. From the standpoint
of the extra labor involved, it is regrettable that there is no
alternative but to try to explain the added complexity that
the presence of sex differences thrusts upon us.

My general stance, then, in regard to sex differences is
that they constitute empirical facts in search of appropriate
psychological interpretations. I frankly believe that the level
of uncertainty regarding the facts of sex differences in cognitive functioning is so great at the present time that any effort to bring a single comprehensive conceptual scheme to
bear on the issue can be considered premature. It is only fair
to note, however, that others have taken quite different, more
committed, stances.

Conceptual Bases for Sex Differences

Psychological sex differences have been conceptualized within
two broad perspectives. One perspective maintains that the
differences between men and women are pervasive and deeply
rooted in early experiences, or possibly even in biology. The
other perspective, represented by social learning theory,
places heavy emphasis on the learned acquisition of sex-role
behaviors and implies that sex-typed behaviors are not intrinsic to the organism but can be modified through the use
of appropriate reinforcers. It is not surprising that women
liberationists are attracted to the latter perspective whereas
psychological researchers in the individual difference tradition lean toward the former trait-oriented point of view.
A further discussion of these issues follows below.

Pervasive Psychological Dispositions. Investigators working within psychoanalytical or broadly psychodynamic frameworks—whether Freudian, Jungian, or ego psychological—
share the view that maleness and femaleness are sharply
distinguishable and all-pervasive, affecting almost every conceivable area of psychological functioning. For example, in a
conference held several years ago on women and the scientific professions, Bettelheim (1965) emphasized that although
men and women might achieve identical solutions to sci-

entific problems, the affective component in problem solution was characteristically male or female. In other words,
males and females are presumably experiencing differentially sex-linked emotions while working on identical problems. The nature of these emotions was unfortunately not
clearly specified.

Other investigators working within psychodynamic
frameworks have been more explicit in their formulations of
processes presumed to underlie sex differences in cognitive
activity. Silverman (1970) subscribes to the view outlined in
a book by Wickes (1963) that there exists a masculine and
feminine principle or genotype designated as Logos and
Eros, respectively. Logos is described in reference to such
cognitive characteristics as discrimination, compartmentalization, and analytic separation and refinement. According
to Silverman (1970), the following adjectives represent instances of Logos: "objective, active, tough-minded, analytic,
rational, unyielding, intrusive, counteracting, independent,
self-sufficient, emotionally controlled" (p. 75). In contrast,
Eros is described in terms of wholeness and relatedness, of
intuitive perceptions, of sensitivities to the feeling component
of situations. Silverman ascribes the following adjectives to
Eros: "subjective, passive, tender-minded, diffuse, sensitive,
impressionistic, yielding, receptive, empathic, dependent,
emotional" (p. 75). From these overarching categories, Silverman maintains that it is possible to deduce prototypical masculine and feminine attentional styles in infants, children,
and adults. The critical question, of course, is whether or not
the available empirical data can be made to support the kind
of high-level abstractions represented by Logos and Eros
principles.

A conceptualization somewhat similar to the Logos-Eros
distinction has been offered by Neumann (1954) and adopted
by Helson (1967, 1968, 1970) to account for sex differences
in creative style. Neumann distinguishes between patriarchal
consciousness and matriarchal consciousness, distinctions
which are presumed congruent with physical procreative
roles. As described by Helson (1967): "Patriarchal conscious-

ness is assertive, objective, analytical, purposive. The intellect functions as an organ for swift registration, development, and organization. In matriarchal consciousness what is to be understood must first 'enter' in the sense of a fructification. The psyche is filled and permeated with an emotional content over which it broods until an organic growth 'comes forth' " (p. 214). I should note that both Wickes's (1963) Logos-Eros distinction and Neumann's patriarchal-matriarchal dichotomy are loosely derived from the personality theory of Jung (for example, 1963). Helson has employed the Neumann schema to account for differences between the creative styles of male and female mathematicians and between the kinds of fantasies contained in children's books that were written by male and female authors. Two other groups of subjects—male architects and female college seniors, both having varying ratings of creativity—have also been employed in Helson's studies. In any case, it seems important that we ask if the relevant empirical data require such high-level abstractions as patriarchal versus matriarchal consciousness.

Finally, within the category of psychoanalytically derived theories, I should like to mention the contribution of Gutmann (1970). Gutmann has adapted Schachtel's (1959) concepts of allocentric and autocentric modes of object-relatedness to refer to ego styles characteristic of males and females, respectively. In the masculine allocentric style, external events are presumed to have a direction and logic of their own, whereas in the feminine autocentric style, external events are perceived in relation to the self. In other words, masculine allocentricity is distinguished by sharp boundaries between the self and the external world of objects and persons; feminine autocentricity implies ego diffusion, or lack of boundaries, between self and object. The evidence that Gutmann (1970) offers to support the foregoing sex difference is largely derived from responses to Thematic Apperception Test (TAT) cards. Males apparently approach the TAT as a puzzle or imaginative exercise, with the result that their stories are personally acknowledged to be only a possible interpretation of the TAT stimulus; distance is maintained between one's imaginative productions and the actual features of the stimulus card. Females, it would appear, are more likely to respond to the TAT situations as if they represented actual occurrences, with the consequence that the stories produced are endowed with an objective reality transcending that of the storyteller. In sum, Gutmann maintains that boundaries between self and other are considerably more tenuous and permeable for females than for males. It should be noted that these ego-style differences between males and females are asserted to be more a matter of nurture than nature. In fact, Gutmann describes changes taking place in contemporary society that are responsible for shifts away from masculine allocentricity toward feminine autocentricity on the part of a segment of young American males. Such trends, if more than a short-term ephemeral phenomenon, are quite relevant to research on sex differences. They reinforce other evidence suggesting that sex differences in cognitive functioning have been steadily declining.

In strong opposition to the psychoanalytic viewpoint are those who claim affiliation with the women's liberation movement. Weisstein (1971), for example, has maintained that psychologists (particularly the male members of that discipline) have constructed the female in the image of the sexist norms characterizing our society. Generalizing from the Rosenthal (1966) studies of experimenter bias, Weisstein implies that psychologists may be finding sex differences because their cultural conditioning has led them to expect such differences. There is undoubtedly some merit in Weisstein's argument, but it does not echo my particular experience. As I indicated earlier, the problem of sex differences for me and my collaborators has involved considerably more post hoc rationalization than a priori theorizing. Of course, it is conceivable that the content of such rationalization is derived from what the contemporary feminists might call sexist norms. The only response I can make to such an argument is that some effort must be made to explain empirically observed sex differences, and for anyone to equate such explanations with sexual stereotypes in the culture is to blur the distinction between what is and what ought to be. Although it is difficult to take seriously the claim that the myriad sex differences reported in the psychological literature reflect the biased perceptions of psychologists, there is another side to the issue that deserves some consideration. We must entertain the possibility that psychologists find differences intrinsically more interesting than similarities. Indeed, the branch of psychology with which many of us may be identified has often been called differential psychology. In terms of the cognitive style designated cognitive complexity versus simplicity (see, for example, Bieri, 1961), the cognitively complex individual assumes people are fundamentally different from one another, whereas the cognitively simple person assumes that people basically resemble each other. Hence, psychologists concerned with individual differences very likely score at the complex end of a complexity versus simplicity dimension. That may well be to our benefit, but there is the danger that we may be too complex for our own good. Bieri and his associates (1966) have in fact shown that cognitive complexity—the attribution of interpersonal differences—is not necessarily associated with interpersonal accuracy. If the "stimulus persons" being judged are in fact quite similar to each other, the cognitively complex judge will differentiate among them excessively, and hence perform more poorly than the judge with a more simple cognitive outlook.

Perhaps this is an appropriate time to ask if the cognitively complex style of the psychologist has not had some effect on the body of theory and research in the domain of sex differences. You will notice that the term used to designate the topic of my paper is "sex differences," not "sex similarities" nor even the more neutral "sex comparisons." There is an obvious reason for the emphasis on differences. An observed sex difference sets off in the mind of the psychologist a stream of conjecture from which the most conceptually reasonable inference as to the basis of the difference is selected. In short, the presence of a difference touches a responsive chord in the psychologist, for it leads him to engage in the kind of cognitive activity that lies at the core of the discipline—namely, making sense out of data. In striking contrast, a sex similarity will be scarcely noticed, unless the investigator fails to find a sex difference strongly anticipated on the basis of prior work in the field. This is the well-known failure-to-replicate phenomenon, an event that all too frequently generates only marginal interest and often evokes suspicions of methodological inadequacies or carelessness.

It is not difficult to imagine how this disparity in value and interest between sex differences and sex similarities can affect publication practices. Research that reports differences is written up, submitted to journal editors, and, if sound in design and conceptualization, eventually published. If no sex difference is obtained, the research, if published at all, will be focused on some issue other than sex comparison. That such a comparison has been made will not be evident from the title of the paper, and hence the article may never be added to the burgeoning psychological literature on sex differences. Since so much of this literature involves differences that are quite small in magnitude, even though statistically significant, the resultant distortion in favor of sex differences over sex similarities may be considerable.

Social Learning. A prevalent theme in the literature of the women's liberation movement concerns the suppression of women's potential on the basis of sex-typed stereotypes dictating what women can and should do. To the degree that psychologists accept the existence of broad pervasive dispositions differentially linked to masculinity and femininity, one can expect to do ideological battle with an articulate and outspoken segment of movement women. Does psychology offer any alternative? The question can be answered affirmatively, for the last decade has witnessed the growth of social learning theory as a major contributor to personality and developmental psychology. It is a theory with enormous appeal to advocates of sex equality, for it deemphasizes psychological constructs located within the person in favor of an examination of the contingencies during socialization that are responsible for the acquisition and performance of specific social behaviors within specific social contexts. If the aim is one of enhancing overall equality between the sexes, a theory stressing the extrinsic, as opposed to the intrinsic, determinants of behavior obviously has much to recommend it. Theories committed to sex-linked biological determinants or deeply rooted pervasive psychological dispositions carry the implication that no matter what the environmental contingencies, certain fundamental sex differences in cognition will necessarily remain. As we shall soon see, however, the great promise of social learning theory in pointing the way toward sex equality must be tempered by the indication that the cognitive domain is the most resistant to social learning principles.

Mischel (1970) is the psychologist most closely identified with the study of sex differences from the perspective of social learning theory. If I understand Mischel's position correctly, he is essentially claiming that broad dispositional characteristics on the order of masculinity and femininity represent nothing more than stereotypes. There is a presumption, in other words, of greater consistency and generality in the mental constructions of typical sex-linked behaviors than one can expect to find in the actual behavior as such. Accordingly, Mischel recommends that if we are interested in what people actually do as opposed to what others think that people do, we should abandon the search for generalized trait differences such as masculinity and femininity and search instead for the determinants of specific behaviors. Thus individuals in our culture are presumed to learn through observation of parents, teachers, peers, and other sources the behaviors appropriate to one's sex role. Since such behaviors are generally reinforced, they will in the majority of cases tend to be adopted. Social learning theory emphasizes, however, that behaviors appropriate to the opposite sex are also learned through observational processes, and these cross-sex-typed behaviors are hence in the repertoire of individuals and will be carried out if positively reinforced. The domain of aggression provides a case in point. Though females are supposed to be especially inhibited in regard to the expression of physical aggression, Bandura (1965) and Taylor and

Epstein (1967) have shown, in the case of children and adults, respectively, that females are capable of as much physical aggression as males when the inducements and provocations are sufficiently strong.

We should note here that social learning theory has been concerned almost exclusively with personality characteristics (aggressiveness, dependency, persuasibility, resistance to temptation, and so forth). Mischel's (1968) treatment of the ability and cognitive style domains can best be described as equivocal. On the one hand, the evidence for temporal stability and generality within the cognitive domain is noted. On the other hand, he notes findings suggesting that performance in the cognitive domain may be susceptible to alteration in the face of particular environmental contingencies. Mischel appears to be uncomfortable with cognitive dimensions, for he treats them as neither fish nor fowl and retreats to the safety of noncognitive social behavior, a domain where social learning principles are presumed to apply with maximal force. It is only natural that Mischel should experience this conceptual difficulty given the intrinsic nature of the variables under discussion. Cognitive styles have conceptual and measurement roots in both the ability and personality domains. This complicates the sex difference issue from the perspective of a social learning theorist because part of the variance distinguishing males and females in cognitive styles may be in the biological realm and hence is at least partially resistant to modification in the face of various situational contingencies. Whereas females can be induced to manifest as much aggressiveness as males through appropriate reinforcements, it is possible, for example, that females will perform more poorly than males in the mathematical arena no matter what experimental inducements may be offered. If the requisite skills have never been in the subject's repertoire, reinforcements are hardly likely to put them there. In short, capacities are only partially under extrinsic control.

Possibly, the strongest evidence against a social learning interpretation of sex differences in ability is in the spatial domain. Three independent investigators (Corah, 1965;

Hartlage, 1970; Stafford, 1961) have reported that parent-offspring correlations for spatial abilities assume the cross-sex form. Mother-son and father-daughter correlations are modestly positive, whereas mother-daughter and father-son correlations are negligible. If parental models contribute to the acquisition of spatial abilities, it is hard to understand why, for example, the son should be using the mother rather than the father as an appropriate role model. The findings are, however, consistent with a genetic explanation based on a recessive gene for superior spatial ability carried on the X chromosome (Buffery and Gray, 1972; Gray and Drewett, 1973).

Where creativity is concerned, the issue is complicated by the fact that more than test performance is implied. Though creativity in the real world is undoubtedly anchored in capacities, important motivational dispositions are also involved. The latter may well be susceptible to modification through relevant reinforcements, and here social learning theory may have something to contribute. It is also obvious that the issue of sex differences in real-world creativity extends beyond the merely psychological to matters more sociological in nature. A thorough treatment of all of the sociocultural forces that differentially influence the creativity of men and women in our society is beyond the scope of this chapter. As much as I should like to attempt such a broad multidisciplinary effort in the sections to follow, the constraints of my academic discipline necessarily bias me toward the psychological aspects of the issue.

Interpretation of Sex Differences:
Some Complicating Factors

A search of the empirical studies reporting on mean sex differences in cognitive functioning has led me to the following observation: the investigation of sex differences demands a high tolerance for ambiguity. A bewildering inconsistency of empirical findings across studies is the rule rather than the exception. The most reasonable inference that can be drawn from the array of empirical evidence available at the present time is that there are no systematic, overall sex differences on any cognitive dimension that has claimed the attention of psychologists. A possible reason for this is that sex interacts with age, socioeconomic status, cultural background, and possibly with other demographic variables. Sex differences absent at an earlier age appear at a later age, or vice versa; differences between males and females in middle-class samples often are absent or assume a different form in relatively disadvantaged samples; sex differences observed in one nation or culture are lacking in another nation or culture. The presence of these interactions between sex and other demographic characteristics necessarily complicates interpretation. At the same time, the presence of such interactions constitutes a strong argument against any all-pervasive biological explanation of sex differences. Biological factors— genetic, hormonal, or neurological—may play a role in sex differences in cognitive functioning, but the role will obviously not be an exclusive one (Maccoby and Jacklin, 1974).

Variation in sex differences with age may be maturational in nature or reflective of generational or cohort differences. Thus Jacklin and Maccoby (1972) have observed that sex differences obtained in past studies have diminished in magnitude or disappeared entirely in the findings of more recent investigations. Conceivably, a paper on sex differences prepared twenty years from now would have to be written from a sociohistorical perspective. Such a paper might trace the disappearance of sex differences in a diversity of cognitive and other psychological characteristics as a function of the growing equality between the sexes, an equality fostered by progressive reduction in sex-typed socialization practices in the home and school.

Another factor complicating the interpretation of sex differences in cognitive functioning is the differential dropout rate for boys and girls in the schools (Fitzsimmons, Cheever, Leonard, and Mancunovich, 1969; Jacklin and Maccoby,

1972). Girls are more likely than boys to finish secondary school. This implies that cross-sex ability comparisons carried out on secondary school samples will favor boys, since they represent a selective sample relative to the remaining heterogeneous sample of girls. Jacklin and Maccoby do not remark, however, on the likely reversal of the foregoing pattern at the college level. Where financial resources of families are limited, it is the male offspring who tend to receive the support necessary for college admission. Also significant is the practice in coeducational institutions of setting aside more places for males than for females in an entering freshman class. If the number of applications is approximately equal, greater female selectivity will necessarily result. I need hardly point out that differential selectivity by sex reaches its peak for admission to graduate and professional schools. Where the assessment of abilities is concerned, then, sex differences favoring males during high school and earlier should tend to disappear and possibly reverse in direction for samples of undergraduates and graduate students. Such reversals favoring females should be most prominent where, for whatever reason, greater selectivity is practiced in regard to female applicants. Since many of the mean sex differences on cognitive dimensions have been relatively small in magnitude, it is possible that the kind of selectivity discussed is largely responsible for whatever differences have been observed. Certainly, psychologists will have to find the means to take account of the relative homogeneity or heterogeneity of their male and female samples before advancing psychological explanations for observed sex differences. At the same time, self-initiated reforms, federal legislation, and executive edicts concerned with sex equality may ultimately eliminate differential selectivity by sex in institutions of higher education. The time may come, then, when the psychologist can blithely ignore the selectivity problem when inquiring into sex differences—presuming, of course, that cultural change has not proceeded so rapidly as to render the study of sex differences in cognition outdated as a significant area of psychological research.

Distinctions Between Cognitive Styles and Creativity

Before treating the distinction between cognitive styles and creativity, it may prove helpful to distinguish cognitive styles from the more general ability domain. Whereas the latter is concerned with *level* of performance—high (or accurate) at one extreme and low (or inaccurate) at the other—cognitive styles are purported to deal with the *manner* in which individuals acquire, store, retrieve, and transform information. This distinction in definition between abilities and cognitive styles is somewhat blurred in actual practice. Elsewhere (Kogan, 1973), I have proposed a threefold distinction among cognitive styles on the basis of their distance from the ability domain.

Classes of Cognitive Styles. Closest to the abilities are those styles whose assessment is in fact based on accuracy versus inaccuracy of performance. Most of the tests that constitute the cognitive style of field independence versus field dependence have the foregoing property. Field-independent subjects perform better than field dependent subjects on tasks with properties of spatial embeddedness. This similarity between ability measures and the field dependence versus field independence dimension in terms of an accuracy criterion for performance is in no way intended to detract from the importance of the cognitive style at issue. Witkin and his associates (Witkin and others, 1954; Witkin and others, 1962) have related their construct to a vast array of developmental, personality, social, and cognitive dimensions. It is hardly surprising, then, that we have a greater fund of knowledge about field dependence versus field independence than about any other cognitive style. (A recent critical review of field-independence literature, especially Witkin's work, is available in Vernon, 1972).

In the second type of cognitive style, the relevant measures employed yield indexes that cannot be characterized in terms of accuracy of performance. Nevertheless, a value distinction is imposed upon the stylistic dimension: performance at one extreme is considered superior to performance at the other. Earlier, I made passing reference to the style designated as cognitive complexity versus simplicity (Bieri, 1961). The cognitively complex individual differentiates his personal world to a greater extent than does the cognitively simple person. Though complexity in no sense implies greater accuracy in discriminating the characteristics of other people, investigators have nevertheless placed a greater value upon that end of the dimension.

The third class of cognitive style involves tasks for which accuracy is irrelevant and where no value judgments are placed upon the kinds of performances obtained. In these respects, such styles are most purely stylistic. Breadth of categorization (Pettigrew, 1958) is illustrative of such a style. When given the central tendency for a quantifiable category (such as the average length of a whale), individuals will vary in designating the magnitude of the most extreme members of that category (the size of the largest and smallest whales). In the initial conceptualization of this style, category limits placed close to or far away from the given central tendency were not characterized on the basis of more or less valued performances.

I shall not attempt to provide a detailed description and discussion of all of the various cognitive styles that have been the subject of psychological research. Nine such styles have been delineated by Messick (1970; see also the glossary at the end of Chapter One), and a comprehensive review of the conceptual and measurement status of each of these styles is available in published reviews (Kagan and Kogan, 1970; Kogan, 1971). Since the focus of the present chapter is on sex differences, I shall concentrate on those styles for which there is some evidence that males and females in the young adult period do not perform similarly. Sex differences have been reported for all three classes of cognitive style, but I strongly suspect that the attention given to such differences in the case of field dependence versus independence exceeds that given to all of the other cognitive styles combined. The evidence suggesting that females are more field dependent than males has been for years the subject of widespread speculation and controversy regarding the possible source of the difference. It is a topic that must be dealt with, and I shall turn to it shortly. Before doing so, however, I would like to consider the other major topic of this chapter—creativity.

Creativity as Divergent Thinking. What is creativity's link, if any, to cognitive styles? In order to inquire into the nature of this linkage, we must first clearly specify how the term *creativity* is to be defined. If the term is confined to test performance (and we should clearly put quotes around it in such a case), "creativity" consists of what Guilford (1967) has designated as the divergent-thinking abilities. It is quite clear, however, that most of these abilities cannot be psychometrically separated from the domain of convergent abilities. This is the well-known issue of the creativity-intelligence distinction. After almost ten years of research on that topic (Hudson, 1966; Wallach and Kogan, 1965; Wallach and Wing, 1969), we can be quite confident that it is the ideational fluency measures within the divergent-thinking domain that are independent of conventional intelligence indicators. A typical task of ideational fluency requires that the respondent list as many uses as come to mind for a series of common objects. The larger the number of such uses listed, the higher is the individual's ideational fluency score. The theoretical meaning of such a score has been discussed by Wallach (1970), who believes the overall evidence supports an underlying construct of breadth of attention deployment. The ideationally productive person seems better able than his ideationally constricted peer to scan and retrieve remote, though appropriate, information for use in new contexts.

Let us return now to the question of the linkage to cognitive styles. For all practical purposes, creativity, when defined as ideational fluency, belongs to the second class of cognitive styles discussed earlier—those for which accuracy is not the critical element in performance yet for which greater value is attached to one end of the dimension than to the other. Alternate responses in a task of ideational fluency are not generally evaluated for quality (though such analysis is feasible), and the prevailing value is the more ideational fluency the better. In short, where test performances are at issue, the borders between intellective abilities, creativity, and cognitive styles are highly permeable. It is quite likely that cognitive styles of the first class—those for which an accuracy criterion holds—are more closely tied to intellective abilities than they are to cognitive styles of the second and third type—those for which accuracy criteria do not apply.

There is an important respect, however, in which the creativity construct can be differentiated from intellective abilities and cognitive styles. Whereas the meaning of the latter domains is exhausted by test performances alone, this most certainly does not apply in the case of creativity. There would be no special problem, of course, if ideational fluency were a near-perfect predictor of real-world creativity. Regrettably, ideational fluency is at best a distinctly imperfect predictor of talented accomplishment, though a decidedly better predictor than standardized tests of verbal and mathematical ability. Both concurrent (Wallach and Wing, 1969) and predictive (Kogan and Pankove, 1972) validity have been established for ideational fluency measures in relation to extracurricular activities and talented accomplishments at the level of secondary school. These validity coefficients are modest, however, and they can obviously not be generalized to accomplishments in the college, university, and postgraduate years.

Sex Differences in Creativity. How do sex differences fit into the foregoing picture? Where creativity refers to such dimensions as divergent thinking, ideational fluency, associative productivity, originality, uniqueness, or spontaneous flexibility—all of which reflect performance on open-ended tasks—the evidence appears to give a slight edge to women (Guilford, 1967; Maccoby, 1966; Wallach and Wing, 1969). It should be noted, however, that these sex differences are not substantial. Exceptions as well as reversals have been reported (Hudson, 1968). In general, however, the empirical outcomes for creativity viewed as a special kind of thinking process indicate a modest advantage for females over males in what might be called creativity potential. I employ that term quite hesitantly, of course, since we simply do not have long-term predictive studies linking ideational fluency assessed at an earlier point in time with genuine, real-life creativity assessed at a considerably later time. In the case of concurrent validity data, that is, the Wallach and Wing (1969) investigation of high school seniors admitted to Duke University, there is little indication of sex-linked differential validity for ideational fluency measures where extracurricular activities and accomplishments constitute the criterion. No one will maintain, of course, that high levels of ideational fluency or uniqueness represent the only, or even necessarily the major, cognitive capacities underlying creative performance in adulthood. Obviously, there are specific abilities associated with particular disciplines that are essential if the individual is to make creative contributions to his field. There is even evidence (Hudson, 1966) that talented adolescent males in Britain who concentrate in the science area may actually have an aversion for tests of divergent thinking. We may be dealing with a transnational difference here, however, for the Wallach and Wing data give no indication that ideational fluency is less strongly linked to scientific accomplishment than it is to artistic achievement.

Sex comparison of adult creative performance constitutes a most hazardous undertaking. Given the progressively increasing differential selectivity in recent practice for males and females beyond the high school years, we can expect that sex comparisons at present will involve samples more heterogeneous in the case of males than females. The extent of this difference in heterogeneity-homogeneity will also vary across disciplines, of course, with the maximal discrepancy very likely occurring in the physical sciences and engineering, where the proportion of women, according to census data, generally falls below 10 percent. Part of this selectivity is clearly a matter of self-initiated choice (few women spontaneously choose engineering as a profession), and the remaining part is likely to reflect differential admission standards for men and women. Whatever the source of this selectivity, however, the ultimate consequence in terms of creativity criteria (such as productivity and recognition) should favor women. The Radcliffe (1956) study did not find such female superiority, however. Radcliffe Ph.D.'s published less than their male counterparts in academia even though unmarried and without alternative demands on their time.

In contrast, a more recent inquiry by Simon, Clark, and Galway (1967) yields findings that are not consistent with those obtained in the earlier Radcliffe study. The authors mailed questionnaires to almost all of the more than five thousand women who received Ph.D.'s between 1958 and 1963 in the natural sciences, the social sciences, the humanities, and education. A sample of male Ph.D.'s about one third of the size of the female list and reflecting the same proportion by academic field also received the questionnaire. The rate of return was about 60 percent for both male and female respondents. The data on differential publication rates by men and women in the sample revealed nothing to suggest male superiority in respect to quantity of publication. Somewhat surprisingly, it was the married women in the sample whose output exceeded that of unmarried women. Furthermore, children did not seem to constitute much of a handicap for the married women as far as publication is concerned. The Simon, Clark, and Galway study strongly suggests, then, that those women who make it to the Ph.D. level do not cease to produce scholarly work. Unfortunately, the quality and influence of this published work for males and females constitute an unknown. Such studies are certainly feasible and would be highly relevant to the issue of sex differences in creativity, but, thus far, no such investigations have been carried out.

Beyond measures of productivity, the data indicate that women Ph.D.'s seem to get their fair share of grants, consultantships, postdoctoral fellowships, and appointments and elections to committees and offices in professional organizations. Despite the similarities between male and female Ph.D.'s in all of the foregoing respects, it is distressing, but not too surprising, to find differentials in salary and aca-

demic rank favoring males. Simon and her associates also
report that women's spontaneous comments on questionnaires indicate that the atmosphere in which they work is
not one of full cordial acceptance. Interestingly enough,
however, their productivity does not seem to be adversely
affected by it.

The research by Simon and her colleagues is highly significant in the sense of demonstrating that a highly selected
sample of women who successfully achieve the Ph.D. subsequently perform at a level equal to male Ph.D.'s. The critical
issue—one that is considerably more difficult to study—concerns the differential dropout rate for men and women with
Ph.D. potential. We could argue, of course, that there should
necessarily be fewer women than men in academia and the
professions (the percentage difference varying across field)
because women are less likely than men to possess the requisite abilities and cognitive styles for successfully pursuing
certain fields. For such a reason, among others, it is important
to take a close look at the psychological literature concerning
sex differences in abilities and cognitive styles.

Sex Differences in Abilities and
Cognitive Styles

It is the rare textbook in differential psychology that does not
feature a chapter or section devoted to the issue of sex differences. The two standard works in the field—Anastasi
(1958) and Tyler (1965)—both feature reviews of differences between the sexes in average performance on tests of
abilities. In addition, Maccoby (1966) in his collection has
published an excellent chapter on sex differences in intellectual functioning that attempts to account for both mean
differences and differences in correlational patterns between
the sexes on the basis of an integrative conceptual model.
This early work has been emended by reviews of a number
of recent conceptualizations advanced to account for sex
differences in the ability domain (Jacklin and Maccoby, 1972;
Maccoby, 1972; Maccoby and Jacklin, 1974). With this for-

midable array of prior work on the sex differences issue, it is really quite difficult to say anything particularly novel about it. Hence, a review of the major findings and the diverse interpretations offered for them will suffice, along with some comments on the practical implications of the findings.

In the period of secondary school and beyond, the intellective domain reveals few consistent differences between the sexes. The one exception is mathematical ability, and in this area findings reveal male superiority. This superiority is not confined to the United States, as Husen (1967) has shown in an investigation spanning twelve industrialized countries. Even with level of instruction held constant, males achieve at higher levels than females. At the same time instruction apparently has some effect on the sex difference; the discrepancy between male and female achievement is considerably greater in single-sex schools than in coeducational ones. Husen also found that females in one country outperform males in another country, again suggesting that instructional quality and/or differential selectivity are of some importance.

Rather surprisingly, the sex difference in mathematical ability has received considerably less psychological attention than the sex difference in spatial abilities, even though the latter, in my judgment, is less pronounced and consistent. Conceivably, spatial abilities have received disproportionate emphasis because they articulate with the analytic versus global (or field dependent versus independent) cognitive style. Hence, the spatial abilities hook up with the host of psychological dimensions that form part of the foregoing cognitive style, whereas mathematical ability stands apart from any body of psychological theorizing concerning cognition-personality interrelationships. In terms of spatial ability, then: since Witkin's criterial measures of the field dependent versus independent cognitive style are spatial in nature and strong significant relations exist between that style and other spatial tasks, there appears to be little warrant for treating them separately (Sherman, 1967). The evidence that verbal tasks with the property of embeddedness do not relate to

Witkin's analytic cluster (Podell and Phillips, 1959) offers further justification for a single dimension of visual-spatial ability cutting across analytic and nonanalytic tasks.

Where do sex differences fit into the foregoing picture? Despite evidence that males perform better than females on many spatial tasks, the magnitude of the difference tends to be quite small. In selective college samples (Bieri, 1960; Goldstein and Chance, 1965; Kogan and Wallach, 1964), the difference sometimes disappears entirely, possibly reflecting the greater selectivity for female admission to college discussed earlier. It must be granted that no one has reported women doing better than men in the spatial domain. Even in the case of samples indicating male superiority, however, the ratio of within-sex to between-sex variance tends to be on the order of 95 to 5. Given the weakness of the sex difference effect, it is truly astonishing to find such a great emphasis placed upon it in the relevant literature. We now have hormonal (Broverman, Klaiber, Kobayashi, and Vogel, 1968), genetic (Garron, 1970; Stafford, 1961), brain lateralization (Knox and Kimura, 1970), and cultural (Kagan and Kogan, 1970) explanations for male superiority in the spatial analytic domain. Jacklin and Maccoby (1972) find none of the explanations fully adequate when taken alone, and nothing has been published more recently to alter that judgment. Since the complexities surrounding the issue are documented elsewhere (Jacklin and Maccoby, 1972), it would seem to make most sense here to sidestep the underlying basis for the small sex difference and to consider instead its practical implication.

Implications of Sex Differences for Real-World Functioning

It appears to me that we should be asking an important question: Can the observed mean sex differences in mathematical ability account for the fact that a study of female mathematicians deemed creative by their peers (Helson, 1967) yielded a grand total of eighteen individuals throughout the United

States? The 1960 census figures listed more than seventy-five hundred female mathematicians, slightly more than one fourth of the total number in the country. We should also be asking whether the reported sex differences in spatial capacity and analytic style can account for the 1960 census figures indicating that the ratio of male to female physical scientists and engineers was on the order of 10 to 1 and 99 to 1, respectively. If such practical questions are posed, we must face up to the realization that variation between males and females in choice of such fields as mathematics, physical science, and engineering—as well as talented accomplishment in those fields—is considerably greater than is to be expected on the basis of spatially based capacities and cognitive styles alone. If these two variables constituted the most powerful determinants of occupational choice and performance, the representation of women in physical science and engineering would have to be many times greater than the census figures indicate to be the case. Quite clearly, it is much more than a lack of spatial ability and/or an analytic cognitive style that is keeping women out of the scientific and engineering professions.

There is now considerable evidence indicating that the global, or field dependent, cognitive style is associated with enhanced sensitivity to people and interpersonal relations (Messick and Damarin, 1964; Wallach, Kogan, and Burt, 1967). Davis (1964) has shown that female college seniors, in picking a job or a career, place great stress on opportunities to be helpful to others and to work with people. Such aspirations are not those of potential scientists and engineers, as Rossi (1965) has demonstrated. The exceedingly low proportion of women in the physical sciences and engineering strongly suggests, then, that occupational values and cognitive style are more likely to be conflicting for females than they are for males. An analytic style will receive more cultural reinforcement in a male than in a female. Such conflict may also account for the fact that women are more likely to be teaching mathematics and science than to be in more theoretical and creative areas of these disciplines. Alternatively, women may choose to become research assistants, thereby helping and supporting their male supervisors' creativity. Such solutions offer a compromise between an analytic style and people-oriented values, but at the price of sacrificed creativity. Such countervailing pressures are less likely for males; abilities, cognitive styles, and occupational aspirations tend to be more in harmony, with the consequence that males have a better prospect for a potentially creative career.

There is also a motivational issue here that cannot be ignored. Women may deliberately choose (and be chosen for) the more feminine parts of various professions—teaching as opposed to research, for example. In that respect, numerous women with advanced degrees have dropped out of the running as far as creative productivity is concerned. We are not dealing here with a matter of job discrimination, but with the socialization of women in regard to occupational possibilities. Such sex-typed channeling of career choice is no easy matter to change, if the Swedish experience is any guide. Despite a vigorous campaign in Sweden to change sex-typed stereotypes regarding careers, Dahlstrom (1971) reports that sex continues to be the major factor in career choice.

Within the domain of cognitive styles, the field independent versus dependent dimension has a special status because it is possible to envision real-world criteria against which the style can be validated. No doubt, the strong link between that style and spatial ability contributes to such validation efforts. The association between other cognitive styles and real-world behaviors is considerably more tenuous. There is the work of Kagan and his associates (Kagan and Kogan, 1970) on the reflection versus impulsivity dimension. A relation between impulsivity and indexes of school failure has been found, but virtually all of this research is based upon elementary school children. The only other cognitive style yielding a consistent sex difference at the young adult level is breadth of categorization. Men appear to favor broader categories than women; that is, women adhere more closely to category midpoints. In the language of cognitive strategies, men are more willing to risk inclusion errors in setting category limits; women are more inclined to risk exclusion errors in establishing category boundaries. The psychological explanation for the foregoing sex difference remains murky (see Kogan and Wallach, 1964; 1967). There is some evidence that broad categorizing is associated with higher mathematical ability (Messick and Kogan, 1965); hence, it may be contributing to the observed sex difference in this area. To the best of my knowledge, no effort has yet been made to relate category breadth to real-world criteria. It is entirely possible that other mean sex differences in cognitive functioning have been reported in the literature, but none has shown sufficient generality or linkages to outside criteria to warrant detailed treatment here.

Earlier, I asserted that within-sex differences are considerably greater than between-sex differences. The matter becomes complicated, however, by the evidence that within-sex correlations are not the same for males and females. Maccoby (1966) has reviewed these findings and has built a conceptual model to accommodate them. The general trend in the pattern of outcomes is one in which inhibition, passivity, and fearfulness are negatively related to intellective functioning in females, whereas impulsivity, aggressiveness, and boldness are negatively related to intellective functioning in males. The model presumes a mean sex difference on a hypothetical inhibition-impulsivity dimension, with girls being more inhibited and boys being more impulsive. The implication of these results is that optimal cognitive development would result from males becoming more inhibited and females becoming more impulsive—that is, from the sexes becoming more similar to each other. To the degree, then, that stereotypes of appropriate masculine and feminine orientations and behavior are broken down, each sex can expect to profit intellectually. One is entitled to ask, of course, how such changes can be brought about. I really do not have an answer that falls short of tampering with the family structure, or possibly undertaking a massive educational intervention for parents and children. Such drastic steps will probably prove unnecessary, however, for the sociocultural forces presently at work, some initiated by the women's liberation movement, are already undermining numerous sexist stereotypes. If Jacklin and Maccoby (1972; Maccoby and Jacklin, 1974) are correct in their assessment of diminishing cognitive sex differences in recent years, advocates of sexual equality have good reason for continued optimism.

It is my firm opinion that the data on sex differences in cognition at the young adult level are too limited in nature to warrant the application of a broad masculinity-femininity dichotomy. Whether such a dichotomy employs terms on the order of Logos/Eros principles, patriarchal versus matriarchal functioning, or allocentricity versus autocentricity is immaterial. The findings of note consist of a substantial male superiority in mathematical skills, a possible slight male superiority in spatial-analytic capacity, and a possible slight female superiority in verbal fluency and interpersonal sensitivity. A slight increase in female selectivity seems capable of eliminating the male-female discrepancy in the spatial and interpersonal domains. Such a body of data is not really sufficient to support claims for masculine and feminine world views. On the other hand, defenders of pervasive sex-linked dispositions may claim that the foregoing polarity extends well beyond strictly cognitive dimensions to encompass motivational and emotional characteristics. I cannot quarrel with such an assertion, and can only remark that the relevant research literature on such noncognitive dimensions also deserves careful scrutiny.

One may further argue that the basic masculine and feminine orientations will be more apparent for genuine, real-world creativity than for test performance. Helson's (1967) patriarchal-matriarchal distinction was applied to creative mathematicians. It is worth remembering, however, that these data consisted of self-attributions concerning mathematical thinking rather than mathematical thinking as such. Male and female mathematicians may describe their thought processes differently, but the crucial test is whether or not their actual mathematical thinking is, in fact, distinctive. Matriarchal self-report items may appeal more to female than to male mathematicians for reasons not directly linked to mathematical activity.

In my view, broad-gauged abstract concepts or principles of masculinity and femininity may well have outlived their usefulness in psychology. Though most psychologists have taken special pains to employ the terms in the strictly descriptive sense—the extent of deviation from male and female norms—the ease with which one can slide into a prescriptive mode is a cause for concern. Researchers are not entirely free of this tendency, but the dangers are especially acute for teachers, counselors, and therapists. Such practitioners are likely to promulgate values focused on interpersonal relations, values that are considered especially relevant for females. As Roe (1953b) has observed, natural scientists give a rather low priority to the interpersonal domain. One can only wonder about the fate of a socially withdrawn girl inclined toward natural science who seeks advice from professional psychological sources.

Notions of masculinity and femininity can be readily replaced by their psychological components. Let there be validated scales, for example, of activity versus passivity, interest in things versus interest in people, and economic versus aesthetic values. Males and females may well deviate from a fifty-fifty distribution on all of these scales, but to combine such values into a composite masculinity versus femininity cluster is to invite normative prescription. If so-called feminine elements contribute to male creativity and so-called masculine elements contribute to female creativity (MacKinnon, 1962), the implication is that the sexes are at their best when they are most alike. Such an assertion is obviously much too general, however, for it is important to ask in what respects the sexes are most alike when they are at their best. Unless such differentiation is spelled out, one runs the risk of advocating a unisex position that stands in ideological opposition to any sex difference not directly rooted in biology. The present chapter has no such ideological intent; it has merely tried to show that the case for sex differences in cognitive styles and abilities may have been overstated. A possible basis for this state of affairs is a psychological view that endows differences with greater interest value and theoretical significance than is attributed to similarities. One cannot help but wonder whether the prevailing state of knowledge on male-female comparisons in cognitive functioning would be the same if investigators had searched for the ways in which the sexes are alike rather than different.

7

Commentary: Complexity of Sex Comparisons

ELEANOR BERNERT SHELDON
DAVID JENNESS

Nathan Kogan's chapter is an instructive, though inconclusive, one. In his opening paragraphs he notes that the empirical evidence strongly suggests that there do, indeed, exist sex differences along a number of psychological dimensions; but he also states that we are not yet ready to examine the issue from the point of view of a single comprehensive conceptual scheme. Maccoby and Jacklin (1974) have reached a similar conclusion on the basis of a comprehensive review of literature on sex differences.

Cultural Versus Biological Determinants

After a succinct review of some general—too general—psychological formulations, Kogan then alludes to a basic issue that is of interest to us all, the ever-present, and more recently increasingly heated, debate of nature versus nurture. This

120

issue cuts across considerations of the theoretical adequacy of various formulations that might be expected to have some power in explaining differential cognitive performance.

Thus, Kogan notes that cognitive styles fall within both the ability and the personality domains, exhibiting commonality not only with social and personality variables but also with ability factors, many of which have at least a partial biological basis. According to Kogan, this particularly complicates the sex difference issue for the social learning theorist because part of the variance distinguishing males and females in cognitive styles may be biologically determined and to some degree resistant to modification through control of environmental factors.

It seems clear that, insofar as social learning theory concerns itself with the internalization of learned experiences, this is not the body of knowledge wherein one would seek, let alone find, biological explanations. Rather, we would anticipate (as does Kogan) that an examination of the social learning literature would shed light on reinforcement, expectation, and modeling variables that might explain some of the sex differences in cognition and creativity that derive from environmental sources. Even here, important theoretical issues bearing on generalized reinforcement versus modeling processes need to be addressed before definitive answers can be given.

In this context, the opposition between the biological and the nonbiological appears to be extraneous and dislocated, though, of course, it may be highly relevant in other contexts. Although Kogan points out that simplistic assumptions of universal biologically based sex differences are impossible to maintain in view of known cultural variation existing in the world, it may be that such variation is more substantial in the realms of sex role and attitudes, with their associated social behaviors, than in the realm of cognitive structure and performance. Indeed, he notes that variables in the cognitive domain appear to be highly resistant to social learning principles. For example, cross-culturally, males tend to perform better than females on the Porteus Maze

Test, which taps spatial abilities, and some cross-cultural consistency is found in differential responses to Witkin-type tests involving spatial perception and orientation. Moreover, research on very early sex differences in perceptual behavior continues to show that males are in some sense more at home in the visual mode, that is, they pay more attention to visual stimuli and make finer visual discriminations than do girls. Nevertheless, more work in neuropsychology will be needed to examine whether or not spatial information in all modes is in fact coded in, or relayed to, the predominantly visual centers of the brain. If so, the relative superiority of males in some forms of abstract reasoning—the mathematical-logical as opposed to the verbally based—may also be related to the same visual-spatial advantage. There may be some truth to the age-old suspicion that some of the supposed analytic superiority in males rests on an advantage in visual and spatial abilities that is in some sense neurobiologically based— a position Kogan does not reject out of hand.

Selectivity in Sex-Group Comparisons

Kogan recognizes quite clearly the problems due to sample selectivity in sex-group comparisons. In his brief discussion of the effects of such selectivity, he refers to a wide range of social variables that influence observations about sex differences. The interactions between sex and socioeconomic status, cultural background, cohort effects, and so forth not only address methodological issues, but also imply the importance of nonbiological factors in the obtained comparisons between sexes. It is possible, however, that Kogan focuses too much on fairly gross demographic aspects of selectivity and overlooks some specific, well-studied developmental processes as they affect sex differences in cognition and creativity viewed longitudinally. This is a point we develop briefly below.

Kogan goes on to explicate some distinctions between cognitive styles and creativity. Here, he quite rightly implies that we should assume that both the cognitive and creative

realms involve multiple dimensions and that they are relatively independent of each other—until proven otherwise.
He also emphasizes the lack of predictive and construct validity of measures of creativity and tries to be very clear as
to his working definition of the term. However, though Kogan is careful to point out that the data are contradictory,
even so, he may be bringing more order to them than is warranted when he says that "there is a modest advantage for females over males in what might be called 'creativity potential.' "
One must keep in mind contradictory evidence from well-
done studies, not just Guilford's (1967) book, which Kogan
cites and which supports his view, but a study done at the
junior high school level by Guilford, Merrifield, and Cox
(1961) or a study by Torrance (1961), both of which appear
to show boys superior to girls precisely in ideational fluency.
In reading the literature as a whole it is important to keep
in mind some of the logical possibilities as to the direction
of a sex difference (if any). If one believes, as Kogan tends
to, that creativity is a separate dimension, isomorphic neither
with intelligence nor with specific aspects of cognitive structure, then one might predict that men and women will bring
different but perhaps equal strengths and weaknesses to
achievement, including a broad range of intellectual achievement, defined in real-world terms. However, data from
Getzels and Jackson (1962) appear to show that at the top
end of the intelligence scale, creativity tends to be less highly
correlated with IQ than across the scale as a whole. This may
imply that as educational level increases, women, who presumably are being socially selected for high intelligence, are
likely to be increasingly noncreative as a group.

In his discussion of sex comparisons of adult creative
performance, Kogan cites the Radcliffe (1956) study and the
Simon, Clark, and Galway (1967) study, the latter contradict-
ing the former by indicating that female scientists are as productive as their male colleagues. Unfortunately, we must add
to the ambiguity of these findings: there is further evidence
that women scientists and scholars publish at a lower rate than
men. Zuckerman and Cole (1975) have recently found this

to be the case. Cole and Cole (1973) report that men who are college-affiliated publish more than their women colleagues, a difference that also holds for university-affiliated men and women. In a study that has not yet been completed, Jonathan Cole also finds that women scientists who have no children publish at about half the rate of childless men, that mother-hood—but not fatherhood—results in less publication, and that discrepancies in scientific productivity between the sexes increase in the years immediately following the Ph.D. Cole and Cole (1973), using the frequency of citation as a crude measure of quality, find that women publish less; further-more, what they do publish appears to have less impact in their field than publications of male counterparts. Bernard (1964) finds that men are better integrated into the network of informal scientific communications, and it is now clear that highly productive scientists are more often in close touch with other scientists than are unproductive ones (Price and Beaver, 1966).

To return now to Kogan's discussion of the effect of selective processes on the samples being tested for cogni-tive style or creativity: the question of the comparability of male and female groups may be much more complex than Kogan outlines. The kinds of factors he cites—for example, that males from low-income families tend to gain college ad-mission more easily than females—are more likely to explain the distribution of gross factors such as general ability than to account for the ways in which different intellect structures, cognitive styles, or creative abilities are represented in the samples at various points. With regard to processes of educa-tional sifting and sorting, it is not just the size of the variance that concerns us; we must always ask about specific cluster-ing effects. We need a model that asks at various points in the educational process, what *kinds* of boys, what *kinds* of girls, continue in the sample? We need to map critical sex-related differences in the course of individual development as revealed in an increasing number of comparative studies dealing with differential shaping of so-called masculine and feminine school behaviors at different stages in the educational process—studies showing that children with interests and values more typical of the opposite sex exhibit cognitive ability structures more nearly in line with those of the opposite sex (Milton, 1958); studies showing how intelligence becomes less global and more faceted in development and differently so in the two sexes (Dye and Very, 1968); and the enormous literature, to which social learning theory contributes heavily, suggesting that at quite an early age males and females begin to display different patterns of achievement and motivation, patterns that depend on how they conceptualize their educational and personal futures. Research on the fine detail of these processes is crucial, because at the very broadest level it sometimes appears that what education in our society does—and this is too crude to be scientifically useful—is to feminize males and masculinize females, and increasingly so as educational level increases. If there is any truth at all to this, then Kogan's conjecture—that the sexes are at their best when they are most alike, implying that social and educational arrangements that facilitate splitting the difference may be desirable and achievable—could contain some traps, particularly with regard to ethics and social values. Do we really want to accelerate a process of homogenization, of blurring of sex differences? If some of those differences are as stable as they appear, whatever their origin, the costs of eliminating them could be great.

8

Commentary: Reality of Masculine and Feminine Trends in Personality and Behavior

RAVENNA HELSON

Nathan Kogan has laid out for us with admirable breadth and lucidity the chaotic state of the field in the three areas of sex differences, cognitive styles, and creativity. Both he and Sheldon and Jenness (Chapter Seven) have pointed out difficulties in experimentation, dilemmas in interpretation, and dangers in premature or narrow commitment to any general notion that there actually are psychological differences between the sexes. It would seem to be my role, then, to emphasize the opposite, that is, the obviously different patterns that men and women show in cognitive style—in the acquisition, processing, and transmission of information—in higher education.

If we do not settle ourselves in our ivory tower, but go up to the observation platform on top of it and look out over the campus, what do we see? To the north, there is the law building. Of every ten students going in or out of the door, nine are men. Nearby is the physics building, where the same

126

is the case; and so it is also in the engineering, geology, forestry, agriculture, business, and medical schools. In contrast, if we look to the south, we see that three of every four students going into the library science building are women, and the same is true of elementary education and home economics. If we put a dime into the telescope on the observation platform and look into these various buildings, we see that many of the buildings to the north have expensive equipment and that the textbooks and blackboards are full of mathematical equations. The buildings to the south have little mathematics and little expensive equipment, but they do have a door that says "Women" on every floor.

Where men predominate, there are high salaries, a high level of research activity, and emphasis upon the inventive, analytical, abstract, quantitative, instrumental, and technological. Where women are relatively numerous, there are lower salaries, a lower level of research activity, and emphasis upon conservation of knowledge, socialization of the young, and upon appreciating and bringing into relationship the insights, expressions, points of view, and ways of life of people in different times and places. Therefore it is not farfetched, I submit, to say that the campus is a community of patriarchal and matriarchal subcultures, each characterized to varying degrees by masculine and feminine cognitive styles, but with patriarchal values generally dominant. As a matter of fact, Feldman (1973), whose analysis of the Carnegie Commission data I have used in my sketch of the campus, asked undergraduates to rate forty-five academic disciplines on the masculinity-femininity dimension. He obtained a correlation of .97 between femininity rating and the proportion of female graduate students in the department.

The representation of men and women in various fields is related, of course, to roles ascribed to the two sexes in other areas of life. Because of these sex roles, women students have a different status and a lower status than that of men. The different status and the low one are related, but to distinguish them is convenient because it allows us to make points which have different implications for action.

Women have a different status because of the old expectation that a majority of them will spend the best years of their lives in child rearing and in holding the family together. Despite changing social realities and some unfreezing of women's options, there will continue to be many gifted women who are not career oriented. There is some evidence that women students with high potential have greater intellectual interests and fewer technical interests than do comparable men (Heist and Yonge, 1968). Especially for women without clear career expectations, our course offerings often seem pedestrian and narrow; this evaluation seems to be associated with dropout phenomena among the more able young women (Rossmann and Kirk, 1970). Since our own best scientific conscience makes a similar criticism (Lerner, 1968), it seems clear that we should not try to shunt such women elsewhere, but welcome the pressure that their particular pattern of needs places upon us to improve our course offerings.

Similar considerations apply at the graduate level. Jencks and Riesman (1968) say that women are less likely than are men to fall into sterile patterns of academic gamesmanship, and for this reason they have exerted a healthy educational influence in graduate school, even when their tangible accomplishments may have been modest. Cartwright (1972) believes that women exert a healthy influence in medical school: though she found men and women medical students to be very similar in personality, the women were somewhat more sensitive to interpersonal relationships and to moral issues, and they were less motivated by economic and status considerations than they were by a personal pressure toward individuation.

As mentioned previously, men and women students do not only have different orientations to higher education; women also have a lower status and study under greater handicaps. "Discrimination against women," states the Newman task force report (1971), "in contrast to that against minorities, is still overt and socially acceptable within the academic community." Among graduate students, women are more likely to be attending school part-time, they have less contact with faculty and fellow students, are taken less seriously by the faculty, and have lower vocational aspirations (Cross, 1972; Feldman, 1973). Feldman's dissertation shows that in five scientific fields, the full-time female graduate students entered with higher undergraduate grade-point averages than did the men, but had less confidence, were less likely to think of themselves as scientists or scholars rather than as students, and had a lower level of professional participation than had men. Feldman shows that women students who have close faculty contact or who have done some research differ more from other women in confidence and self-evaluation than their male counterparts differ from other men. Although these findings cannot be interpreted unequivocally, it would seem worthwhile to test the hypothesis that women are in particular need of the apprentice relationship, as described in Chapter Twelve by Wallach (see also Taylor, 1959), and respond particularly well to it. I might mention parenthetically that divorced men seem to be another group of graduate students in need of attention and support.

Kogan suggests that the only important cognitive difference between the sexes may lie in the area of mathematical ability. I find it surprising, as he does, that this area has not received more attention, but I am also surprised that he cites the work of T. Husen and his collaborators (1967) as providing support for the idea that differences between the sexes in mathematical ability may be universal. In this study of mathematical achievement of adolescents in twelve modern nations, significant sex differences were found at the last year of compulsory schooling in Belgium, Japan, and the Netherlands. Some countries reported differences between boys and girls intending to go on in science, and another set of countries, including some from the first set, reported differences between boys and girls *not* intending to go on in science, this distinction being made for samples tested in their last year before attending the university. But the interesting fact was that for none of these samples were differences reported as significant in the United States, Sweden, or Israel, countries where sex roles are most equalitarian. Across countries, boys did much better than girls in single-sex schools, apparently because mathematics was more emphasized in boys' schools than in girls' schools; but there was no difference between boys and girls in coeducational schools. Interest in mathematics, however, showed more difference between the sexes in coeducational schools than in single-sex schools, and of course interest in mathematics was significantly associated with performance. Although it is true that this study reports a substantial overall sex difference in mathematical achievement, the findings seem to me to give rather strong evidence for social and cultural influences.

Except for this digression on the subject of mathematical achievement in adolescents, I have been emphasizing the enormity of sex differences. Kogan says that they are very small. Clearly, we are looking in different directions, he at laboratory studies and I at real life. What difference does it make, then, where we look? Although it is very interesting and useful to have Kogan's opinion that we have been magnifying sex differences in cognition out of proportion, and also to have his analysis of some of the factors contributing to this distortion, I think that we are not well-advised to stop with a minimization of sex differences in the abstract when the observable personal-social differences between the sexes are so large in terms of processes engaged in and outcomes attained. To do so seems to embed many academicians in the comfortable position that, liberal as they may be, there is really nothing to do until society decides to change its socialization practices. In the meantime, "if a gal comes along who plays the same game we do—sure, why not give her a try?"

The assumption that nothing can be done until women are "brought up" to be men is unnecessarily condescending. Furthermore, it grossly underestimates the importance of programs which can be put into effect now. As Sanford (1972) said, "if in an institution of higher education the women are treated like girls in a mining camp, . . . new experiences are simply organized according to old stereotypes." Indeed, there seems to be a blindness to the arbitrariness of many of the conventions and assumptions of masculine academia.

Let me give one recent example of such blindness in psychological research. An investigator reports an attempt to show that students who have an internal locus of control, using Rotter's conceptualization, enjoy different leisure activities from students who have an external locus of control. The hypothesis was confirmed for men, but the women students responded in a random fashion. When one considers the list of activities which was employed, the results are hardly surprising: handball, flycasting, chess, basketball, glider piloting, gambling, bowling, and so forth. Let us do the investigator justice; retrospectively, in his discussion, he did ponder for a moment whether his list might have impinged differently on the women subjects.

What a bore to deal with subjects who have to be pampered and given special consideration! But what should we do about it? Throw the women out? That is often done. Try to socialize them to be interested in handball and flycasting? Or do we make our research designs—and our educational designs—more adequate. Carlson (1972) says "it is not particularly helpful to dismiss the conventions and findings of psychological inquiry as 'male chauvinism.' Rather, our current inability to deal with the psychological problems of femininity is best construed as a symptom of a far more general impoverishment of current personology" (p. 19). By looking at sex differences, not overlooking them, and by admitting the best feminine values into our system, we will not only do better by women but improve our entire enterprise.

Of course, as Kogan notes, one wants to avoid normative prescription. He finds it ludicrous that men and women engineers might be found to have different affective components in their problem-solving methods. And yet no one, I think, who has compared male and female personality in depth and detail would find this idea even controversial. Study, for instance, the charts in Bayley's (1970) discussion of the development of mental abilities. Certainly, creative men and women mathematicians show many differences in personality and work style (Helson, 1967, 1971). The main point is not that one style is better than another or that people

behave according to a stereotype; it is the very opposite. Some
women have such creative commitment that they achieve
their individual destiny in spite of stereotypes and adverse
environments, and their cognitive styles reflect the adaptations that they are making.

Cognitive style is shaped by the circumstances of the
individual's history, present situation, and expectations for
the future. For a given area or situation, some styles seem
more likely to work out than do others. I think that we might
achieve more success in guiding the development of talent
if we use constructs which take into account some of the recurrent main forms of interaction between intellectual processes and their inner and outer environments. Patriarchal
and matriarchal styles are concepts of this sort, since they
are double-rooted in the biological and in the cultural. But,
of course, we need more specific constructs too. In my work
on mathematicians and writers, I have relied heavily on Q
Sorts of the type originally developed by Gough (Gough and
Woodworth, 1960) but adapted for more intensive assessment of what might be called the phenomenology of cognitive-
motivational patterns. We do not find that all the creative
women work in a matriarchal way and that all men operate in
a patriarchal way. It is not that simple. But since academic
disciplines have the strong connotations of masculinity-
femininity that I alluded to previously and since creative
work involves a relationship to what we may refer to, over-
simply, as the unconscious, one can expect that an individual's sex-related traits and imagery, his or her intrapsychic
communication structure, will be involved both in the choice
of field and in the development of cognitive strategy in more
specialized intellectual endeavor. We have had some success
in showing stages and types of cognitive style within fields
(Helson, 1973) and to a modest extent across fields (Helson,
1968, 1976). It might be worthwhile to investigate whether
this approach could be used with graduate students in different intellectual disciplines. One would want to study in-
tensively the interactions between types of cognitive style in

men and women, their creative products, and characteristics of both personal history and academic environment.

I agree with Kogan that abstract masculine and feminine principles are likely to be constricting—unless one takes into account their patterning in relation to each other and to the rest of the personality and social group or, in other words, unless one brings the "feminine" principle of relatedness into conjunction with the "masculine" abstractions. After which, of course, there are no longer two opposed principles but a variety of patterns. Why bother, then, with masculinity and femininity at all? Because, as Octavio Paz has said, "What sets worlds in motion is their interplay of differences, their attractions and repulsions." We don't want a psychology that is a secondhand dry goods store of scraps and samples of patterns. The alternative is to find the poles that define the worlds and the forces that set them in motion.

From the point of view of the individual and the academic institution alike, the goal, I believe, is nothing simpler than differentiation and integration of masculine and feminine traits, achieved through graded challenges, flexibility, patient suffering, and recognition of diversity. This goal of psychological androgyny—not the poorly differentiated condition of hermaphrodism—is an ancient one and has long held a prominent place in Jungian psychology. Recently it seems to have gained acceptance in other quarters (Bakan, 1966; Bem, 1974; Block, 1973; Sanford, 1972). The working out of an individual personal identity is particularly important for young men and women with creative potential (Mac-Kinnon, 1963), since they are especially reluctant to give up the opposites in their nature, since the search for identity may be intense during the college and graduate years, and since this process of finding and expressing the self may be the prime motivator in creative work.

Part Four

Cultural Impacts on Cognition and Education

Unlike sex differences, which are manifested more in motivation and social behavior than in cognition and intellectual skills, cultural groups appear to differ markedly in patterns of ability. In Chapter Nine, Gerald Lesser reviews the accumulating evidence that ethnic groups, independent of socioeconomic status, display characteristic patterns of specific abilities that are strikingly different from one another. This confronts us squarely with an educational/political dilemma. Education responsive to individual differences in ability patterns may very well yield program groupings predominated by particular ethnic groups. Not only might this produce educational outcomes that differ by cultural group, but the tailored treatments may actually magnify group differences in the face of a countervailing social and political emphasis upon equality. The educational and political ramifications of this dilemma are extensively explored in Chapter Nine.

One way out of the dilemma would be to find grounds for reconceptualizing abilities so as to eliminate any differential patterning by cultural group, thus sidestepping all the ethical and political problems that follow from it. Michael

Cole does this in Chapter Ten by interpreting measured ability, not as an index of fixed status or competence that characterizes the way people are, but as an expression of interaction between task and context. Patterns of ability scores, then, would not reflect differences in competence but, rather, differences in the expression of competence in various domains of activity or interest. From this perspective, individualized education would emphasize the same concepts and competencies in different cultural groups but by means of different materials and contexts.

Another way out of the dilemma is to switch our focus from ability differences, which are the outcome of prior learning, to the processes by which the differences arise. Edmund Gordon suggests such an approach in Chapter Eleven. He argues that individualized education should not attempt to match treatments to ability patterns, which are the product of background and opportunity, but to match treatments to individual consistencies in learning processes, as these are likely to cut across cultural groups. We should not just point individuals toward programs and careers that call for their specialized abilities; we should determine how best to utilize those abilities in achieving whatever educational and occupational ends students choose.

We should recognize at this point that education can be responsive to individual differences in a variety of ways (see Chapters Eighteen and Twenty-One). Treatments can be matched to learner characteristics to build upon strengths or to eliminate weaknesses, or both. The question is not Whether? but Which? Which dimensions of ability differences should be equalized by correcting weaknesses in low-scoring groups? Which differences should be cherished or enhanced as reflections of cultural diversity? In which areas should education attempt to increase all dimensions, at the same time striving to attenuate correlations with prior status, especially with such invidious distinctions as race and sex? From this perspective, it should be clear that the central issue in our educational/political dilemma is one of social values, not pedagogy.

9

Cultural Differences in Learning and Thinking Styles

GERALD S. LESSER

This chapter is based on a single fundamental assertion: people who share a common cultural background will also share, to a certain extent, common patterns of intellectual abilities, thinking styles, and interests. I shall discuss some of the existing evidence for this assertion, its implication for higher education, and the current political pressures that threaten to foreclose (or have already foreclosed) further research on this topic. As research on cultural differences in learning and thinking styles has become increasingly controversial politically, less new research is being done—to the point that almost a total moratorium has developed. We will need to look carefully at how we as social scientists are responding to the present political pressures that have provoked this research moratorium.

The topic of culture and cognition contains so many profound philosophical, political, and scientific issues that

I have been forced to choose carefully between those that I can discuss here and those that I must ignore, or at least set aside. I shall begin with two issues that cannot be treated here in detail; I discuss them briefly simply in order to note their special importance. Both issues are historical. The first concerns the massive direct effects over the centuries of cultural differences on the quality and uses of education in general, and of higher education in particular. The second issue concerns the attempt to reconcile the vast array of conflicting studies on culture and cognition that has accumulated over the last century.

Beginning with our first issue, we meet at the outset the problem of elitism. Cultural differences in degree of elitism have affected education almost from the beginning of recorded civilization, affecting higher education in particular. The more advantaged or elite families within a society are those whose children are expected to proceed to advanced education, those from less elite backgrounds making their way only through exceptional, Horatio Alger-like circumstances. Although the educational systems in many Western countries are moving toward comprehensive education, elite educational systems still are the rule throughout the world. Here, then, is the first clear, direct effect of cultural differences upon higher education: the cultural elite go to college, the poor do not.

Even in the more egalitarian societies, cultural differences always have had massive direct effects upon the quality and uses of all levels of education. In the United States, as each wave of immigrants reached this country, each ethnic group congregated in communities and neighborhoods where they could join relatives and friends who had preceded them. They sometimes established special schools, such as schools for religious education, where their children congregated. When attending public schools, their children were clustered together with other children and teachers with that same cultural heritage, again affecting the nature and use of education within the community. The educational effects of such clustering by cultural group have led, in turn, to plans either to retain the cultural character of the community while improving education within it (community control is a clear example here) or to plans to permit freer movement across communities (our recent agonies over busing and the programs of open enrollment of minority group students at universities are good examples of this direction).

Another example of a profound direct effect of cultural differences upon higher education occurs when young adults from certain cultural groups are forced to leave their communities completely in order to achieve some form of advanced education. This characterizes many rural communities; the Appalachian and the American Indian communities are but two examples. Since students most often do not return to their communities after completing their educations, seeking higher education almost demands the renunciation, or at least the abandonment, of the cultural group. Indeed, in Appalachia, it has been regarded as the highest achievement to leave the region to seek higher education and then to stay away and succeed in the world outside of Appalachia; second best is to show enough gumption and ability to leave for higher education but then return to the restricted opportunities of Appalachia; third, and by far the worst, is to remain in Appalachia and depend on the local higher educational and occupational opportunities. The long-term effects of this cultural pattern upon the community and its institutions of higher education are obvious. In contrast, for young adults in cities—Chinese, Blacks, Hispanics—a different choice is faced. Some remain within their communities while pursuing advanced education, others choose to migrate within the city. Again cultures differ widely and dictate patterns of use of higher education: Some individuals are forced to migrate and to abandon their groups; others face a choice of migrating or not, with their decisions having a profound effect on both the individual and the community.

A few final concrete examples of cultural differences affecting various levels of education will suffice here: at the preschool level, the availability of Head Start programs is contingent upon the family's financial status, which unfortunately is presently equivalent to saying that certain cultural groups will attend and others will not. At the secondary school level, any high school in which students find themselves tracked into honors, general, and vocational lines or, alternatively, into curricula A, B, and C will also show clear clustering by cultural groups. Again at the secondary school level, the predominance of so-called vocational or technical schools in certain areas of large cities indicates that the quality of education offered depends on the particular culture group being served; such schools supply custodial care but little serious vocational, technical, or commercial training to the students. And in universities, the growth of programs of ethnic studies are open to all cultural groups in some instances but restricted to certain ethnic groups in others. The conflicting reactions to the growth of such programs also have cultural determinants. All these instances connect culture and education directly, but they derive from economic and political forces that by far supersede the influence of any scientific theory or any evidence about culture and cognition.

Why have I told you so much about what you already know? Elitism, the congregating of immigrants, community control, busing, open enrollment, migration patterns, Head Start, curriculum tracking, vocational education, patterns of ethnic studies—each stems from cultural differences operating in one form or another, and each has had massive direct effects upon our educational system. Aside from noting their extensive and obvious importance in this way, I shall not be discussing them further here.

I turn now to the second historical issue: the array of conflicting studies of culture and cognition. At different times, anthropologists, psychologists, sociologists, and educators all have seen various pieces of this puzzle as their province; and the resulting bodies of theory and data are bewildering in their diversity and inconclusiveness. There simply is no way to summarize the findings and implications supplied by all these researchers, but perhaps the least I can do is give a partial list of names: Boas (1938), Bruner, Olver and Greenfield (1966), Durkheim and Mauss (1963), Greenfield and Bruner (1969), Herskovits (1948), Levi-Strauss (1966), Mead (1946), Price-Williams (1961, 1969), Sapir (1921), Werner (1948), Witkin (1967, 1969a), Witkin and others (1962), Woodworth (1910). On culture and language, they range from Whorf (1956) to Chomsky (1966); on culture and memory, from Bartlett (1932) to Doob (1960) to Cole and Bruner (1971), and Cole, Gay, Glick, and Sharp (1971); on culture and perception, from Rivers (1901, 1905) to Segall (1966). I think that most of these investigators would share, with some reservations, the fundamental assertion in this paper—that different modes of thinking are characteristic of different cultures. But I am not really certain of the amount of dissent that even that statement would evoke, since important disclaimers of the generalization also exist. For example, Cole and Bruner (1971, p. 868) summarize their argument that "different groups (defined in terms of cultural, linguistic, and ethnic criteria) do not differ intellectually from each other in any important way," by citing as historical precedents for their argument Kroeber's (1948) doctrine of psychic unity and the linguists' assertion that languages do not differ in their degree of development (Greenberg, 1963).

Patterns of Mental Ability

In the face of all this complexity, I shall concentrate on describing the evidence from only one line of research on cultural differences in learning, and then trace some of its implications for higher education. My line of research is a narrow one, with perhaps its most narrow aspect being the limited range of abilities included. We have followed the factorial analyses on the structure of intelligence associated with Guilford's work (1967), and especially with Thurstone's studies (1938) on the organization of what he called the primary mental abilities. The approach ignores the many other definitions of learning and thinking styles and analyses of sensory-modality preferences; in talking about abilities, it also disregards important distinctions between competence and performance. It depends entirely on measuring performance on various tasks that can be grouped factorially around the particular demands that they place upon the individual. Better and broader definitions of abilities must indicate not only how well people actually perform on specific tasks but also how well they can learn when provided with opportunities to practice tasks that are unfamiliar to them. Within our limited definition of abilities, however, the fundamental assertion remains that regular relations exist between a person's pattern of mental abilities and his cultural group background. I believe that some of these regularities can be observed as early as the earliest grades of elementary school, that they continue to operate as children grow older, and that they cannot be ignored within any rational system of higher education.

In 1965, Lesser, Fifer, and Clark reported a study that tested hypotheses regarding the effects of social class and ethnic group affiliation (and their interactions) upon patterns of mental abilities. Four mental abilities (verbal ability, reasoning, numerical facility, and space conceptualization) were studied in first-grade children from four ethnic groups (Chinese, Jewish, Black, and Puerto Rican). Each ethnic group was divided into two social-class components (middle and lower), each in turn being divided into equal numbers of boys and girls. Thus, a $4 \times 2 \times 2$ analysis-of-covariance design included a total of 16 subgroups, each composed of 20 children. The total sample of 320 first-grade children was drawn from 45 different elementary schools in New York City and its environs.

There are, of course, many procedural problems in conducting research of this sort; to illustrate, I shall describe only one: controlling examiner bias. Each child was tested by an examiner who shared the child's ethnic identity in order to increase chances of establishing good rapport and to permit test administration in the child's primary language or in English or, more often, in the most effective combination of languages for the particular child. Thus we had a Black tester, a Spanish-speaking Puerto Rican tester, a Yiddish-speaking Jewish tester, and three Chinese-speaking Chinese testers to accommodate the eight different Chinese dialects encountered among our Chinese children. Each tester had been trained beyond the master's degree level, and each had extensive experience administering psychological tests. Nonetheless, the tendency of the testers to empathize with the children from their own cultural groups demanded careful control of the testing procedures to insure uniform test administration. This standardization was accomplished through extensive videotaped training in which each examiner observed himself, as well as other testers, administering the test materials.

The findings were that each ethnic group displays its own distinctive pattern of mental abilities, significantly different from that of the other groups, and that social class variations within the ethnic group do not alter this basic pattern specific to each ethnic group. In other words, ethnicity affects the pattern of mental abilities. For example, the pattern displayed by the middle-class Chinese children and duplicated at a lower level of performance by the lower-class Chinese children differed strikingly from the pattern specific to the Jewish children; and the pattern displayed by the middle-class Jewish children was duplicated at a lower level of performance by the lower-class Jewish children. Parallel statements can be made for the other ethnic groups as well.

Since these early results were both surprising and striking in magnitude, our next step was to conduct a partial replication with first-graders in Boston. The replication, conducted under the direction of Jane Fort Morrison of the Laboratory of Human Development at Harvard University, used middle-class and lower-class Chinese and Black children (the samples of Jewish and Puerto Rican children who fit our social class criteria were not available). Once again, the results were both striking and surprising. The replication data on Chinese and Black children in Boston duplicated almost exactly our earlier data on similar samples in New York City. The raw mean scores of the Chinese children in Boston and in New York were different by an average of only one third of one standard deviation, and the Black children in Boston and in New York differed from each other by one fifth of one standard deviation. Only one mean difference (numerical scores of Boston and New York Chinese) slightly exceeded one half of one standard deviation. In contrast, the differences in patterns of mental ability between the two ethnic groups were extensive.

Beyond this replication, other confirming data on first-grade children exist in the study by Coleman and others (1966) on equality of educational opportunity. This study includes children from Oriental-American, Black, Puerto Rican, Mexican-American, Indian-American, and White groups, but does not include all our mental ability variables; nor does it provide a good assessment of social class for the younger children. Nevertheless, Coleman's data for first-grade Chinese, Black, and Puerto Rican children on verbal and reasoning tests show patterns very similar to ours. We have some confidence, then, in our earlier findings on the effects of cultural group influence on the development of patterns of mental abilities in young children: at least several mental abilities are organized in ways that are related to cultural background.

Does the major finding of these studies of first-graders, that differential patterns of ability are related to cultural group differences, remain stable across age groups? That is, does ethnic group membership continue to be related to ability patterns as children mature? Do the relative strengths and weaknesses of the subjects represent different rates of learning that eventually level off to a more or less common mean for all groups, or do they indeed represent stable cognitive organizations? What is the role of school experience in modifying distinctive ethnic group patterns? That is, do the different patterns of mental ability persist in spite of the possible homogenizing effects of schooling through the heavy emphasis on verbal forms of instruction and the deemphasis of other intellectual skills? To answer these questions, we completed the construction of an upward extension of the tests of mental ability to provide appropriate measuring instruments for older children; we then relocated and retested 208 of our original 320 children (65 percent of the original sample) when they reached sixth grade.

This study was conducted in 1968 and remains unreported. The collection and analyses of these data coincided with an explosive upsurge of political controversy about research on cultural differences initiated by Jensen's (1969a) paper on the strength of genetic components in racial differences in intelligence and scholastic achievement. We decided that since our earlier data (which actually are mute on the subject of heritability of intelligence) had been inserted into these discussions and since our data on stability of mental ability patterns over time would perhaps suffer a similar fate, we would declare a self-imposed moratorium on the publication of these results. Although my colleagues were adamant in this decision, it was an agonizing one for me personally, and I ventilated this agony by consulting with numerous professional colleagues regarding its wisdom. Almost without exception, they agreed that the political climate—and the likelihood of misuse of the data to support racist causes— warranted this self-imposed censorship. I shall return to this issue later.

I believe that the data on stability over time can be described in a manner that does not permit invidious comparisons to be made among cultural groups. In Figures 1 to 4, each ethnic group's mental ability scores are plotted around its own average normalized score as a zero point. Let me take hypothetical test scores of hypothetical groups to illustrate the data-display procedure. If, for example, the normalized-scale scores for the subjects in ethnic group A were: verbal, 50; reasoning, 55; number, 55; and space, 60 (all scores thus being at or above the median for all groups combined), these are plotted: verbal, −5; reasoning, 0; number, 0; and space, +5. If, in contrast, the normalized-scale scores for ethnic group B were, respectively, 50, 45, 45, and 40 (all scores thus being at or below the median for all groups combined), these are plotted +5, 0, 0, and −5, respectively. The comparative levels of performance of groups A and B thus are not displayed, but their comparative patterns are. In the analyses of variance conducted on the stability data presented in Figures 1 to 4, the Years × Tests interaction term represents the degree of stability of each group's pattern; none of the F-ratios for this interaction term approach significance, and as Figures 1 to 4 indicate, only minor changes in pattern over the first-grade through sixth-grade period have occurred.

Nonsignificant F-ratios represent a negative means of displaying stability; they, of course, show nonsignificant instability. Another way of presenting the stability data shows it in a more positive fashion. Classification analysis allows us to compare the pattern of mental ability scores for each individual subject with the pattern of profiles for his cultural group and other groups. By looking at the degree to which subjects can be classified correctly through knowledge of their mental ability patterns at first grade and at sixth grade, we can get a clearer notion of their stability over time. Looking at the follow-up study, when the 208 cases in the study were in the first grade, 116 (56 percent) could be correctly classified by knowledge of their mental ability scores. This 56 percent is more than twice the chance expectation of 25 percent. (See Table 1.) When these same children reached the sixth grade, 121 of the 208 cases (58 percent) still could be correctly classified by knowledge of their mental ability

Table 1
Classification Analysis of
First-Graders (N=208)

Group	Group Patterns			
	Chinese	Jewish	Black	Puerto Rican
Chinese (N=64)	42*	10	8	4
Jewish (N=44)	6	31	6	1
Black (N=55)	9	15	25	6
Puerto Rican (N=45)	15	1	11	18

*Figures to be read across as follows: The scores of 42 Chinese subjects fit the Chinese pattern, 10 Chinese subjects fit the Jewish pattern, 8 the Black pattern, etc.

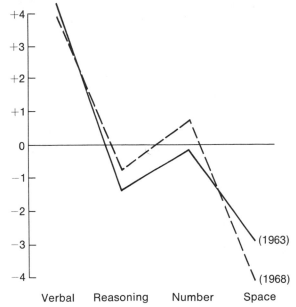

Figure 1. Follow-up data for Chinese subjects (N=64).

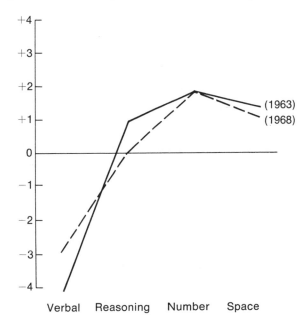

Figure 2. Follow-up data for Jewish subjects (N=44).

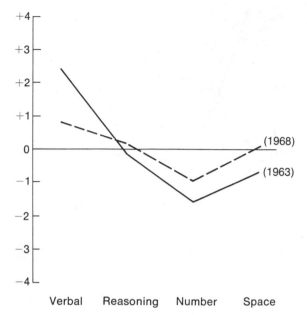

Figure 3. Follow-up data for Black subjects (N=55).

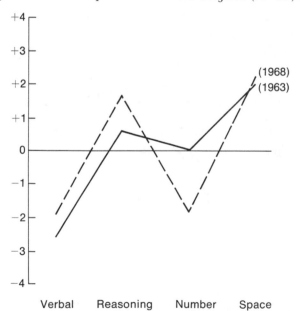

Figure 4. Follow-up data for Puerto Rican subjects (N=45).

scores. (See Table 2.) The distinctive ethnic group patterns seem to be operating at least as strongly as they were earlier in the children's lives.

Table 2
Classification Analysis of
Sixth-Graders (N=208)

Group	Group Patterns			
	Chinese	Jewish	Black	Puerto Rican
Chinese (N=64)	**48**	8	5	3
Jewish (N=44)	11	**23**	9	1
Black (N=55)	10	10	**18**	17
Puerto Rican (N=45)	5	0	8	**32**

When we look at the fate of the 92 children incorrectly classified by knowledge of their mental ability patterns when in the first grade, we can add one other dimension to this discussion of stability in cultural group patterns over time. By the time they reached the sixth grade, 48 of these exceptions were returned to their actual cultural group (for example, a Chinese child who was classified as Jewish as a first-grader was then classified as Chinese as a sixth-grader); 31 stayed in their initial misclassification (a Chinese child, for example, who was originally classified as Jewish remained classified as Jewish in the sixth grade); and only 13 showed no regularity in their patterns (for example, a Chinese child classified originally as Jewish was classified as either Black or Puerto Rican in the sixth grade). The comparison between these observed and expected frequencies is associated with a chi-square value of 53.62 (p<.001), indicating that many more of the cases originally misclassified either returned to their correct group or stayed consistently in their original misclassification than moved randomly from one group to another. (See Table 3.)

Table 3

Classification of Sixth-grade Subjects
Misclassified in First-Grade (N=92)

	Observed	Expected by Chance
Return	48	23
Stay	31	23
Change	13	46

Our follow-up study analyzed data from our original first-grade sample when they reached the sixth grade. Marjoribanks (1972) reported data from children of roughly the same age, eleven-year-olds, for five different cultural groups in Canada: Canadian Indians (Iroquois), French Canadians, Jews, Southern Italians, and White Anglo-Saxon Protestants. Once again, highly significant differences in mental ability patterns were described.

Do cultural group differences in patterns of mental abilities persist beyond the elementary school years? There are two good studies on high school students, one giving remarkable replication to our findings on younger children, the other testifying to clear cultural group differences in mental-ability patterns but finding also that sex differences are a more powerful influence on patterns of mental abilities than are cultural group differences. The first study was done by Flaugher (1971) at Educational Testing Service, using data from approximately two thousand eleventh-graders in Project Access, a program sponsored by the College Entrance Examination Board to provide access to postsecondary education for minority students. Flaugher makes it easy for me by presenting his data on eleventh-graders side by side with my data on first-graders; see Figure 5. In commenting on these data, Flaugher said:

The similarity between the patterns displayed on the two sides of Figure 5 [my numbering] had not been anticipated. Careful inspection of the individual lines shows a similarity of pattern for the two Black groups, for example, with Verbal highest, Reasoning next, Space next, and Number the lowest. The Oriental graph on the left-hand side also looks similar to the Chinese graph on the right-hand side, and the Mexican-American results on the left are similar to those of the Puerto Rican on the right. The most dissimilar are the two remaining lines, that produced by the Project Access students designating themselves as White and those children in the Lesser, Fifer, and Clark study designated as Jewish.

These results are particularly surprising when the nature and number of apparent divergencies in the data are con-

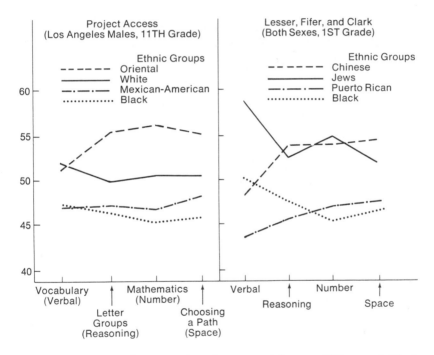

Figure 5. Results from Project Access and Lesser, Fifer, and Clark compared: patterns of test performance for males from each ethnic group.

Reprinted with permission of the author, Ronald L. Flaugher (1971).

sidered: the four ethnic groups are not the same in the two
analyses, though there are obvious relationships between particular pairs; the age span between the two studies is about
ten years over a period in life in which great development and
change might be expected; further, these four measures are
only approximations of each other in the two studies. Yet in
spite of the dissimilarities, the analyses show that the pairs of
ethnic groups which have obvious relationships between them
are those which display similar patterns in the two studies.

The similarity of the findings of the two studies . . . can
be considered as additional evidence of the viability of the
original findings of particular test performance patterns being attributable to particular ethnic groups. (pp. 24-25)

The second study of high school students follows closely
the methodology of the studies I have been describing. Backman (1972) reported data on about three thousand twelfth-
graders who had participated in Project Talent. The findings
indicated that ethnic group patterns of mental abilities among
four groups (Oriental, Jewish, Black, and non-Jewish White)
are significant beyond the .001 level of confidence but are
far less powerful than the sex differences appearing within
each group. Backman looked closely at the specific tests
with high loadings on each mental ability factor in order to
understand the reasons for these unexpectedly large sex
differences and concluded that content-specific test items
were at work. Boys, for example, scored higher than girls on
the factors of verbal knowledge (which included tests of information about the military, aeronautics and space, sports,
and electricity and electronics) and mathematics (reflecting
the fact that far fewer girls than boys had proceeded beyond
ninth-grade algebra when they were tested in the twelfth
grade).

It is true that these studies represent only one narrow
approach to studying cultural group differences in patterns
of ability, and there are not a great many studies at that; but
strong indications exist, nevertheless, that some regular relations exist between a person's cultural group background and
the type of intellectual strengths and weaknesses that he dis-

plays and that these regularities seem to persist as students advance educationally.

Cultural Differences in Higher Education

Let us accept, for the moment, the assertion that certain regularities will exist between cultural differences and individual differences in abilities and styles. As higher education, in order to arrive at a more rational system than we have, begins to respond to individual differences, it will inevitably encounter circumstances where treating people according to these individual differences (perhaps even clustering them for instruction) will create cultural group clustering as well. We either can reject this outcome as undemocratic and segregating or accept it as an inevitable consequence of maximizing each individual's educational opportunity. A trade-off will exist between political and educational consequences. I believe we now are being forced to confront this trade-off, and we will be forced increasingly to face it as we move toward more responsive forms of higher education.

Consider, first, some direct, immediate implications of the data on cultural differences in mental ability patterns. To the extent that past experiences, abilities, styles, and perhaps interests are regularly related to cultural membership, educational outcomes may differ dramatically among these cultural groups. Let us take a specific, if partially hypothetical, case. Our evidence indicates that young Chinese children have their strongest skill in space conceptualization and their weakest in verbal ability. Conversely, young Jewish children are strongest in verbal ability and weakest in space conceptualization. Making maximum educational use of each group's contrasting set of strengths and weaknesses, we may produce proportionally more Chinese architects and engineers than Jewish ones while producing proportionally more Jewish authors and lawyers than Chinese ones. If this plan were followed, serious questions of social policy would be raised. On one level, we would not have put members of these two cultural groups on an equal footing for entering these particular occupations, and this would seem to run counter to our beliefs in providing equal educational opportunities for all groups in all areas of educational and professional attainment. On another level, that of operating programs in higher education, we would have clustered each group in schools and classes directed toward certain types of training. In this hypothetical example, Chinese students would congregate in certain programs of higher education and Jewish students in others. Of course, this already occurs due to natural political and economic forces that we do not understand very well, some of which I mentioned at the beginning of this chapter; but recognizing individual differences in higher education and accepting that some regularities exist between cultural and individual differences may accentuate these tendencies toward clustering. This, I believe, is the nature of the political-educational trade-off that now is coming into clearer focus. Are we willing to accept or encourage this possible consequence of making higher education more responsive to individual differences? Will we accept the possibility that in certain areas of intellectual accomplishment, we may actually magnify the differences among various cultural groups, rather than reduce or equalize them?

To throw further light on this question, I should mention an analogous issue that has been of some importance for many years at the level of early childhood education: the difference between compensatory and supportive educational programs for the disadvantaged. Compensatory programs aim to compensate, to make amends, to eradicate symptoms and causes—to give disadvantaged children what they need to make them like everyone else. In contrast, the aim of what might be called supportive education is to give disadvantaged children what they need and can use maximally in order to learn to cope with and change their particular environments, even if they are made increasingly different from other groups in the process.

There are, for higher education, some less direct and less immediate implications of cultural differences in mental ability patterns. These implications rest on the assumption that higher education, in the effort to arrive at a more rational analysis of what it is doing and why it is doing it, will increasingly inject considerations of individual differences among its students into these analyses. Although some sporadic forays in this direction are reported (for example, McKeachie, 1961), no clear indications exist that this will happen, but surely it makes good logical sense, and things that make good logical sense do sometimes happen.

No studies yet reported take the analysis of stability of cultural group patterns over time into the college and university levels. Assume for the moment, however, that these patterns do continue to operate, even to a modest extent, and then let us trace some implications for higher education. In the absence of useful data at the higher educational levels about the relations between instruction and either cultural group differences or individual differences, the argument now becomes almost entirely theoretical.

As we all know, colleges and universities are in desperate financial trouble and may be forced to retain the large-lecture form of instruction, and perhaps even expand it. But any rational system of higher education must recognize and accommodate to individual differences among its students and contain heavy components of small-group and individualized instruction in order to teach successfully. Both small-group and individualized instruction in higher education have been revealed to be pitifully inadequate; here is a simplified overview of what we have. For small-group instruction, the large-lecture classes are divided into smaller sections, usually themselves composed of from twenty to thirty students. These sections are formed mostly by alphabetical assignment or by some other arbitrary criterion that has nothing to do with shared abilities, styles, or interests of the students—but then these sections operate for the purpose of allowing a greater degree of discussion between students and instructor or among the students than the large lecture can tolerate and not for the purpose of accommodating to individual differences. Alternatively, seminars are formed in which students cluster themselves primarily according to their interest in the content being taught. These sections and seminars probably are the main forms of small-group instruction in higher education; neither recognizes or capitalizes upon individual differences among students.

For individualized instruction, we have had independent study, usually for the advanced students in universities. What this usually amounts to is that the student, in consultation with an instructor, selects a topic that interests him and works on it under periodic and often remote guidance of the instructor. Individualization through computer-assisted instruction also exists in some areas of higher education. Both independent study and computer-assisted instruction do operate effectively in selected cases, but neither has transformed higher education dramatically.

Obviously we will need to go beyond these older forms of small-group and individualized instruction in order to recognize and capitalize more fully and effectively upon individual differences among students. These still pervasive forms of small-group or individual instruction have evolved from what Glaser (1972) recently has described as an archaic "selective" mode of education, which, he argues, will need time to be replaced by an "adaptive" system. In the traditional selective mode, minimal variation exists in the conditions under which individuals are expected to learn, a narrow range of instructional options is provided, and a limited number of ways to succeed are available. The adaptability of the system to the student is limited, and alternative paths that can be selected for students with different backgrounds and talents are restricted. In this selective higher educational environment, the few fixed paths that are available require particular student abilities; and the only abilities that really work well in a selective system range from verbal, abstract, symbolic skills to the ability to read the instructor in order to give him what he wants to hear (which usually is what he has said in the first place). The system is selective in the sense that those individuals who have the particular abilities for success in response to the limited means of available instruction are those who filter through the admission tests and proceed through the system. In the system itself, the selective mode is well protected, and no change in its educational environment is necessary: it selects students who can meet well its particular demands; they do well as predicted, and the only individual differences that are relevant are those that predict success in this particular setting.

In contrast, the adaptive mode of instruction seeks to establish multiple educational options and to provide expanded opportunities for achievement and success. Alternative programs and styles of instruction are adapted to the individual's abilities, styles, and interests. Success here is defined by the extent of successful matching between the student's special abilities and interests and the educational activities he pursues. Admission procedures demand measures of individual differences that help to define the alternative paths that result in maximum achievement for the individual student. We remain a great distance from knowing what forms of an adaptive system in higher education will be effective, and even farther from putting these forms into practice. Some years ago, the research analyses of aptitude-treatment interaction seemed to hold great promise for suggesting how matches between instruction and individual differences could be created (Bracht, 1969; Bracht and Glass, 1968; Cronbach, 1957, 1967; Cronbach and Snow, 1969; Glaser, 1972; Hunt, 1971; Kropp, 1967; McKeachie, 1961; Mitchell, 1969; Snow, 1968). But then an extended period of rather discouraging empirical results ensued (see Chapter Eighteen).

But there still may be positive signs within these aptitude-treatment analyses. Glaser (1972) and Hunt (1971), for example, propose reconceptualizations in which small-group instruction will be developed in higher education to accommodate individuality among students. My point is that any form of recognition of individual differences in higher education, whether it flows from aptitude-treatment interaction analyses, the computer-assisted instruction orientation, or any other theoretical perspective, will encounter regularities between individual differences and cultural group background. These, in turn, will force us to confront serious decisions involving competing political and educational considerations.

Political Considerations

Politics enter this discussion directly when we ask, Should we tolerate or even promote certain inevitable consequences of clustering people in higher educational programs according to their individual characteristics? An equally direct political and ethical question deeply affects, both professionally and personally, all those who do research on cultural differences. That question is, Should we tolerate or even encourage research on cultural differences when there are such great risks of its misuse and misinterpretation to support unjust causes? If we decide that these risks—and the many instances of actual abuse of data on cultural differences—are too great to tolerate, how must that decision affect our image of scientific research as a free, open, and public enterprise?

Objections to continuing research on cultural differences in cognition always have been prominent, and the problems of conducting such research can be so overpowering that it does seem reasonable to question if legitimate scientific evidence ever can be collected in this way. These conceptual and methodological problems have been clarified somewhat in recent years, but they certainly are not solved. Added to these long standing conceptual and methodological problems are the more recent political repercussions, and the combination of all these forces has led to widespread censorship of research on cultural differences by outside agencies and to self-censorship by the researchers involved. The blatant outrages we all have witnessed probably should not be dignified by serious discussion. The disruption of scientific conferences and university classes by demonstrators hurling accusations of sexism or racism and the other personal and private attacks on people who voice their conclusions on culture and cognition are disastrous professionally and personally and seem beyond rational behavior.

But other objections must be taken seriously, and here

are some of them. Scientific research is of no value, and rarely ever has been of any value, in correcting social problems. This objection would challenge us to locate one convincing instance in which theory or evidence from studies of culture have led to real solutions of important social problems. Not only is scientific research useless in providing practical solutions to social problems, but, it is argued, it contains incalculable hidden mischief and is a positive menace to social improvement. It diverts us from the humanitarian approach which is the only possible route to social reform. It acts as an excuse for inaction by claiming that we must wait for all the scientific data before acting. The results of scientific research can be, and will be, misused to further unjust causes such as racism by arming the opponents of social reform and by bolstering the arguments from which social injustices flow (for example, the genetic interpretation of cultural group differences as presumably an objective ground for racism). It is argued that in all these ways scientific research on cultural differences actually impedes progress toward social improvement and harms individuals as well. With all these risks, it also is argued that scientific research on politically controversial topics must be totally valid, totally foolproof, and absolutely beyond question before its results can be reported. That is, when the potentially damaging political and personal consequences of a line of research are clear, the research itself must meet much more stringent criteria of conclusiveness. Yet no research ever will be totally foolproof. Hence, Catch 22.

In the light of these objections, fewer and fewer young social scientists are undertaking research on culture and cognition; the penalties to this research are all too obvious. What I have mentioned before bears repeating: we are facing a self-declared moratorium on research, and until the times change, we will know less and less about the connections that exist between cultural conditions and cognitive growth.

We never have devoted much research energy to discovering how to establish a more rational system of higher education. Despite some explosive agitation in recent years, or perhaps because of it, we continue to do things much as we always have done them. Now, we add to this disregard a dose of deliberate ignorance—what little research we have on cultural differences now sputters on with strong political coloration attached to it. This disregard of an experimental orientation in higher education combined with deliberate ignorance about cultural differences will serve us poorly.

10

Commentary: Cultural Differences in the Contexts of Learning

MICHAEL COLE

Leaving aside the question of the origin of group differences in test performance (the controversy over the role of heritability in producing test scores, for example), we find that data from IQ tests have historically led to the interpretation that such tests in some sense measure fixed competencies characteristic of individuals, revealing the way people are intellectually. At least, most of us talk as if IQ tests measure the way we are intellectually. The line of research pioneered by Lesser and his associates and continued in the other studies which he has described goes beyond overall ability ratings. This work demonstrates that the subtests which constitute most IQ tests yield stable results within ethnic groups and differing profiles across ethnic groups. I believe this work to represent a definite advance over global IQ characterizations of differing ethnic and socioeconomic groups.

Lesser shares with his predecessors, however, a belief that his tests (or subtests) tell us something general about the way people are. In so far as this conclusion is correct (and I should add that it is shared by many psychologists), his discussion of alternatives makes very good sense. I am concerned with many of the problems he raises and just as puzzled about possible solutions. Since this line of discussion poses dilemmas that are political and social rather than psychological, I will not pursue it. Instead, I will try to offer a different perspective on the whole issue of ethnic group differences in intellectual performance and on the concept of an ability.

A convenient starting point is provided by Jensen (1971), who makes the following kinds of observations in his writing on the heritability of conceptual and rote learning capacities: "Why some children do this so spontaneously [make overt, verbal responses where none are required] . . . and why some children have such a high threshold for spontaneous verbal utterance in what outwardly appears to be a non-verbal problem situation is the key question. In social and verbal contexts, one type of child is as verbal as the other" (p. 51). Jensen is discussing the manifestation of different levels of mental ability. As might be expected, he goes on to claim that social interactions involve only lower-order skills, but I think that another point can be taken from his observation—that abilities expressed in one domain of activity may not be expressed in others.

I think that this point goes to the heart of the problem of making inferences about the significance of IQ and other test differences. Such tests are, by definition and design, predictive of school performance as schools have traditionally been conducted. But do they tell us the way people are generally when dealing with certain kinds of topics in decontextualized, symbolic (written) form? Several lines of evidence, including my own research, have caused me to conclude that people are not content-independent information processors with two levels of abilities. Nor are they consistently good reasoners, or good spatial manipulators, in everything they do. Rather, abilities represent the interaction of content, structure, and context. Let me give some examples of the kinds of data that have led me to this conclusion.

First, there is the ingenious work of William Labov, the linguist. In his irritation with the notion that many Black children grow up "linguistically deprived," Labov (1970) set out to demonstrate that the diagnosis depended upon both the test situation and the content of the test. What is striking about Labov's example is the extreme measures that were necessary to modify test performance. It was not enough to have a Black interviewer from the child's neighborhood; it was not even enough to have the interviewer drop in on the child at home. Not until one of the child's friends was present, the situation made informal, and clearly taboo (but exciting) topics introduced did the child's wealth of verbal capacity manifest itself. A somewhat different example comes from the work of Farnham-Diggory (1970). Working on a problem that, I suppose, would fall under the rubric of spatial skills, she discovered that the order of words in the sentence made a vast difference in whether or not her poor Black subjects manifested normal spatial skills or abnormally low ones.

A quite different sort of evidence can be gleaned from those rare anthropological studies in which the intellectual lives of primitive peoples are the concern. I have been particularly impressed by Evans-Pritchard's (1963) description of the exploitation of ambiguous speech as a device for social control among the Azande of East Africa. The Azande have a form of speech, called Sanza, with which it is possible to insult or tease someone in such a way that the target of the attack cannot accuse you of an insult. So successful are they in this practice that Evans-Pritchard (1963) is led to complain: "It [Sanza] adds greatly to the difficulties of anthropological inquiry. Eventually the anthropologist's sense of security is also undermined, his confidence shaken. He learns the language, can say what he wants to say in it, and can understand what he hears; then he begins to wonder whether he has really understood" (p. 222). Note that our Oxonian colleague is describing the behavior of people who perform miserably on IQ tests, on verbal and nonverbal subtests alike.

A hint of the same kind of issue can be gleaned from Lesser's chapter, although the account is quite brief. I refer to Backman's (1972) data on sex differences in IQ subtest profiles. The explanation of her results indicates that certain subtests include items that are of particular interest to boys; therefore boys score higher on those subtests. But where does interest enter into verbal, spatial, numerical, or reasoning ability? Clearly interest enters into subtest performance, as Lesser's discussion indicates, but the relationship between performance and ability is problematic. This point tends to get lost as we proceed toward a view of the implications of test performance for higher education.

In considering the implications for higher education of what I call an interactional concept of ability, I will begin by sharing Lesser's concern about the ability clustering that has been taking shape in our nation's schools. One of the features which makes this kind of clustering so distasteful to many people (aside from the fact that it leads quickly and dramatically to segregation by ethnic origin) is that it smacks of the tracking system used in many elementary and secondary schools. That is, the central, defining characteristic of such clustering programs is not concern about qualitative differences in the kinds of teaching approaches used, but concern about quantitative differences in the amount of so-called ability possessed by the student. In short, the Black children are placed in remedial classes, and the Chinese-American children are placed in accelerated physics.

Another way to attack the problem of providing for differences in ability lies within the interactional framework I have been discussing. If the expression of numerical or reasoning ability depends on the kind of problem confronted and the social-intellectual context in which it is embedded, we would expect that the same concepts taught in different contexts and using different materials would differentially influence students from different cultural groups. Although awkward and abstract, this notion is shared in one form or another by the many educators and social commentators who are urging the opening up of our school curricula and the "deschooling" of society. I do not refer here to the Summer-hillian "do your own thing" approach to education, whose application to the problems of poor people has been cogently criticized by such writers as Kozol (1972). I refer, rather, to those cases where drastic modifications in curriculum have led to equally drastic modifications in the skills manifested by presumably incompetent students. Most of us are familiar with the examples provided by such master teachers as Kozol and Holt. My own favorite example comes from the Italian school children of Barbiana, Italy (Rossi and Cole, 1970). A group of these children, drummed out of the Italian schools as incompetents, put together a scathing attack on the Italian school system, in the course of which they used the concepts and skills of mathematics, economics, history, sociology, and political science. There are, of course, similar efforts going on at the present time within the American educational system. But on the whole, they are marked by their timidity and narrow range. None capture the spirit of Labov's successful interview or the Barbiana manifesto.

These examples are admittedly thin evidence for the viewpoint I have been describing. In an intellectual climate that accepts the notion that low performance in school reflects lack of ability in the student, such departures from tradition are viewed as radical and even anarchical. They may also be the solution.

11

Commentary: Group Differences Versus Individual Development in Educational Design

EDMUND W. GORDON

By means of an extremely interesting and important line of research, Lesser has produced evidence to support the assertion that specific cultural groups tend to be characterized by particular patterns of intellective behavior. He and others have referred to these tendencies as being indicative of stylistic differences in basic cognitive functioning. Probably out of his own biases, as well as out of sensitivity to certain political realities, Lesser gives emphasis in his interpretation of these trends to an association between culture and cognitive function and thus avoids questions as to any possible relationship between genetic factors and cognitive style. As he moves further to discuss possible implications of these trends, he suggests that schooling might well be made more sensitive to group differences in cognitive style by directing learners toward those learning activities and developmental-vocational goals which are most dependent upon the respective cognitive styles. Finally, Professor Lesser turns to the political context in which his work must be viewed and finds himself in conflict with respect to the behavior of research scientists concerned with the problems of cultural and ethnic differences in mental function. I will direct my remarks to each of these issues.

In response to concern with the development of more sensitive analyses of intellectual behavior in human subjects, several investigators have proposed procedures for factorial analysis of standardized tests of intelligence. Each of these procedures permits us to use data from standardized tests of mental ability, collected under standardized conditions, to categorize patterns of intellectual function and the relative strengths of persons tested. It appears that Lesser has used this work as the basis for his approach to the determination of stylistic variation in the mental behavior of several ethnic groups. This clearly must be regarded as an advance in the development of the field of psychometry. Before one draws implications from these findings that are too specific, however, the limitations of these efforts must be considered. Standardized tests have been criticized from many sources on the basis of their inappropriateness or insensitivity to the assessment of groups with differential patterns of intellectual function. In response to these criticisms, I have advocated a qualitative, as opposed to a quantitative, approach to assessment. I have argued that a detailed description of cognitive and affective function in a variety of performance situations is essential to what I consider to be the major pedagogic purpose of assessment: to understand learning behavior in ways sufficient to allow for individually prescribed instruction.

What seems to be missing in Lesser's psychometric procedures is sensitivity to the qualitative aspects of behavioral function, as opposed to the quantitative characterization of demonstrated status. For example, using items that seem to require a relatively high level of competence in spatial relationships as his indicators, he assigns high status in this modality to examinees performing well on these items. Since no attention is given to analysis of the process by which mastery of these items is achieved, the characterization of function can only be inferred, based upon the status of the examinee's responses. If cognitive style is considered to be an important aspect of intellectual function, and particularly if we are to draw implications from such stylistic variations, cognitive style as reflected in the processes of mentation must be more sensitively analyzed.

There is a long tradition in psychometrics of attention to the assessment of the more stable aspects of human function. Since our concern has focused primarily on the predictive value of assessment data, our instruments of measurement have been designed to tap those achievements which reflect relatively stable functions and from which we can infer status with respect to the intellective categories represented by those functions. Our concern with relative position and prediction of future achievements has resulted in a heavy dependence on the numeric value and normative position assigned to demonstrated achievement and inferred status. Although I do not question the administrative utility of these quantitative data, I seriously question their value in understanding human behavior in learning or their value in the design of learning experiences.

It is for these reasons that even though I welcome the advance in the application of psychometry represented by Lesser's work, I cannot view it as an important contribution to the advancement of pedagogy. I want to make it clear that I have no problem with his assertion that persons who share common cultural backgrounds may also share common patterns of intellectual behavior. I fully support the idea that differences in learning style may be due to differences in cultural experience. I'll even go further than Lesser seems willing to go and assert that differences in patterns of intellectual function may be, in part, a reflection of differences in genotype. We know that all children do not grow alike or look alike and that these differences are based in part on genetic differences. I concede that it is entirely posssible—even likely—that children's differences with respect to mental function are based in part on genetics. But that is another issue. Let us return to differences attributable to cultural variation. There is increasing evidence to support the conclusion that patterns of cognitive function are associated with cultural group experience.

Greenfield and Bruner (1969), Witkin (1969a), and others have found differing patterns of intellectual function in a variety of cultural groups in the United States and in other countries. Greenfield and Bruner point out that culture can affect the very basic functions of perception and sensation as well as more complex behaviors such as conservation. So powerful is the relationship that these investigators have been led to conclude that "intelligence is to a great extent the internalization of 'tools' provided by a given culture" (1969, p. 634). While I support the findings that differences in learning patterns may be due to culture, gene pool, or some other characteristic, I do not feel that the pejorative connotation usually assigned to the fact of difference is either appropriate or useful. Learning differences are important, and in spite of political and social consequences, they must be recognized in the educational process. It is only when these differences are ignored or dealt with inappropriately that certain groups may suffer. The problem for education, then, is to find an appropriate match between differential learner characteristics and differential characteristics of the learning experience. Lesser tends to focus on a match between the dominant pattern of intellectual characteristics and the outcome, rather than the process, of the learning experience, emphasizing a relationship between preferred mental modalities and vocational choice. He suggests that it is maximally efficient to have students choose those careers that are related to their special abilities or preferred cognitive styles. This relationship, however, is a questionable one and represents a weakness in Lesser's position. In drawing implications from the characteristics of learners, we may find that the nature of the learning experience is more important than its goal. The issue is not whether Chinese-Americans are likely to make better architects than they would lawyers, but whether the functional advantage that some Chinese-Americans may have in dealing with spatial relationships ought to be utilized in the learning processes that allow them to achieve an educational or vocational end of their own choosuing, rather than an end dictated by that particular proclivity.

In speaking of the relationship betwen preferred mental modality and vocational choice, it is important to consider the role and importance of the level of criterion mastery necessary for adequate function, as opposed to excess competence or potential. Abstract thinking, for example, is a necessary ability in law and in some aspects of medicine, but it is not necessarily true that one has to be superb in that area of function in order to master these fields and excel in them. Berg's (1972) work clearly demonstrates that superiority with respect to entry requirements bears little or no relationship to on-the-job criterion mastery. Analyses of college admissions data and subsequent achievement produce similar findings. In many fields, there may be an essential level of competence beyond which any excess potential contributes very little. Until we have dealt with this problem in teaching, learning, and vocational development, the determination of educational and vocational choice based on some identifiable preferred cognitive style will be dangerous; there will be a tendency to select only those people who function best in an area when people who are functioning adequately in the area could achieve the goal just as well. In planning for groups of people in relation to their preferred cognitive style or the cognitive styles in which they show the greatest strength, we may be ignoring the fact that the height of one's competence in that area may not be as important as the fact of adequate competence.

Another consideration: one ought to explore the possibility that the level of ability an individual has attained may be related to the opportunity he has had to develop it. Given Lesser's interpretation that cognitive abilities are probably culturally determined, it seems that the opportunity to function in an area may contribute to the quality of subsequent functioning in that area. Whether one argues as a genetic determinist or as a cultural determinist, it seems clear that the interaction of the individual's basic cognitive pattern with the opportunity to express that pattern may enhance its function. Further, the opportunity to utilize an alternative function may result in the alternative's accelerated development. A prediction made simply from having determined status at a particular point in time may not be adequate. One needs to look at the interaction of the basic pattern with the environmental support for its expression and its possible subsequent level of expression.

Lesser's work seems to have neglected the noncognitive factors involved in learning. Without demeaning or deprecating Lesser's contributions, I feel that it is important to recognize that the strictly cognitive aspect of intellectual functioning is only one aspect of such functioning and that all behavior, including cognitive behavior, occurs in the context of an integration of affective and cognitive factors. There is some evidence to suggest that the quality and nature of cognitive function is influenced by the quality and nature of the affective experience; thus in investigating stylistic differences in cognitive function, it may be a mistake to isolate them from the context of the affective conditions in which they are called into play. More specifically, Lesser fails to consider the compensatory role of motivation. Even though an individual's ability to perform certain cognitive tasks may not be extremely high, his desire to excel may be strong enough to enable him to persevere and master the field requiring the particular skill. In vocational choice, interest and motivation are frequently as significant as are ability and aptitude.

In educational planning as well, one has to consider other factors in addition to the child's cognitive ability. Lesser states that since cognitive abilities are determined by culture, the schools, in grouping youngsters according to abilities, have isolated cultural groups from each other. This situation would be rectified if the separation of youngsters were related to self-determined goals so that the grouping is functional and purposive with respect to those self-determined goals. The role of cognitive styles in the planning of learning experience is an important consideration; it is not, however, the only consideration in planning the ways in which we group people, and it ought to represent only one element in the learning equation. Lesser implies that grouping people according to their particular cognitive strengths and weaknesses has been the most efficient way to educate them. To achieve humanistic goals, however, the easiest or most efficient route may not be adequate justification for the choice of treatment. If our goal is to develop all people in a society, we must consider in our educational planning the relationship between the ease of program implementation and the goals we are trying to achieve. For some people, we may have to take a harder route because the goal we are trying to achieve requires it.

Related to this problem of the easiest or the hardest choice is the issue of group development versus personal development. Although we are concerned with the development of both individuals and groups, the relative weight given to one or the other at different times is a function of the social values in operation. There may be times in history when we would place the greatest emphasis on development of unique individuals because of some long-term goal of the society. At other times we would place the greatest emphasis on the development of groups, again because of some societal goal. In early periods, for example, when resources were much more scarce, it was very important that societies, particularly in their developmental stages, produce at least a few people who had exceptional leadership ability. We may now be reaching a period in which there is little need for such leadership development; instead the society may need to assure itself that there are not large numbers of people who are underdeveloped. In highly complex societies, survival of the society and the people may depend on everyone's functioning at what we might call a social-intellectual survival level. If that is the principal need, then group development becomes the primary issue. Under such circumstances, the choice with respect to the easier or the harder route can better be made. If it is most essential that a few members of the society function at a particular level, certainly we will take the easiest route to get there; but if the goal is to ensure that everyone functions at an adequate level, it may be that we are going to have to take the harder route to achieve that goal.

Allow me to return to an earlier point. Although group data are important to policy decisions and total group planning, group data are contraindicated in prescriptive curricular design. Individual, not group, differences are important for this purpose. Lesser's data speak to the characteristics of groups, and if one is primarily concerned with policy decisions for the total society, it probably is useful to understand different trends in the several groups in the society. But if one believes, as I do, that in this particular period in the history of education the primary problems have to do with individual differences and their implications for the prescriptive design of learning experiences, then this work becomes less important in its implications for groups and has to be examined in the light of its contribution to helping us to better understand the functioning of individuals. As we make more progress in solving learning problems relating to individuals and in better understanding the mechanisms of attribute-treatment interactions, we may be able to generalize to groups of people. But it is probable that those generalizations will be more appropriate to groups that share learning characteristics than to groups that share racial traits, social class, or culture; for the differences within cultural groups with respect to patterns of intellectual functioning are probably more extensive and more important than the differences among cultural groups. I suspect Lesser's data would substantiate this, since there is no uniformity in the patterning of functioning within his groups. He is simply showing that there are group trends, but the range of functioning within these groups varies, suggesting, for example, that within the Chinese-American group some people are functioning much more like Puerto Rican, Black, or Jewish children. It is not really at issue, then, which ethnic group an individual belongs to or resembles; nor is it essential that his pattern of functioning indicate what his educational or vocational goal should be. The essential question is: What does the nature of the individual's pattern of functioning tell us about helping him to develop and learn.

I would like to conclude with a few remarks about the moratorium on the investigation of cultural differences. I can sympathize with Lesser's anguish on this point, but I think he was poorly advised in his decision not to publish, particularly if he was reasonably certain that his work reflected the best he could do with current knowledge and techniques. What his experience, and that of others, indicates is that things are tough out here, and there are fewer and fewer places for serious workers to hide. I see no alternative for the investigator but to carefully examine his own motives to be sure that he is willing to stand with them, to apply the greatest competence, skill, and compassion that he can muster, and then to come out prepared to fight. Research on cultural and individual differences is terribly important, and we need Lesser's contributions. It is true that some people, for the wrong motives, have seized upon the issue and have tried to use the results to political advantage. But despite this, the area remains an important one, and it is incorrect to discourage research or to refuse to publish good research simply because it is politically sensitive. It is essential that we not quit or hide, that we join in the humanizing task of creating the conditions that make such research and the social environment in which it should occur both possible and respectable. Maybe we can no longer afford to separate science and politics. For honor and science are not alone at stake; for some, what is at stake is a more equitable chance to live and to learn.

Part Five

Diversity of Creative Talent and Delimitations of Higher Education

The value issues highlighted in the previous section have always been present in higher education but in somewhat different form. The traditional issue has not been one of differential placement into assorted programs or treatments but rather differential selection into higher education itself. Selection is just as much a response to individual differences as is differential instruction, and the same questions of equity arise for individuals and for groups.

Historically, selection into higher education has favored those high in scholastic aptitude as reflected in test scores and grades, and the justification for such a system has long been taken for granted. In Chapter Twelve, Michael Wallach now challenges the basis of this system, charging that it is fundamentally at odds with the psychology of talent. Neither test scores nor grades, Wallach argues, are very good predictors of significant career achievements or real-life

175

creativity. Earlier talented accomplishments, in contrast, are quite good and highly specific in predicting later excellence in the same field, suggesting that "persistence forecasting," as Wallach calls it, would be a defensible alternative to general scholastic aptitude as a basis for college and graduate school selection. Since such a system would select students having specialized talents (as well as a required minimal level of scholastic aptitude, of course), specialized programs would need to be made available to enhance and extend those talents. To accomplish this, Wallach calls for higher education programs that have focused vocational purposes, that follow an apprenticeship model matching talented students with talented practitioner-professors in specific fields. Persistence forecasting in higher education, then, capitalizes on student strengths in both selection and training.

Both the premises and the conclusions of Wallach's argument are debated in Chapters Thirteen and Fourteen. In Chapter Thirteen, Liam Hudson argues that some individuals are not very predictable; neither their academic performance nor any other attainment can accurately predict their level of success in higher education. Thus, for important segments of the potential student population the appropriate model might not be persistence but development and change. If so, one should be wary of selection and training procedures that restrict individual opportunity on the basis of accomplishment to date. Hudson further warns that the apprenticeship system, in addition to the desirable features ascribed to it by Wallach, also serves to perpetuate orthodoxies. The intellectual control of the master needs tempering to facilitate, or even permit, challenges to dogma and to foster innovation and creativity.

In Chapter Fourteen, Jacquelyn Mattfeld reminds us that Wallach's proposals have been made before and that, although many of them have been put into practice in experimental colleges over the years, they have been generally eschewed by the bulk of higher education institutions, especially the elite ones. The problem, as Mattfeld sees it, is not Wallach's recommendations, although they are indeed controversial, but rather the multiplicity of ways in which faculties resist such notions. A different kind of persistence holds sway institutionally—a perpetuation by the faculty, usually in the name of excellence, of the same system of selection and training that produced *them*.

The basic issue in this argument concerns the values underlying any educational system that aims to capitalize on student strengths. To what extent should education strive to exploit talents already possessed? To what extent should it develop talents not yet shown? Should education extend and enhance existing individual differences or attempt to erase or reshuffle them? Such value issues are persistent and pervasive, and in a very real sense every educational program takes a stand with respect to them, even if only tacitly. Attempts such as Wallach's and those in subsequent chapters of this book to expand the range of viable educational alternatives responsive to individual differences should help to confront and clarify many of the value issues so often ignored.

12

Psychology of Talent and Graduate Education

MICHAEL A. WALLACH

Two basic issues exist in regard to graduate education. First, who shall be selected for access to the training programs offered by the more advantaged universities, programs that constitute inevitably scarce resources? Second, what shall these training programs involve as their pedagogical content? Traditionally, the answer to the first question has been treated as rather obvious, and attention has focused on the second. We would propose, however, that the answer to the first question is not so obvious at all; in fact, the obvious approach to answering it turns out to be inappropriate in terms of the psychology of talent. At the same time, the most natural way of affecting the form and character of training probably arises from the nature of the trainees themselves; it is easiest, after all, to train them along the lines already established by the skills they possess. Thus, the answer to the first question influences the answer to the second. In addition, the nature of talent seems to carry some direct implications for the form and substance of training.

That admissions requirements play a crucial role in the qualities displayed by the graduates of an educational institution is well recognized. Astin and Panos (1969), for example, have found the type of student input to be more determinative of the results a college achieves with its students than anything the college may try to do in its teaching programs. Applying the same point to graduate education, Keppel has put the matter this way: "Recruitment and selection of personnel for the professions are major responsibilities of a university in American life. . . . By the success or failure of their programs of recruitment and selection, [graduate and professional schools] tend for a generation to influence the activity and the stand of the profession they serve. . . . One can even argue that the policies and programs which bring such future leaders to the profession may be more important than the academic training programs themselves" (quoted in Berelson, 1960, p. 137). And the same general idea has been stated by Jencks and Riesman (1968): "Professional schools have their students for only a few years, and they can do only so much with whatever raw material they get. But to the extent that they are overapplied and can select their raw material according to some preconceived plan, they can influence the profession they serve decisively" (p. 254).

But what kind of selection plan should be put into effect? The answer typically provided is that intellective ability test scores and academic achievement are the appropriate bases for choosing candidates. To make admissions decisions on bases other than these, it is argued, is to be nonmeritocratic in one's selection procedures. Jencks and Riesman even advance the seemingly widely accepted view that true meritocracy calls for more emphasis on nationally normed tests and less on teachers' grades: "School teachers can also give good grades to students who have made a good impression in class but have done poorly on quizzes and tests, and can thus improve both the student's class rank and his college chances. Educational Testing Service has no such device for rewarding poise, politeness, and the like" (p. 64). In the same general way, Berelson (1960) quite automatically assumes that the results of intellective aptitude tests provide an essentially veridical reading of a student's potential for occupational or professional competence. Thus, for example, to determine which lines of graduate training are populated with students of the highest caliber, Berelson looks at information comparing students in law school, medical school, and various fields of graduate study in the arts and sciences in terms of IQ scores. He seems to believe that talent for becoming a meaningful contributor to any of a diverse panorama of specialized skills is adequately predicted from scores on intelligence tests. It seems particularly ironic for Berelson to take this approach, since he argues that the appropriate objective of graduate education is the training of the skilled specialist rather than of the liberally educated person.

Is it so clear that merit is most appropriately defined by a student's scores on the verbal and mathematical aptitude sections of the Scholastic Aptitude Test or the Graduate Record Examinations—with the possible inclusion of more subjective estimates provided by a student's grades in conventional courses? If not, then the answer to the question of how admissions selection should be carried out is by no means an obvious one; nor is the answer predetermined by the mere fact of subscribing to a meritocratic value scheme. In order to address the two issues of how selection for graduate education should proceed and what kind of training such education should provide, two prior tasks await us. First, we must consider the nature of talent: How does it relate to measures of academic achievement? How can we assess it? What can we consider evidence of a person's merit when making preferential decisions regarding educational opportunities? Second, we must examine admissions processes in higher education and consider the extent to which the selection procedures seem congruent with the nature of talent.

Talented Attainments and Academic Measures

Talent does not consist of scores on national tests or of most of what forms the basis for grades in school. If these interest us, it is because they are presumed to predict a person's probable accomplishment when he is not in the role of a student carrying out assigned tasks. With the occasional exception of intrinsically meaningful scholarly papers or projects that consolidate an area of thought or treat a topic with insight or imagination, proficiency at the usual sorts of academic tasks is valued not in itself but rather as an indicator of what the person can do when on his own—when he sets his own goals of excellence in terms acknowledged by the outside world instead of meeting demands set by teachers or test makers. From various sources of evidence, however, it has become clear that for students scoring within the middle and upper part of the range for the usual indexes of intellective ability and academic achievement, little or no relationship exists between their scores and talented attainments in real life—whether viewed during the student years or later on in occupational settings. Of course, it is precisely for candidates scoring within this part of the range that discriminations tend to be made concerning acceptability for attendance or scholarship support at the high-quality (and hence high-prestige) graduate and undergraduate institutions, where competition is most keen. Moreover, attainments in one domain, such as excellence at creative writing, cannot predict attainments in another, such as skill at composing music. We shall first review some evidence for these points obtained from work with students and then turn to results concerning occupational attainments after the school years are past.

How do we assess talented accomplishments? We look at what the world takes as evidence of intrinsic merit in products or performances that a person contributes to the environment. For merit evaluations it is most feasible to rely upon the judgments of those who are experts at a given type of endeavor. Ideally, we might want to bring representative samples of the person's work before these experts, and sometimes this has been done. Often, the most practical and efficient approach is to obtain reports of external evidences of quality, such as the winning of awards in competitions or the recognition of merit implied by acceptance for publication. Such reports seem to qualify as usable evidence (Maxey and Ormsby, 1971; Richards, Holland, and Lutz, 1966, 1967).

As evidence of high quality contributions, students have been asked to provide retrospective information concerning signs of public recognition of their achievements outside the classroom in such areas as art, creative writing, dramatics, debating, music, scientific projects, and the exercise of political leadership. These attainments constitute environmental contributions of direct significance in their own right, and they provide a rather good basis for predicting future accomplishments, thus constituting a suitable means of selecting students who can be expected to excel at cognate activities in times to come. Such attainments reflect a relatively free response by the individual to the real-life circumstances offered by his world, rather than a response constrained by the necessities and demands of the academic treadmill.

When we consider directly meritorious accomplishments such as winning competitive awards for achievement or performance in the arts and sciences, the general finding is that little or no relationship exists between display of a talented accomplishment and a student's location on the academic skills measures—at least for students scoring in the middle to high range of these measures. Contributing to the now rather extensive collection of evidence documenting this basic point are studies by Holland (1961, 1964), Holland and Nichols (1964), Holland and Richards (1965, 1966, 1967), Menges (1972), Nichols and Holland (1964), Nichols (1966), Richards, Holland, and Lutz (1966, 1967), Wallach and Wing (1969), and Wing and Wallach (1971).

Richards and others (1966, 1967) examined the talented attainments outside of school of several thousand college freshmen and sophomores who had also reported on such attainments during the high school years. The findings were unequivocal. Intellective ability and academic achievement assessments from high school intercorrelate and predict grades during college, but they fail to predict talented real-life accomplishments. Real-life accomplishments during the high school years, on the other hand, predict similar accomplishments during college, but they do not predict college grades and are not related to academic skills measures from the high school years. The predictability over time of talented attainments was quite specific: early artistic excellence predicted later artistic excellence, but it did not predict later literary or scientific excellence; early excellence at scientific pursuits predicted the later manifestation of scientific excellence, but not later literary or artistic excellence; early excellence at creative writing predicted that a person would go on to do significant writing later as well, but it did not predict later excellence at scientific or musical activities; and so on.

Parloff, Datta, Kleman, and Handlon (1968) had scientists judge the quality of research projects that were conducted by high school students on their own and not as part of school assignments. Substantial quality differences emerged, but these had nothing to do with the students' intellective ability test scores or academic achievement levels. There is nothing inherent in the nature of schooling that precludes its concerning itself with direct indications of talent and merit as the outside world defines these. The next two studies illustrate this reality; both involve the bringing of undeniably meaningful displays of talent within the purview of the academic curriculum.

In one study (Morrison, 1963), results indicated that talent at theater arts, with particular reference to the skills that would make for high competence as an actor in dramatic productions, was not predictable from scores on intellective ability tests. In this instance, dramatic skill was the specific concern of the academic program in question—a rare case where competence in the eyes of the world and in the eyes of the school coincided. The very unusualness of this case reveals the divergence of so much of academic work from what constitutes merit in any direct sense that would be in agreement with real-life standards. Morrison also found that excellence at dramatics outside of school during the high school years predicted excellence in theater arts within the given college curriculum, where the performance skills of acting were made part of the definition of academic achievement.

In the other study (Mednick, 1963), which involved graduate students, talent for scientific research in psychology was brought within the graduate curriculum. Since excellence at independent research at least purports to be the goal of much graduate instruction, it is, of course, ironic that special note must be taken when tasks having that aim are incorporated into the curriculum. Faculty members applied an evaluation schedule used to judge the quality of research of professional scientists (Taylor, 1958) to research projects carried out on an independent basis by graduate students. The faculty members in question were ones who were well acquainted with the students' autonomously undertaken research endeavors, and the ratings concerned the imaginativeness of the research and the degree to which it contributed to knowledge in its area—just the kinds of considerations that would in fact be brought to bear upon scientific work in real life. While these ratings varied across a considerable range, they were not at all correlated with intellective ability test scores or with grades in graduate school courses. On the other hand, the test scores predicted the course grades quite adequately.

The lack of relationship found to obtain between real-life definition of talented attainments and course grades causes one to question the end toward which the courses are directed, or at least to question the bases for grading the students' achievement in those courses. Indeed, as Heiss (1970) has found in her surveys of graduate school faculties and students, both groups voice criticism of the ways in which grade distinctions are made in such courses, and it is just this lack of validity which the Mednick (1963) study documents. That faculty members know how to evaluate in ways that possess validity for real-life accomplishment criteria is evident from their ability to make sharp distinctions in terms of quality among their students' research undertakings. What graduate programs must do is provide students with the right sorts of tasks as the basis of their graduate training—tasks as similar as possible to, and judged in the same terms as, the scientific work students are supposed to engage in later as professionals.

When we consider real-world merit criteria for adult professionals engaged in their occupational tasks, do we find the same lack of relationship to academic skills indicators as we have noted for directly meaningful talented attainments of students? By and large, the answer is yes. Marston (1971) found that for psychology graduate students who obtained their doctorates from a given graduate school over a fourteen-year period, subsequent publication output as professionals was unrelated to their intellective ability scores as assessed upon entrance to graduate school. While the number of publications is, to be sure, imperfect as a criterion of professional competence, it has been found in fact (Bloom, 1963; Harmon, 1963; Helson and Crutchfield, 1970) to relate substantially to expert judgments about the quality of the contributions to knowledge contained in the publications—critics of the publish or perish doctrine to the contrary notwithstanding. That this should turn out to be the case is not surprising, after all, when we consider that standards of editorial merit, often quite stringent ones, must be satisfied for most professional publication and that a certain amount of publishing must of necessity occur if a person is to make significant research contributions to a field.

More or less the same conclusion obtains in a study by Bloom (1963). Chemists and mathematicians chosen as significant contributors by their peers were matched for such characteristics as age, educational background, and professional experience to controls not so chosen. The peer selections, which were made with high consensus by two groups of experts working independently, related strongly to publication output, but the significant contributors were no higher on intelligence test performances than their controls. Similar results were reported by Helson and Crutchfield (1970) in the area of mathematics. Studies by Harmon (1963) of physical and biological scientists yield the same conclusion yet again. The scientists' intelligence test scores and academic achievement indicators were quite unrelated to the quality of their professional work. Expert judges, working independently, evaluated professional accomplishments in terms of a carefully worked out criterion involving the quality of contributions to scientific knowledge. While unrelated to academic skills measures, excellence as a scientist was strongly related to publication output. It is a matter of some irony that faced with results of this sort, Harmon nevertheless refrains from concluding that something may be wrong with using aptitude scores or academic achievement as criteria for selecting candidates for preferential educational treatment. So strong is his commitment to these academic yardsticks that he questions instead the validity of the evaluations made by the expert judges. If we look at quality differentiations among professional artists (Barron, 1963) and among architects (MacKinnon, 1968), the same story emerges. Sizable contrasts regarding professional eminence based on evaluations by knowledgeable experts find no parallels when it comes to intellective ability or academic achievement data. Grades obtained in high school do not relate to quality of later professional contributions; nor do grades obtained in college. But, once again, talented attainments as students, outside of school, do predict strong contributions later as adult professionals.

Consider one more example from yet another domain of professional activity. Ulyatt and Ulyatt (1970, 1971) evaluated women graduates of a medical school in Britain over a ten-year period in regard to a quality index of their occupational activities as physicians. This quality index was the number of specialist qualifications that the physician went on to obtain in the course of occupational work. Two indexes of academic achievement in medical school were obtained, one reflecting actual course grades and one embodying teacher views of which students were superior. The two academic skills measures correlated highly with each other, but neither predicted the quality level of the person's subsequent occupational work as a physician, as indicated by the number of specialist qualifications obtained. Such findings led Ulyatt and Ulyatt (1970) to conclude: "It is clear that using academic standards is unlikely to help in the choice of appropriate candidates and, by reducing the variety of applicants, this trend may perhaps be actively harmful" (p. 34).

Certain methodological queries raised by Werts (1967) about some of this evidence have been dealt with by Holland and Richards (1967) and by Wallach (1971a). Werts has argued that the kinds of talented accomplishments described are rare and for that reason difficult to predict from academic skills measures. Evidence has been cited, however, showing that such accomplishments, no matter how rare, are quite predictable from information about earlier accomplishments of similar kinds. If, in turn, one wishes to criticize such evidence as the foregoing on the ground that range restriction applies for the academic measures (Weitzman, 1972)—that one is dealing with groups which are too select to begin with—it seems relevant to consider the following points. Some of this work (Harmon, 1963) found negative coefficients for almost half of the correlations that were computed between the academic assessments and real-life accomplishment. Statistical adjustments for attenuation of range, which would increase the size of all correlations, negative as well as positive, would still leave the overall result near zero. Moreover, where college-applicant populations, rather than already selected groups, were studied (Wing and Wallach, 1971), the same picture of minimal predictability from academic skills indicators to criteria of real-life attainments also emerged. In any case, we are generalizing only for the upper part of the academic skills range, the point being that this sector is sufficiently extensive that selections for further educational advantages still take place within it.

In sum, the evidence in hand casts strong doubts on the utility of making academic skills distinctions within the upper sector of their range when seeking to understand who is likely to exhibit meritorious attainments in occupational or professional contexts. This was suspected by McClelland (1958) when he perceived a lack of correspondence between the criteria defining academic aptitude or school achievement and merit as defined by the quality of one's occupational contributions. In an extensive literature review considering the relationship between academic achievement in college and professional contributions manifested later on, Hoyt (1965, 1966) reached the same conclusion as has emerged here. Even in fields where the needed skills clearly must include rational-analytic powers of the kind that academic curriculum designers could not possibly view as beyond their coverage or concern, such as scientific research, Hoyt's review indicates that students earning the higher grades are not more likely to show stronger occupational achievements. This general outcome is especially impressive in light of the self-fulfilling prophecy expected to operate in the direction of producing a relationship between academic skills indicators and subsequent occupational attainments. To a certain degree, after all, preferential advantages in recruitment for superior occupational opportunities are given to those who can present a dossier of superior academic credentials to their prospective employers. From the findings in hand, it thus seems fair to say that the case for the lack of such a relationship is the stronger one.

Thus, there is substantial evidence that the way to predict whether a person will manifest a given line of talented attainment later is to determine whether he or she manifests a similar type of attainment earlier. We have called this type of prediction persistence forecasting (Wallach, 1971b), taking our usage from meteorology, where it turns out to be fairly reasonable to use the weather today as a basis for predicting what the weather will be like tomorrow. The best candidates for graduate students would seem to be those who already show forms of competence which the graduate program hopes to nourish toward ultimate display in professional roles, not students who have the edge over their peers on intellective aptitude tests or who earn the best grades in courses (where high grades often accrue from exercising skills, such as memorization of material for exams, which have minimal transfer to the real-world competences in question).

Persistence forecasting of talented attainments has its analogue in the study of other aspects of human functioning as well. In the sphere of personality assessment, for example, it has been argued that the best way to predict whether someone will manifest particular forms of behavior in the future is to determine whether the person has displayed those or similar behaviors in the past, not to use an indirect test which presumably taps the disposition to engage in such behaviors. This leads one to focus attention on forms of conduct which possess intrinsic significance—which are themselves of interest to us—rather than on responses which obtain meaning or become of interest only if they validly function as signs of something else (Wallach and Leggett, 1972). The analogous point in regard to personality is nicely put by Mischel (1972): "Predictive validity tends to decrease as the gap increases between the behavior sampled on the predictor measure and the behavior that is being predicted. On the whole, research regarding the relative specificity of behavior suggests that sampled predictor behavior should be as similar as possible to the behavior used on the criterion measure. . . . For example, to predict someone's chance of success in response to a treatment, it would probably be more efficacious to observe the individual in a sample of the treatment situation than to analyze his responses to inkblots" (p. 323).

Persistence forecasting implies, of course, that if talented attainments during a person's student years are essentially independent of academic skills measures, this independence should also obtain when we look at displays of such talent in occupational tasks after the student years are over, namely, in the carrying out of professional roles. Talent should be defined, then, in terms of accomplishments—scientific, literary, artistic, or any other—that we view as intrinsically meritorious. Viewed during the student years or after, attainments that the outside world recognizes as inherently meaningful are essentially unpredictable from the grades a person earns in the usual kinds of academic courses encountered during high school or college and are unpredictable as well from intellective ability test results. But, earlier manifestations of talent, accomplishments which the environment judges to be significant, predict the continuation of contributions of the same kind. With most admission selections for preferred higher educational opportunities being made among students who score in the upper sector of the academic skills range, we next must consider the basis of the selection processes typically used in the light of the preceding evidence concerning the nature of talent.

Admissions Decisions in Higher Education

It is of more than historical interest to note that the use of intellective aptitude tests for selection in higher education can be traced back in a lineage extending to the Army Alpha intelligence test developed by Arthur Otis in World War I (Schudson, 1972). At the time of the First World War, the United States Army sought help from psychologists in developing a way to screen out recruits whose general intelligence was too low for them to be good potential soldiers. The response of the American Psychological Association to the army's request was to appoint a Committee on Classification of Personnel in the Army under the direction of Otis. The product of this committee's work was the Army Alpha test. Consider, however, what this test's function was. The Army Alpha test was used for rejection, not for acceptance. It served as a basis for rejecting those candidates who presumably would not be able to function usefully from the army's viewpoint. The expectation thus was that the validity of such a test for predicting forms of conduct relevant to the outside world—in this case, the ability to serve as a competent soldier—resided in distinctions to be made at its low end. As the use of intellective ability tests subsequently made its way into educational circles, however, and particularly with the growth in applicant pressure for admission to higher quality undergraduate and graduate programs after World War II, a significant change took place in the way in which decision makers used test scores. Rather than limiting the function of such tests to the rejection of applicants for admission and/or financial aid, the tests came increasingly to be used for making distinctions among candidates who scored within the middle to high part of the distribution. As the preceding pages have suggested, this change in use from attaching significance to the low end of such tests to attaching significance to the high end is not justifiable; those upper-end score differences do not seem to possess the implications for real-life proficiency that commonly are imputed to them. What implications do they possess? They tend to be valid bases for predicting academic achievement differences, again within the upper part of the range, on conventional types of course materials.

Returning to a historical perspective, we find that the power of score differences within the upper part of the range on intellective tests to predict grade achievement differences has traditionally been invoked as the warrant for making selection distinctions in terms of these test scores. This genre of justification can be noted as early as 1941 in the Carnegie report (Carnegie Foundation for the Advancement of Teaching, 1941) on the validity of GRE scores. Academic achievement in conventional courses was accepted virtually without question as the appropriate validity criterion for intellective aptitude measures such as the GRE's verbal and mathematical aptitude tests. Justification in these terms has proceeded in an unchanged fashion to this day. There is an ironic circularity, of course, to this custom. Researchers (Jencks and Riesman, 1968), for example, urge the ascendancy of intelligence test scores over grades for making selection decisions because of the belief that grades are more open to the effects of teacher bias, yet those very records of grades constitute the validity criterion invoked as the rationale for using the intellective ability tests in the first place.

Clinical observations by persons acquainted with student-selection processes suggest an awareness that something is awry with the situation just described. For example, a report on graduate education at Radcliffe (Radcliffe Committee on

Graduate Education for Women, 1956) concluded that the Graduate Record Examination "threw little light on [the candidate's] originality, creativeness, or ability to reason" (p. 80). As another example, Sears (1964) pinpointed in an intuitive way what he believed present practices to be like and presented his method of reforming them. Noting that "measures of academic intelligence are the most frequently used aids in selection" (p. 21), he then offered this suggestion: "If you have the right kind of information blanks for your graduate school admissions, you will find out whether [the candidate] has had any hobbies, that is, whether, in the best sense of the word, he has been a dilettante of intellectual, social, and emotional experiences. A well-integrated dilettante with wide experience and high standards is a promising character for graduate school" (p. 22). Sears seems to feel that when making selection appraisals of students, one should seek evidence of competence at something done extracurricularly and hence for its own sake. But is Sears correct in his view that "academic intelligence" still is the basic criterion for selection at such institutions? If he is, then he is referring to a practice which seems quite adequate to the faculties in question. In a survey of ten universities with strong graduate programs, Heiss (1970) reported that graduate faculties express considerable satisfaction with their admissions practices. The relative absence of specific information on these matters led Wing and Wallach (1971) to explore actual admissions processes at highly selective undergraduate institutions, and it seems likely that their findings apply as well to the graduate admissions situation at such institutions. It is precisely the practices at highly selective institutions that concern us, of course, since we can be confident that the relatively less selective institutions are using academic skills indicators to screen out those scoring below some threshold of acceptability which is just the way such measures should be used.

In brief, Wing and Wallach (1971) found that even at those institutions which select their admittees from candidates ranking within the upper part of the range for conventionally defined academic skills, intelligence test score differences and academic achievement differences are heavily weighed in deciding which candidates to accept and which to reject. The more selective institutions simply tend to require that higher test scores and higher grade averages be exhibited for the candidate to gain admission. Although we did not find it practiced, there is an alternative: once a candidate demonstrates a certain level of academic skills, his chances for admission would not be increased by higher performance in those skills. Admission would then depend upon ways of evaluating the candidates that do not covary with measures of academic skills within this upper part of the range.

Wing and Wallach (1971) studied the effect on class composition of selecting candidates on the basis of talented accomplishments rather than on academic skill. They found that had real-world attainments received prime attention—once the candidate had shown that his or her academic skills were strong enough to succeed in the program—the admitted class would have differed in membership by some 50 to 60 percent from the class actually admitted. By contrast, if we consider what the class would be like had it been selected exclusively on the criterion of maximizing traditional academic proficiency, the admitted class would have differed in its membership by only some 20 to 30 percent from the class actually admitted. In other words, while knowledge of academic skills credentials predicts actual acceptances for fully 70 to 80 percent of the admitted class, knowledge of meritorious talented attainments by the candidates predicts actual acceptances for only 40 to 50 percent of the admitted class.

Further, the primacy of academic skills performance over real-world forms of talented accomplishments in admissions decisions is shown in a comparison of the rates of admissions found to occur for each of four groups of applicants characterized by different sorts of qualifications (Wing and Wallach, 1971). In the comparisons that follow, the absolute frequencies of candidates falling within each group are substantial. Among applicants showing neither the highest academic forms of proficiency nor significant real-world attainments of some kind, the acceptance rate found was on the order of 15 percent, representing a kind of floor likelihood of acceptance for candidates. That this floor is greater than zero may indicate that some decisions are made on grounds other than those just mentioned, and may also in part reflect a quite natural element of unreliability in the decision-making process. As a kind of ceiling at the other end of the scale, the acceptance rate found for the group whose members showed both the highest academic skill levels and also some kind of substantial real-world attainments was on the order of 80 percent. That the ceiling operating for this group is less than 100 percent most likely reflects the same factors that account for the floor likelihood being greater than zero for the previous group.

Having specified these floor and ceiling rates of acceptance, the crucial question is where, in relation to these rates, the two remaining groups of candidates fall: those with significant real-world attainments to their credit but lacking the strongest academic skills credentials and those with the highest academic skills credentials but lacking significant real-world accomplishments. The rate of acceptance among members of the former group is found to be approximately 20 percent. By contrast, the acceptance rate for members of the latter group turns out to be approximately 70 percent. These results provide a rather clear picture. Applicants with substantial real-world attainments who lack the highest academic skills credentials are admitted at a rate only slightly higher than the floor rate found for applicants who are without either type of qualification. On the other hand, applicants with the highest academic skills credentials who lack substantial real-world attainments are admitted at a rate only slightly lower than the ceiling rate found for applicants characterized by both types of qualifications. Clearly, having those somewhat higher intellective aptitude test scores and secondary school grade averages counts for a great deal, raising the applicant's chances of admission almost five times the floor rate—from 15 percent to 70 percent—a level almost as high as would be reached if the candidate were also characterized by significant real-world attainments.

With regard to college admissions procedures at highly selective institutions, then, direct evidence of talent counts for considerably less than does scoring a few points higher in traditional academic skills measures. Since academic skills distinctions in the upper part of their range do not predict real world attainments, we are forced to conclude that selection processes for high quality higher education give considerably more weight to fine distinctions at the upper end of the academic skills range than can be justified in terms of the nature of talent. Sears' (1964) general intuition about these matters appears to be confirmed by the Wing and Wallach (1971) findings, and it seems reasonable to expect that admissions procedures at prestigious graduate institutions will be comparable to the admissions procedures we have found at prestigious undergraduate institutions. We apparently have come full circle in that academic proficiency indicators whose basic justification resides in their presumptive validity for predicting environmentally meaningful attainments have in fact supplanted those very attainments as criteria of selection in higher education. Armed with the information contained in the preceding pages, we now are in a position to return to the questions with which we began, namely, how selection should proceed for those graduate education opportunities that are most contested, and what should be the character of the education that is provided by these opportunities.

Selection and Training in Graduate Education

Throughout the last decade or so, from writers as diverse, for example, as Berelson (1960), Levi (1969), and Campbell (1971), one can sense a growing disillusionment with the concept of liberal education in relation to graduate work and a growing regard for the idea that such work should be oriented toward developing skilled specialists, people possessing specific competencies, with the acquisition of these skills defined as the purpose or goal of the given program of study. In a sense, what this trend suggests is a movement toward rehabilitating the notion of vocational training in relation to graduate education. This position is not a form of antiintellectualism; it is simply a request that there be clarity of goals for the educational enterprise. With clear goals one would not have the commonly encountered situation of a graduate education being irrelevant, or even antagonistic, to the occupational activities expected of the holder of an advanced degree.

Apparently, as the apprenticeship method lost its respectability toward the end of the Middle Ages, the concept of training for a vocation fell increasingly into disrepute in the history of Western education. Status came to depend instead upon book learning—a form of education that did not have any specific practical purpose as a goal. However, if one admits the desirability of explicitness of occupational goals (whether practical or not) in relation to graduate training, the heterogeneous nature of talent as we have described it earlier indicates the need to establish good matches between a person's competences and what he is being trained for, between the nature of the training and its goal.

The first requirement in connection with any graduate program, then, would seem to be clarity as to vocational purposes. Once these purposes have been delineated, we can address the issues of selection criteria and the character of the training itself, mindful that answers for these issues require specific reference to the occupational purposes that have been established. For a distinctive thing about any vocation, after all, is that one knows the activities which define it. A person's potential for success reflects how well he can match the necessary activities, and training consists of induction into ever closer approximations of these activities. Once the occupational goals of a given graduate education enterprise have been specified, we then should sample those behaviors of a candidate that would be directly relevant to fulfilling these goals—the persistence forecasting idea—and decide accordingly whether the individual is likely to achieve these goals.

Since talent, as we have seen, has been found to be diverse rather than unidimensional, talent for becoming one kind of specialist cannot really predict talent for becoming another kind. To predict success we must therefore know and agree upon a given program's goals in terms that are as concrete and specific as possible. For example, if the goal is competence at teaching—something one hears espoused with increasing frequency as an area that should receive more attention in graduate education—then one should look for past evidences of teaching skills as such. If necessary, one should fashion miniaturized samples of the goal situations (for instance, one can create actual teaching situations and evaluate how the candidate performs in them). Self-report of past performances, concrete products, societal recognition in the form of awards or publications, assessment of performance in contexts that involve the very competences whose development and continuance one is trying to predict—all of these are relevant ways of anticipating the quality of a person's future activity within the same domain.

We must emphasize again that the goals which the graduate training is to fulfill need to be shaped by consideration of the actual occupational or vocational roles into which the student is expected to move. Thus, for example, high grades on examinations of the usual sort would be a reasonable goal only if the person would be expected occupationally to take tests of that kind and earn high grades on them when scored in the conventional manner—obviously a silly job description. If the person is to teach, he needs practice at teaching; if he is to do scholarly research of a particular kind, he needs practice at that. Such practice most appropriately should be offered to those candidates who start out with the greatest competence at the same or similar activities, as judged from the best evidence available concerning past accomplishments at those activities.

It has been widely noted (for example, Grigg, 1965) that current selection practices result in the better graduate schools competing with one another for the same students—those with the highest scores on intellective aptitude tests and the highest grade point averages. Candidates not in that category tend to be denied admission and/or financial support and are therefore obliged to enter lower quality graduate programs or are put out of the running entirely. Clearly, however, it is not access to just any graduate training that matters; it is access to the higher quality forms of such training that is important when one considers the influence of admissions practices on the composition of professional and leadership groups. It is, after all, the graduates of the more prestigious institutions that are more readily conveyed into positions of power. The growth in the number of graduate programs of relatively low quality over the years, largely for reasons of institutional image enhancement, has been commented on in various places (Hollis, 1945; Mayhew, 1970; National Science Board, 1969). In the face of this array of weak graduate offerings, appropriate admissions practices for the better institutions become all the more crucial. If we are mindful that talent is diversified rather than unidimensional (see also De Haan and Havighurst, 1957, for corroborating evidence from younger ages), our use of selection procedures emphasizing talented attainments that conform with the occupational goals defined by each graduate program should result in enlarging the pool of candidates deemed attractive by the more prestigious graduate schools. Rather than all seeking the same candidates, the programs and departments in question can search more explicitly for candidates with competences tailored closely to the vocational purposes of the training. To say however, that the talent pool will be broadened by this kind of change in selection criteria presupposes that some variation will take place in the goals that different programs will set up for themselves. What should these goals be?

In general, the most appropriate goals of these prestigious graduate programs would be to promote and foster activities that preserve, integrate, transmit, and add to knowledge in each of the fields. Because of the influential role of graduate education on professional and leadership groups, the effects of the systematic neglect or overcultivation of educational domains or functions will be apparent, as Berelson (1960) puts it, not only in the value system of American education but also in American life. Certain kinds of systematic neglect and overcultivation can, in fact, be readily identified. In the overcultivation category, one can point to the almost magical significance taken on by the term *research*, in whose name activities are sometimes carried out that are so lacking in perspective as to seem more like the exercise of pedantry than of genuine scholarship. In the category of systematic neglect, two areas stand out: concern for teaching skill and for practitioner skill. In considering these lines of vocational endeavor, there are many ways in which programs can differentiate their mandates from one another and thus select students with different kinds of talents. Let us take each of these neglected areas in turn.

By now, the point that preparation for college and university teaching receives short shrift in graduate education has been made numerous times (Chase, 1970; Heiss, 1970; Nowlis, Clark, and Rock, 1968; Strothmann, 1955). That it is important for at least some high-quality graduate programs to adopt college and university teaching as an explicit vocational goal seems difficult to deny. Integration, preservation, and transmission of knowledge are intimately connected with the teaching function, and they are of central importance within the spectrum of vocations for which graduate education has responsibility. Concentration on adding to knowledge at the expense of these other activities seems often to have resulted in the kind of pedantry mentioned above. What tends to be ignored in such discussions of teacher preparation as the studies mentioned above, however, is the idea that selection has a role to play here. If training for teaching is to become a serious goal of some graduate programs, then such programs will need to select candidates for admission and financial aid who in fact possess teaching skill to a substantial degree. And this means basing selection decisions on past performances which sample as directly as possible the candidate's competence as a teacher. While it may not be as easy to sample teaching competency as to have the can-

didate take an intellective ability test, there is every reason
to believe that the most competent teachers, based on evidence concerning actual teaching behavior, will not be efficiently identified by recourse to such a test.

Practitioner Skills. Also subject to systematic neglect in
graduate education's customary value system has been the
cultivation of practitioner competences. When we speak of
graduate education's need to reflect the full spectrum of
vocational activities concerned with integrating, preserving,
transmitting, and adding to knowledge, there is no justification for limiting one's definition of knowledge or meaning
to that which can be treated in already codified form. On the
contrary, direct practice also constitutes part of knowledge.
There is a strong tradition of emphasis upon the practitioner
skills involved in research in the natural sciences, but this
tradition seems to be quite foreign to the humanities as they
are customarily treated within academic circles. Practitioner
expertise in the creative skills of the artist, musician, dancer,
actor, or writer, are part of knowledge and meaning in the
fields of art, music, dance, drama, and literature; these fields
are not just the domain of art critic, musicologist, literary
historian, or philosopher of aesthetics.

Practitioner activities have been receiving increased attention these days in other fields: witness such activities as
conducting interviews in clinical psychology, giving practical
legal advice and carrying out community advocacy and arbi-
tration activities in law, practice teaching under extensive
supervision in education, and a greater emphasis on practi-
cum experience with various aspects of the study of medicine. These experiences have become part of the training
program itself, that is, the student receives academic credit
for them. And as our reference to the natural sciences suggests, scholarly research itself often involves a range of skills
extending well beyond the bibliographic ones; but in many
cases this range receives relatively little emphasis in graduate
training until the dissertation, by which time it may be too
late. Predissertation graduate work in the social sciences, for
example, does not involve extensive experience with empiri-

cal skills used in the research enterprise, in spite of the fact that the student is supposed to be able to manifest such skills later on as a professional.

The desirability of greater concern with the kinds of practitioner skills described above has been pointed out by such writers as Berelson (1960), Jencks and Riesman (1968), and Heiss (1970). Once again, however, it is only in relation to curriculum that this has received emphasis. No attention has been paid to selection. We have seen, however, that orienting one's selection procedures toward candidates who have demonstrated significant levels of competence yields different groups of students than those siphoned off by recourse to the traditional indicators of academic skills (Wing and Wallach, 1971). If one is serious about including practitioner skills within graduate education's purview, the place to begin would seem to be at the admissions end of the picture; thus there will be students in attendance who would profit maximally from such curricular changes as are introduced.

Since the student demand for them will be greater, reforms bringing greater emphasis on practitioner skills are more likely to take place, and the presence of groups of students who are explicitly talented at one or another of these skills means that pedagogical reforms are likely to be more successful. For example, candidates for law school with histories of high competence in political leadership activities and debating probably are more likely to make meaningful contributions to the advocacy, mediation, and advice-giving aspects of legal work than are candidates who possess only the highest academic records. The English literature or art department that is willing to view practitioner activities as falling within its occupational mandate will not use academic skills indicators as its sole selection criterion; in all probability it will most effectively select students by examining prior evidence of the writing or art work that the candidate has produced. When graduate departments are unwilling to view practitioner skills as within the appropriate definition of knowledge in their particular fields, however, such broadening of selection procedures will be difficult to come by.

Resistance to Change. If knowledge in its various aspects includes forms that emerge from practitioner activities—if besides adding to knowledge we agree that its integration, preservation, transmission, and, therefore, the teaching of it are significant parts of graduate education's province as well—why is there considerable resistance to changing selection procedures in such a way as to better reflect these occupational goals? For one thing, institutions tend to imitate one another in the selection criteria they utilize, and any one of them is loathe to make admissions changes of a kind that could be interpreted as a lowering of standards which would downgrade its position on the status hierarchy. Barzun (1968) has noted this in terms of the general inertia encountered in an educational institution when there is an attempt to introduce serious changes in the way things are done. Wing and Wallach (1971) have observed that intellective ability test scores have become imbued with large amounts of the surplus meaning that adheres to the term *intelligence* in its common-sense application, and who could quarrel with the desirability of selecting candidates who are the most intelligent? The only trouble is that recourse to traditional types of academic skills measures in the upper part of the range does not in fact identify applicants who are the most intelligent in the common-sense meaning of the term; rather it pinpoints students who are specialists in doing well on certain kinds of tests and in certain kinds of classwork. Given the lack of transfer from such skills to environmental attainments calling directly for the exercise of talent, one can only conclude that the commonsense meaning of intelligence is more appropriately reflected in the kinds of work samples we have considered than in those measures of academic skills that go by the name of intelligence tests. Faced with the kind of problem to which Barzun alludes, it seems appropriate to suggest that testing agencies themselves need to play an active role in directing assessment into new channels of the sort described. This would, to be sure, call for the mustering of a considerable amount of disinterestedness on their part, for it involves downgrading the degree of utility claimed for forms of information that they have become particularly adept at providing.

Another reason for resisting change in selection procedures arises from the cumulative effects over time of the use of the customary selection procedures themselves. This point was well put by Campbell (1971): "To the extent that the faculty controls admissions policy, they will sway the policy in the direction of admitting the students that most closely resemble them" (p. 645). The same point concerning graduate school faculties was put in more general terms by Berelson (1960): "Perhaps more here than in other professions, present practice is perpetuated precisely because the judges of the product are themselves earlier products and present producers, so there is a closed system at work" (p. 218). In their student days, faculty members were selected for preferential educational advancement in ways that resulted in their being a relatively homogeneous group, characterized by test scores and grades at the upper end of the academic skills range; their own values and competencies are biased in favor of these same criteria and away from the kinds of neglected goal areas that we discussed before. Once again, however, testing agencies have a potentially significant part to play. Such agencies could identify those occupational goals and facets of occupational performance for which the customary selection criteria tend to have little predictive significance. In those instances where faculty members come to agree upon and accept a broadened range of vocational goals, it will become clear that use of the traditional selection procedures must be severely curtailed in favor of the kinds of alternatives that we have described. For otherwise, substantial numbers of candidates will be passed over even though they are more likely to achieve success in the occupational goals in question than are the candidates who receive favored treatment.

Apprenticeship System. Once one accepts the view that graduate education should be oriented toward the achievement of particular vocational competences, certain implications regarding training follow. The apprenticeship idea mentioned earlier can be said to underlie the selection philosophy proposed above. In the medieval apprenticeship system, the potential aptitude of a neophyte apprentice for a particular craft was assessed through a probationary period of work at samples, rudiments, or scaled-down versions of what the craft entailed, that is, through performance of activities akin to those the apprentice would be expected to master (Eby and Arrowood, 1940; Good, 1960; Myers, 1960). In theory, at least, the master craftsman would not accept an apprentice until satisfied that the boy was talented enough at the particular craft to be worth the effort and worth the cost of the apprenticeship to the boy's father. This, of course, is persistence forecasting once again—the master predicts that if the boy does well enough on the work samples during the period of probation, further training should lead to his becoming a master craftsman in his own right. But the apprenticeship idea also carries with it a philosophy of training or pedagogy which makes it just as relevant in its implications for graduate education as in its implications for selection.

When selection emphasizes the use of intellective ability test scores, the shape taken by pedagogy tends naturally to emphasize the conventional types of courses, where memorization and regurgitation of content are called for, since such tests are valid predictors for this kind of academic achievement. It does not matter which came first, the courses or the tests, because the system, once in motion, perpetuates itself. However, when selection is based on a representative sampling of those very skills or attainments which define the vocational role, it becomes evident that training should provide practice in these skills under the guidance of someone proficient at the given vocation, thus enabling the student to move by successive approximations toward levels of competence qualifying him for carrying on that occupation. Pedagogically, graduate education should provide training by a competent mentor that gives students apprenticeships in the occupational roles that serve as the goals of the program.

To do this is expensive of resources, of course, since an apprenticeship involves a close relationship between someone whose behavior reflects a high degree of mastery of the vocation in question and a student who aspires to that vocation. The best faculty members will be able to give meaningful training only to small numbers of graduate students, thus making selection practices all the more relevant. There is some modern psychological parlance for referring to this matter—terms like *modeling* and *identification* as applied to education (Bandura, 1969) convey something of the apprenticeship idea. Sears (1964), a student of modeling processes who has also been involved in the administration of graduate education, has expressed the belief that the most pedagogically effective function of graduate faculty is to serve as models, encouraging the student to identify with, and thus behave like, the professor. The mechanisms underlying an apprenticeship involve motivation or inspiration as well as tutelage in cognitive skills. Its cardinal characteristic, however, is the establishment of a one-to-one relationship that permits the apprentice to become privy to all aspects of the mentor's occupational activities. In this way the mentor is able to provide corrective feedback that allows the apprentice to make closer and closer approximations of those activities.

There has been increasing awareness that a large part of the academic preparation required for certification to carry on various occupations is, in fact, irrelevant to competence at the lines of work in question, while forms of training that would be relevant often receive minimal attention (Berg, 1972; Mayhew, 1972). That this describes the nature of much graduate education in the West probably reflects the supplanting of the apprenticeship system over the last several centuries through acceptance of the notion of liberal education as the definition of high-status educational preparation. In our effort to give the apprenticeship idea a central position as the training paradigm for graduate education, it may be instructive to consider why it fell from grace in earlier times.

The guild system's power resided in its fairness and relevance. Apprentices were selected on the basis of apparent skill to perform tasks required for a given type of work. Training consisted in practice at those tasks, first as an apprentice and later as a journeyman working for wages from a master. Ultimate certification as a master depended upon demonstrated competence at the repertoire of activities in question as attested to by the production of an acceptable "master-piece." Thus, selection, training, and certification all were based on manifestations of the vocational competence defining the given line of work—not on tests or learning tasks of doubtful or minimal pertinence to that vocation, and certainly not on ascriptive considerations. As the Middle Ages evolved into the Renaissance, the guild system with its use of achievement criteria gave way beneath the onslaught of new wealth to the use of ascriptive criteria. The guild system lost its credibility as the practice of nepotism rose: the son of a master could by virtue of that fact expect to become a master himself, while a journeyman could be an excellent craftsman yet never attain certification as a master with a shop of his own.

As an educational method, apprenticeship became consigned to the low-status function of providing government with a means of keeping poor and orphaned children from becoming too much of a burden on the state (Brubacher, 1947; Butts, 1947; Pounds, 1968). As reflected in such documents as the English Poor and Apprenticeship Law of 1601, children from the lower echelons of society were funneled into apprenticeships to reduce the amount of relief needed, reduce pauperism and crime, supply employers with workers who would remain in low-status employment categories, and, in general, help preserve the existing social order. Training for a vocation through apprenticeship thus lost its standing as an educational approach—a far cry from its heyday several years earlier when it served to define the expected training regimen for occupations extending across a wide spectrum of competences. Respectable education turned instead into the notion of education that was *liberal*, that is, inapplicable and unbound to a vocation. With little clear connection between what now was learned and particular occupational objectives, education in this new era came increasingly to function as a status-defining ritual rather than as a specific preparation for adult roles. It is this heritage that set the stage for the contemporary evolution of higher education in both its undergraduate and graduate forms—and, interestingly enough, for the low standing frequently accorded to the apprenticeship method by historians of education (Eby and Arrowood, 1940).

If apprenticeship is to become the training paradigm for graduate education, then the vocations to be taught must be reflected in the activities of the faculty. Apprenticeships are available, in other words, only in those areas for which faculty members can serve as suitable models. This quickly brings us back, of course, to the question of systematic neglect and overcultivation in graduate education. If it is agreed, for example, that teaching and various practitioner competences have not received enough attention, then it is not alone sufficient for students to be selected for admission and financial support on the basis of such competences; in addition, the faculty must provide mentors who in their vocational behavior exemplify the competences in question. And it does not seem to be sufficient from this point of view to arrange, as Heiss (1970) seems to recommend, procedures for the temporary residence of practitioners as guests or visitors on campus rather than as regular faculty members. While Heiss declares that practitioners of various kinds, such as creative artists and performers, should be welcomed to the campus, what she has in mind for them is an enrichment function "while they find a temporary haven" (p. 279). The point, however, is that unless these people are granted full faculty status with the usual tenure provisions and unless their presence is felt in sufficient numbers, the vocations they represent will be downgraded in terms of the payoff matrix facing the graduate student, and the practitioners will be to that extent less relevant and less available as models for prospective apprentices.

That even Heiss, who accepts the idea of giving practitioners more of a role in graduate programs, can suggest awarding them no more than second-class citizenship in this regard testifies to the difficulty of bringing about genuine broadening of the range of vocational skills acceptable as training objectives. Berelson, writing in 1960, felt that he detected a movement on the part of graduate departments in the humanities toward increased hospitality to practitioners, but Jencks and Riesman (1968), surveying the same scene some eight years later, did not find that much had happened in that direction. They pointed out, for example, that if graduate schools really "wanted students to write poetry as well as read it, they would offer writing courses for graduate credit and weigh the results heavily in awarding degrees" (p. 521). To carry out such an objective seriously, however, means apprenticing the students to writers, and that in turn means having enough good writers occupying regular faculty slots as members of the English department to allow a low student-faculty ratio to be maintained for this purpose. This situation is clearly distinct from having a writer-in-residence for a year, while the regular faculty positions are devoted to specialists in literary history and criticism. The issue for the humanities is whether practitioners in fields such as literature, art, and music will receive substantial numbers of bona fide faculty positions and whether fields that are more devoted to practice per se, such as drama and dance, will be invited into the academic structure and have departments and programs of study founded on their behalf. As Wing and Wallach (1971) have noted, such changes require the ceding of power by academic groups whose self-definition as professionals tends to place practitioners at a distance from the university or, at least, from what is considered to be part of the academic disciplines. Thus, while generally applauded as a positive current trend by Parsons and Platt (1972), increased faculty professionalization has its constricting effects as well. These groups of academicians need to be persuaded, therefore, that the practitioner skills are legitimate parts of the corpus of knowledge.

The same general point holds as well concerning the other neglected domain mentioned before—that of teaching. Those who teach skillfully would need to be on hand in sufficient numbers to exemplify, or model, such behavior for graduate student apprentices. This implies, of course, the need to reward faculty members for devoting time and effort to teaching so that it will be adequately represented to the graduate students as a viable occupation for them to emulate.

For training, the student would need to function as a teacher who at the same time is in an apprentice relationship to a mentor. The apprentice status would be reflected in the student's observation and imitation of the mentor under the latter's supervision, in much the same way as someone learning to be a therapist carries on therapeutic sessions, which are usually recorded and reviewed subsequently with a supervisor whose own therapy sessions are also observed and studied by the apprentice. This is, of course, worlds apart from the customary situation of teaching assistants, a situation which allows the faculty to slough off unwanted duties onto graduate students.

When the vocational goal is research competence, it is practice in research that is needed. An appropriate apprenticeship in this occupational direction is one that will veridically reflect the professional role expectations to be encountered later. By and large, the natural sciences seem to have been best at providing this kind of apprenticeship, while the humanities have been worst; but even in the former case, the degree of slippage between the training program and the presumed vocational criterion often can be considerable. Such slippage is most obvious, of course, when even the doctoral thesis is not required to reflect the kind of investigatorial acumen that is expected to characterize the researcher's professional activity. When a Ph.D. is awarded in such instances, we simply have a situation where certification has been provided by the guild, even though the masterpiece presented did not have the attributes it should have had.

In the last analysis, we would maintain that invoking the apprenticeship paradigm as central to the nature of pedagogy in graduate education simply amounts to enlightened common sense. It seems natural indeed that we should arrange for maximal continuity to exist between the skills a student is expected to possess in the vocation for which he seeks certification and the training that is provided. Apprenticeship appears to be the method par excellence for doing this. It seems natural to select for such training those candidates whose past behavior best exemplifies the kinds of vo-

cational attainments that are the goal of the program. Yet
selection and training in regard to the more sought-after opportunities for graduate work rarely seem to take these points
into account. An unapologetic return to the idea that it is
eminently respectable for education to train people for vocations—and hence to specify rather concretely occupational
competences—may offer the means of remedying this situation. By forcing in this way the achievement of greater clarity with respect to purposes, graduate education should be
brought into better alignment with the psychological nature
of talent.

13

Commentary: Singularity of Talent

LIAM HUDSON

With admirable candor Michael Wallach has pointed to the lack of correlation between students' examination results and what they achieve subsequently. Predictively speaking, the emperor is naked, or almost naked, and Professor Wallach has had the courage to say so. Very properly, he emphasizes the multidimensional nature of human talent and advocates a policy of persistence forecasting, rather than one of mystic divination, whether based on ink blots or IQ scores or the grade point average. He also voices a certain disillusionment, one that many of us share, with graduate education that is self-consciously broad and liberal but that lacks any satisfactory anchorage, either in the requirements of society or in the demands that a rigorous search for truth make upon us. He proposes instead that we return to the idea of apprenticeship. This is a formula, whatever its hidden complexities, that comes like a breath of fresh air to a debate in danger of stifling itself in its own good intentions.

I propose now to complement Wallach's thesis with evidence from the other side of the Atlantic, and to draw to it certain caveats and qualifications. My purpose in doing so is in no sense to blunt the points he seeks to make but quite the reverse, to ensure as best I can that they are pushed the more resolutely home.

Let us begin with the poor correlation that exists between what happens inside the school and college system and what happens outside it. As Wallach and many others have observed, IQ scores, grade point averages, and aptitude test results are one matter; achieving something competent, exciting, or original in the world at large is another. Both the time-honored and the more up-to-date arguments that have subsumed the many different kinds of human accomplishment under ideas of general excellence or intelligence are, I am afraid, essentially mythological. As a profession, we psychologists have, in all conscience, some dismantling of false impressions to do. So allow me to add some British evidence to the ritual pile.

Some years ago, I made a retrospective analysis of the academic records of distinguished men who had been students at Oxford or Cambridge: scientists, judges, politicians (Hudson, 1960, 1961). While there did seem to be a positive association between academic record and subsequent achievement, among judges and politicians especially, there could be no question that many men of outstanding intellectual distinction in British public life had academic records that we would nowadays view as catastrophic. Most of the scientists in my sample had been students at Cambridge, and among them there was no relation at all between degree class and subsequent eminence. Once a Cambridge science graduate moved into research, there was absolutely no relation between his degree class and his chance of becoming a Fellow of the Royal Society. Among judges, only one of the five Lords Justice had gained a First Class degree, and two of the most intellectually powerful of the judges at the High Court level had records that today would preclude them from graduate study anywhere in the United Kingdom.

terms of specific skills, when most of those we now possess will in fifteen years time be obsolete. If this argument holds for the future doctor or the future electronic engineer, it must hold a hundred times over for those forms of graduate education that do not lead directly to a socially established profession. Wallach is absolutely right when he says that we must think in an orderly and rational way about what such courses exist to do. But, I suggest, we cannot and should not expect our conclusions to be couched in too literal or specific a form.

As for the model of the master and the apprentice, this enjoys my loyalty and support. It is, after all, the model on which Oxford and Cambridge teaching is based. But to adopt it is to confront not only its immense virtues—the close contact, week after week, between teacher and student and all the benefits that this tutorial arrangement carries in its wake—but also its characteristic snags. These are three. First, it is vastly expensive of teachers' time; hence, if they are to adopt this style of teaching, American graduate schools must surely either cost more or shrink in size. Second, being expensive, it tends to be elitist both in its patterns of recruitment and in its influence on the assumptions of those who are taught. Third, the model of apprenticeship is one which has built into it the tendency to perpetuate orthodoxies. The relation of master to apprentice is one of close intellectual control; as a result, the contents of the master's mind usually pass to his apprentice in an undisturbed flow—skills, insights, prejudices, blind spots, and all. I have recently published a somewhat autobiographical account of the way this process works, both in Oxford philosophy and in British experimental psychology, and I am convinced its potency is something we underestimate at our peril (Hudson, 1973a). In this regard, perhaps the greatest of the many virtues that Wallach's chapter displays is the clarity with which he has called to account certain orthodox but mistaken assumptions of mental measurement. The facts, he points out, deny the dogma. But if he had been apprenticed to a psychologist who held these dogmatic beliefs and who was in a position to require from him as evidence of craft skill and craft allegiance proficiency in just those technical operations which have distracted us so successfully from the obvious truth, he could scarcely have written the chapter he has produced. He would either have knuckled under and accepted the orthodoxy or he would have been excluded from this particular trade altogether, and sent to learn another.

These drawbacks, however, should not distract us from the virtues that the model of apprenticeship unquestionably possesses. It remains, in my view, superior to any of its rivals and categorically superior to the cafeteria system, which offers students a broad conspectus of specialized knowledge but no firsthand experience in acquiring it. These anxieties off my chest, let me return to supplementing Wallach's case with evidence from overseas.

The Demography of Accomplishment

Exciting results have been emerging from demographic studies of academic and professional life, illustrating the truism that the universities transmit not merely habits of thought but ways of life. This leads us to consider what one must call, for lack of a better phrase, the "deep structure" of the professions themselves. Allow me to summarize a great deal of this evidence in a few relatively simple propositions.

We have found that:

(1) When purely academic members of American universities are compared with their professional colleagues—when arts and social science specialists, biologists, and physical scientists are compared with members of staff who are also lawyers, doctors, and engineers—distinct demographic profiles emerge. The differences are by no means massive, but they are surprisingly consistent. The academics are more likely than the professionals to remain single, to be infertile, to have small families, to divorce, and to have highly educated wives (Trow, 1971). In other words, the academics are more removed than are the professionals from the conventional mores of upper middle class American life.

(2) Among academics, there are marked tendencies for groups of specialists to possess their own characteristic demographic patterns. The most striking found so far is the tendency of specialists in the arts, on both sides of the Atlantic, to remain single as compared to groups of biologists and physical scientists (Hudson, 1973b; Hudson and Jacot, 1971b; Hudson, Jacot, and Johnston, 1972).

(3) Among eminent British academics there are sharp fluctuations in rates of divorce from group to group. Eminent physicists, for example, prove six times as likely to divorce as chemists of the same status. There seems some indication, too, that rates of divorce may be tied to the states of the disciplines in question, decade by decade. The data seem to support the view that rates of divorce among the eminent may well be high when a discipline is in a turbulent or revolutionary phase (Hudson and Jacot, 1971b).

(4) Among eminent British doctors, there are quite close connections between the individual's social background and the part of the human body on which he works. The privileged were much more likely than the unprivileged to specialize in work on the head, as opposed to the body below the waist; on the male body, as opposed to the female body (to be urologists, that is, rather than gynecologists); on the living body, as opposed to the dead body; and on the outside of the body, as opposed to its insides (Hudson and Jacot, 1971a). I do not need to remind you, I am sure, that these analytic categories are the ones that emerge from work of structural anthropologists like Lévi-Strauss. The implication, clearly, is that such distinctions—ones between "clean" and "dirty" work—may well embrace all cultures, economically sophisticated and economically primitive alike.

All this evidence, however, deals with students and universities considered at arm's length. It deals with inputs and outputs, and we can only hypothesize about the processes that intervene. Almost all research in higher education has had this character, perhaps because those in authority have been shrewd enough to keep the details of their activities to themselves. But now that our early, proselytizing enthusiasms are behind us, there is a case, I believe, for research on universities that is at once more experimental and more intimate.

It is a simple matter, for instance, to envisage experiments in admissions policy. Elsewhere, I have described a study made at King's College, Cambridge: a number of students were admitted whose academic qualifications were very poor, but some of them had excelled on open-ended questions designed to tap their fluency and imaginativeness (Hudson, 1968). The colleges that undertook this experiment are among the world's most fiercely competitive academically. The results of the experiment at the end of the first year were initially lamentable; but in the long run, the high scorers on the open-ended tests improved beyond all recognition, and at the end of three years the experiment paid handsome dividends, even in the most narrowly academic terms.

But even this small study was based on the model of inputs and outputs, of the "black box." There is, in the United Kingdom, a growing dissatisfaction with this approach—what is known disparagingly as "agricultural botany," or "agric bot" (Hudson, 1973b; Parlett 1972; Parlett and Hamilton, 1972). Enthusiasm is mounting, in contrast, for a more anthropological style, in which research, as in the bush, consists of an outsider approaching an academic institution and attempting to reach some understanding of its inner workings. It is just this that the Nuffield Foundation's "Anabas" Project attempts. (Anabas is defined by the *Oxford English Dictionary* as a genus of acanthopterygian fish; these fish sometimes leave the water and even climb trees.) We are making a number of detailed studies of innovations in university teaching: efforts made by medical schools, for instance, to teach aspiring doctors that people are people, not conglomerates of symptoms or lumps of meat; efforts made to teach electrical engineers about the society in which they are to exercise their professional skills; and, in the arts, efforts made by historians and literature specialists to teach in an interdisciplinary fashion (Sheldrake and Berry, 1975).

Already, we are embarrassingly aware how often the "agricultural botanist" in each of us addresses the wrong issues. At the pragmatic level, for instance, one makes no sense of a certain course in the behavioral sciences, until one sees it as a compromise reached between a number of university departments, each of which has a legitimate interest in its content. The curriculum, simply, is a by-product of a process that is starkly political. And at the conceptual level, we find ourselves continually confronting mysterious notions, like that of a "discipline." To begin to grasp what happens inside universities, we find ourselves compelled to grapple with the boundary rules which surround bodies of knowledge like history, medicine, chemistry, or psychology and to make interpretative sense of their function. We need, too, to come to terms with what one might describe as the politics of knowledge—that territory in which such disciplines take shape, in which schools of thought do battle one with another, and in which certain views of mankind are rendered legitimate, while others are cast beyond the pale.

Such insight cannot be gathered by means of postal questionnaires; nor is it gained by gazing at the correlations between students' IQ scores and their grade point averages. Still less can it be found by exercising the rhetorics of reliability and validity or by discussing the virtues of the multiple-choice test. Important though such technical considerations may well be in their proper context, they do not help us address the prior issues of what it is that universities, at both the undergraduate and the graduate level, can, do, and should transmit.

Happily, as Wallach has shown, we are not entirely without relevant professional expertise. We have specific experimental and analytic techniques, and the beginnings of more appropriate theory are quite rapidly making themselves evident. What we need above all is a new kind of research worker: the kind of young man or woman who can fulfill the role of outsider that the anthropological paradigm requires, who can cope with the research techniques and their attendant theory, who can inspire the trust that access to confidential information imposes, and—most essential—who is sufficiently open-minded to realize that, as yet, we know relatively little. Such paragons do exist, I am happy to say; we have found a few and are training more. Their existence is perhaps the best guarantee we have that we will not again fall too readily into a posture of self-sufficiency: a posture in which we encapsulate ourselves not only from the requirements of policymaking, nor even solely from the rest of behavioral and social science, but from the kinds of evidence that give beguiling orthodoxy the lie.

14

Commentary:
Needs of Talent
and Problems of
Institutional Change

JACQUELYN A. MATTFELD

>0⊂⊃0⊂⊃0⊂⊃0⊂⊃0⊂⊃0⊂⊃0⊂⊃0⊂⊃0⊂⊃0⊂⊃0⊂⊃0⊂⊃0⊂

Although the title of his chapter is "The Psychology of Talent and Graduate Education," Michael Wallach has ranged widely in his extensive presentation and touched on many facets of that self-contradictory phenomenon, American graduate education. While I share all of his concerns (though, as a cultural historian, not the language in which he couches them), I was disappointed to discover that Wallach had no more practical suggestions than the rest of us had on how to persuade our colleagues, who are enmeshed in the very system of selection and training that produced their own academic careers, that both society's needs and pedagogical common sense dictate change.

Wallach has, in fact, reviewed for us a considerable body of recent study that reinforces the validity of the observations and educational principles which led to the curriculum design of a number of experimental undergraduate colleges in the 1920s and 1930s. These colleges, which have developed along lines close to their original purposes and practices, have been the first to suffer from severe financial problems and must still, after forty years, continue to fight a persistent image of being dilettantish and nonprofessional in the eyes of the nation's ranking institutions of higher education. In the calls for reform in prestigious conventional institutions, one can observe with interest, and some irony, the rediscovery of so many of the hallmarks of these pioneering colleges. Let me single out three of Wallach's main recommendations as confirmation that this is so: his recommendations about admissions criteria, the use of practitioner skills, and improved selection and training of teachers.

Wallach emphasizes that admissions decisions in the "quality" universities continue to be based on academic aptitude as measurable on standardized tests. Furthermore, although the professions entered by recipients of higher degrees from graduate schools all require a generally high level of intelligence, each calls for specific abilities of superior quality (talents) which are unrelated to the relatively small differences in aptitude scores that applicants to graduate school from selective colleges display. In addition, although Wallach does not address himself to this, specific personality traits and behaviors are as persistent as the meritorious work he refers to as evidence of talent and appear to be as essential to success in various fields. Thoroughness, patience, enthusiasm, or even competitiveness appear to be as closely correlated with real-life success in certain professions as are early evidences of speaking ability, organizational talents, manual dexterity, instructional ability, or perfect pitch. Although this has been thoroughly documented and has been demonstrated in the early experimental colleges, conventional selective graduate schools and the colleges that support them virtually ignore personality differences of this sort among candidates, even though they are more valid predictors of career success than traditional academic indicators. The experimental colleges, in contrast, used evidence of meritorious work and both subjective and objective evidence in selecting their students.

In his discussion of the need for practitioner skills, Wallach correctly points out that in the university tradition, theorists have viewed practitioners as inferior as far back as the medieval period and that this viewpoint has not changed in the twentieth-century academic world.

It is certainly true that inclusion of fieldwork in the social sciences or in the humanities as bona fide components of the curriculum of either an undergraduate liberal arts degree or a graduate school advanced degree (as distinguished from the degree requirements of professional schools) is considered by conventional educators as a bastardization and lowering of the institutions' standards. However, Wallach fails to mention the success of the fieldwork programs in the experimental colleges like Bennington, Sarah Lawrence, and Antioch. The universities, unlike these colleges, bowed to practitioners by adding separate professional schools under the university's umbrella and in this way preserved the assumed superiority and purity of the "arts and sciences."

Wallach emphasizes the need for teachers who will work closely with individual students and who will serve as models and mentors in more areas than ivory tower research. But the old myth persists, that those who can, publish; those who can't, teach. Few persons combine the qualities of a research scholar with those of a humane and accessible teacher. In general, the traditional institutions have hired the researchers, and the experimental colleges have hired the teachers. Repeated calls for better teaching have been met by singular unresponsiveness from universities.

Wallach's recommendations regarding admissions criteria, inclusion of practitioner skills and experience, and restoration of the lustre of teaching (with specific emphasis on master-apprenticeship modes of instruction in the graduate schools) have all been made countless times before. They have always been strenuously resisted by faculty, especially the faculties of those quality institutions where he would most like to see change instituted. Wallach has mentioned only briefly the specific barriers that would have to be overcome before the elite universities would rethink the objectives

of their graduate programs or redesign their degree requirements and student selection processes in accord with the
wider vocationalism he advocates. These barriers to change
bear repetition and emphasis because until these basic obstacles are removed, the prestigious universities cannot evolve
and will, I believe, be doomed to slow ossification and demise.

One barrier is the continuing confusion about the several functions of the university and about the priorities among
these functions. Wallach's view that preserving, integrating,
and transmitting culture or knowledge is as much the university's responsibility as adding to knowledge or training future
scholars is not widely held by modern university faculties.
Most faculty members would rather add to knowledge and
train scholars than preserve, integrate, and transmit knowledge. The men and women now teaching in these liberal arts
facilities actually speak often of professionalism as a virtue,
while giving only lip service to the virtues of nonutilitarian
education; they prefer to teach graduate courses or, at the
very least, those for advanced and specialized undergraduates, rather than introductory or general courses for the
nonmajors.

Another strong barrier is the power of faculty through
their governances and their high percentage of tenured,
research-oriented scholars to prevent rapid adoption of any
new priorities. The rewards for teaching and counseling are
not comparable to the rewards for research and publication.
Moreover, as jobs become scarcer, faculty members are more
zealous in guarding their ranks from professionals (practitioners) who have had different training and experience,
and who might better embody the qualities Wallach has established as essential in a master-apprentice relationship.

The identification of conservatism with excellence is a
third barrier to change. Past modes of teaching and curriculum organization are retained in the name of excellence but
are in fact preserved because of the human reluctance to accept change in the institutions and practices that formed us
and are therefore familiar to us. Most faculty members are
reluctant to admit the inevitability of the evolution of edu-

cation and society; and it seems, unfortunately, that the more prestigious the institutions, the more they claim excellence and thus retain their status quo.

The diminution of private and public aid to higher education, the general economic recession, is causing several kinds of reactionary trends which militate against the changes Wallach advocates. These trends have also begun to root in the early experimental colleges, in part also because of the recession. Older faculty cling more tenaciously than ever to the conditions that drew them to the university originally (emphasis on graduate rather than undergraduate instruction, minimal teaching loads, maximum time for research). Younger faculty, who in affluent times felt freer to experiment in their teaching and in the development of their course content, now march more closely to the tune of the older faculty because their security, promotion, and tenure depend upon publication rather than experimentation in teaching and because there is a dwindling national market for college teachers. Fewer fellowships are available for students, and thus smaller numbers of them can be accepted for graduate work; and since the power of the senior faculty is relatively greater in a recession, it is they who are more influential in the selection of graduate students, selecting them in their own image. Finally, the economic recession dictates a search for cheaper, or at least not more expensive, mass means of instruction; more personalized teaching programs are expensive and thus are bypassed.

On the other hand, there are forces working for change even in some of the most tradition-ridden prestige universities, and the changes Wallach asks for may yet come into favorable environments. These forces include the dwindling market for new college teachers and the financial exigencies that are changing university working conditions for faculty already on hand. Together these factors may bring persuasive pressure on graduate schools to consider creating new programs designed to train for professions other than university teaching and research. In addition, the predictions of a smaller college and graduate population in the next fifteen years and the need of private universities to compete for students against state universities that may be more responsive to the changing requirements of various occupations and professions may make the private universities more receptive to new self-definition to ensure their survival.

Those of us who have long sought a broader definition of talent and a happier relationship between liberal and professional education (and believe it possible) had best learn more about how to change long-held convictions, if not human nature. And the work of Wallach, his predecessors, and colleagues will continue to remind us that more sophisticated and comprehensive assessment strategies are required if graduate schools are to be persuaded to lay aside old myths and seek to identify and educate those who possess the multiple talents and personality traits needed for prominence, high achievement, and service in our society.

Part Six

Environmental Influences on Creative Performance

In the search for effective means of adapting higher education to the kinds of individual and group differences highlighted earlier, the remaining sections of this volume extend the reconstructionist arguments introduced in Part Five beyond a call for administrative changes, however radical, to an insistence upon more basic environmental and pedagogical changes. Part Five stressed the need for administrative alternatives in selection and training to provide means of capitalizing upon specialized talents in higher education, especially those creative skills already operative in primitive form in prior real-life accomplishments. Now, Part Six takes up the question of environmental influences on creative performance, raising the possibility of designing novel institutional and interpersonal environments to stimulate creativity and educational development.

In Chapter Fifteen, Donald Pelz points out that two somewhat antithetical conditions are required for creative problem solving: security and challenge. Since important sources of both of these characteristics are rooted in individual personality, the major problem of environmental design is to create educational systems that strengthen and exploit these internal resources with sufficient flexibility to accommodate their personalistic nature. Pelz considers the primary personal source of security to be self-confidence, a combination of intellectual independence and self-reliance reinforced by competence. The major internal source of challenge derives from the personal quality of curiosity. An educational environment that strengthens these personal qualities would, Pelz argues, both protect the student from unmanageable demands on the one hand and expose him to provocative demands on the other. The protective features are those that serve to reinforce self-confidence and competence, such as social reward structures giving visibility and recognition to individual accomplishments or the availability of technical resources that are adequate to the tasks at hand. In addition, however, the system must regularly expose the student to new problems and challenges as a means of stimulating curiosity and encouraging long-term involvement. Hence the ideal educational environment, it would appear, is both matched and mismatched to current learner characteristics, simultaneously offering support with one hand while facilitating change with the other.

Pelz thus stresses the joint contribution of personal and environmental factors to creative productivity. But, to use an analysis-of-variance analogy, he tends to treat them more as additive main effects than as interactions, thereby emphasizing optimal environments for the generality of students rather than differential environments for different kinds or levels of personal functioning. In contrast, Norman Frederiksen, in Chapter Sixteen, highlights the importance of multivariate interactions between personal characteristics and organizational factors to point up the contingencies and complexities that must be taken into account in specific environmental prescriptions for creativity and learning. In Chapter Seventeen, Proshansky further elaborates the point that research environments must be highly differentiated in order to be responsive to individual differences in the scientific talents displayed by researchers and graduate students. Of special importance in this regard is the development of an interpersonal climate fostering patterns of collaboration and colleagueship that capitalize upon differential research skills.

15

Environments for Creative Performance Within Universities

DONALD C. PELZ

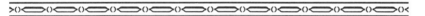

Several years ago a colleague and I published a study based on eleven research and development organizations conducting basic and applied research in industrial, government, and university settings (Pelz and Andrews, 1966b). Our book examined a number of social-psychological factors with the aim of detecting and identifying the kinds of social environment that are likely to foster a high level of scientific effectiveness. In the present chapter, I intend to speculate on what the results of that study might imply for institutions of higher education. It will not be possible to give more than a brief reference to some of the findings; a good summary of these, however, can be found in Pelz (1967). Mainly, I shall use the findings to construct a framework of principles delineating how creative performance can be nurtured, and I shall then speculate rather freely on how these principles might be translated into operating procedures within the university.

Some of the illustrations will be drawn from a survey conducted by James Kulik and others at the University of Michigan on undergraduate education in some six hundred departments of psychology throughout the country (Kulik, Brown, Vestewig, and Wright, 1973).

In our study of scientific organizations, we used several criteria of scientific effectiveness, including judgments by colleagues as to who in the department had contributed the most significant advances to his technical field in the past five years and the number of technical publications, patents, and unpublished reports produced by each individual in the past five years. I like to think that our findings on scientific effectiveness apply more broadly to any type of creative problem solving, and I shall use the two terms interchangeably. The question for this chapter thus becomes: By what procedures can a university help to develop in its students and in its staff a vigorous capacity for creative problem solving?

Conceptual Framework

Various findings supported the view that creative problem solving requires the presence of two somewhat contradictory conditions: on the one hand, there must be some source of security—some condition or conditions which serve to protect the scientist from demands of his technical environment; and on the other hand, there must be some source of challenge—some condition or conditions which serve to expose the scientist to demands of his environment. A major source of security, for example, is a large amount of autonomy or freedom in determining the direction of one's own work. This may take the form of control over resources. A man who controls a five-year grant has more protection from his environment than does a man with a one-year grant. If someone asks him to take on a new project, the man with the five-year grant is freer to say no.

The concept of challenge is illustrated by the following. We asked each scientist how much of his technical work was directed toward five kinds of research and development activity: basic research (the discovery of general principles), applied research (the discovery of answers to particular questions), invention of new products or processes, improvement of existing products or processes, and technical services for other staff members. We found that even in basic-research laboratories the most effective scientists did not concentrate on only one or two of these five research and development activities, but gave some attention to as many as four. The same was found in applied-research laboratories. It seems probable that the scientist who diversifies in this way is likely to be exposed to more different kinds of problems than is the nondiversified scientist and that this diversity will be a source of challenge.

We should note that neither security nor challenge alone is sufficient for effectiveness; nor can scientists be particularly effective if they are only moderately secure and challenged. Rather, according to the concept of creative tension, scientists are most effective when they have high levels of *both* security and challenge. The question now arises: Just how are security and challenge linked with scientific accomplishment? Which comes first? If a scientist is given more autonomy and is also exposed to diverse problems, will he become more effective? Or is it the case that after having proved his effectiveness, the scientist will insist on greater autonomy, or will be sought out to help on diverse problems? Let me propose an answer to the question in terms of a diagram (Figure 1). This represents a personal synthesis of how I think a number of principles link together to generate creative problem solving.

First, consider the components on the left side of the diagram—competence, curiosity, self-confidence, and involvement. For problem solving to occur, whether the problems originate in either a practical or a theoretical puzzle, there must be at least three essential qualities that are characteristic of the individual. The researcher must first have some degree of competence, based both on his intellectual abilities and on his technical training. Second, he must have a quality of curiosity, that capacity to detect technical prob-

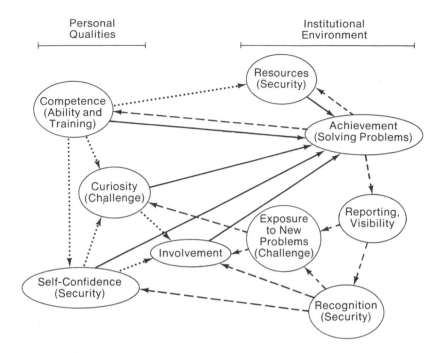

Figure 1. A conceptual framework on conditions for creative
problem solving.

lems and to enjoy trying to solve them. The curious individual
supplies his own challenge by exposing himself to unan-
swered questions. A third essential quality—one that is perhaps not sufficiently recognized in the creative process—is a
rugged self-confidence (or self-reliance), the individual's
conviction that he can solve the problems that he undertakes.
This is an internal source of security, and a good scientist has
a large measure of it. As shown by the arrows, these qualities
reinforce each other. Competence reinforces the individual's
self-confidence, and both of these in turn sustain his curiosity. To become an effective researcher, I think, it is essential

that a technical man either possess or acquire all three qualities at an early stage.

The fourth quality is involvement (other terms might be enthusiasm or commitment). In our study of research organizations, we found that the sense of being absorbed in one's work was widely related to technical performance in various kinds of research and development (Pelz and Andrews, 1966b, (chap. 5). On the diagram, involvement is placed between personal qualities at the left and institutional environment at the right. Involvement is nourished by the personal qualities of curiosity and self-confidence, but it is also a relationship between the individual and the technical tasks which form a part of his environment.

Next, consider the components at the upper right of the diagram—achievement and resources. The latter comprises part of the institutional environment. The competent individual is likely to command resources in the form of money, staff, and equipment; and control of these is another source of security. The conditions now exist for the next step: the solving of technical problems. For simplicity, we can call this achievement. Each of the previous elements plays an essential part in this process.

We turn now to visibility, recognition, and exposure to new problems—the components at the lower right of the diagram. If the system is operating effectively, certain important steps will follow from achievement. The achievement will be reported publicly, either internally through seminars or technical reports or externally in the form of published papers. This step in turn leads to recognition for the investigator—a further source of security. Because of the reporting and the recognition, other people will expose him to new problems, and these will be a fresh source of challenge. The recognition in turn will enhance his self-confidence; the exposure will stimulate his curiosity and his involvement in new problems. Also, the achievement adds to his knowledge and thus enhances his professional competence; it also assures him of continued resources. And thus the conditions are reinforced for another cycle of successful problem solving.

What is represented in this diagram, then, is a process of cyclical feedback, in which the personal qualities necessary for achievement are strengthened by that achievement.

Implications for Student Development

If such a conceptual framework is valid, what does it imply for colleges and universities that wish to nurture the capacity for creative problem solving in their students and staff? In attempting to answer this question, I will consider, one by one, the four ingredients at the left of the diagram, as they apply to higher education.

Competence. Selecting for ability and imparting knowledge are, of course, the traditional concerns of the university. We are all familiar with the conventional procedures for doing so. A professor (or perhaps a committee) determines what the student ought to learn; the professor transmits much of this material himself in the form of lectures or in the form of carefully structured laboratory exercises; he or his assistants give examinations to test mastery of the assigned information, and he grades the student's performance accordingly. Students who fail to show the required performance are weeded out. But in its emphasis on competence, the traditional system of university education may have failed to build curiosity and self-confidence. One indication is the substantial number of doctoral candidates who will complete all of the qualifying requirements for the Ph.D. but will never finish the dissertation. I have heard it estimated that the number of dissertation dropouts may run as high as 30 or 40 percent. The candidates are technically trained; but do they possess the other qualities necessary for the independent problem solving of the dissertation itself? We may also ask whether the conventional system is particularly effective in building competence per se. It has some major drawbacks. For instance, it stresses teaching rather than learning, that is, it assigns the larger part of responsibility for education to the instructor rather than to the student. All students are

expected to move at about the same pace, which is, by necessity, too fast for some and too slow for others.

A radical solution to these and other problems is offered
by what is often called the Keller plan. Named after its de-
signer, who labeled it "self-paced supervised study" (Keller,
1968), it draws on B.F. Skinner's concepts of immediate reinforcement and programed instruction. Keller used this approach initially to teach introductory psychology, and it has
been extended to engineering, biology, and physics. In a
given domain (such as the context of a one-semester textbook), the material is divided into specific units, each of which
must be mastered completely before moving into the next;
mastery is determined by a short essay exam monitored by
an advanced student. The individual may take each exam
when he feels ready and may take it as often as he needs to
pass, with immediate personalized feedback. He thus moves
as rapidly as he is able. Lectures are infrequent and optional,
and are used to motivate rather than to inform. The self-
pacing feature puts the initiative on the student rather than
on the professor, and the close contact with the proctor gives
personal recognition and encouragement. Preliminary evidence (Kulik, 1972) indicates that students spend more time
with this method than with the conventional one and that
they perform at least as well; the student proctors in particular seem to benefit from the plan. Note that evaluation is
shared among three sources: the proctor, the course instructor, and the student himself, since he can repeat each exam
up to mastery.

My impression is that as a means of imparting competence, the Keller plan represents a distinct advance over traditional methods. It makes learning a process of active seeking
rather than passive absorbing. However, it still presents a
course content that is completely specified by the instructor,
with a rigid sequence of units. I would judge it to be effective
in transmitting a known body of coherent knowledge, but I
suspect it would do little to arouse curiosity or to develop the
strategy of creative problem solving. It seems more useful
for an introductory course than for an advanced one.

In these days of rapidly changing technology, the university must do more than impart a fixed body of knowledge; it must also train for flexibility, the skill of learning how to learn. This approach starts with recognizing the fact that no curriculum, however sophisticated and farseeing, can hope to prepare a student with all the skills he may need for a lifetime, or even for the next seven years. If a graduate has been trained for flexibility and is faced with a technical problem for which his present skills are inadequate, he will know how to dig out the necessary background from the technical literature or from consultation with colleagues. If this type of learning is its objective, let the university provide early training in flexibility. Already there exists more knowledge than can be crowded into the available semester-hours. At the same time, there are pressures for more problem-focused instruction (see below), field experience, and independent research. How can the university accommodate all of these competing pressures?

Let me repeat a suggestion I offered some time ago (Pelz, 1970a). It has parallels with the Keller plan but is more suited to an advanced course. Consider a certain subject which is normally taught in one semester. Suppose that the area includes a dozen subspecialties that can barely be crowded into one semester and that more advances are emerging every year. Let the professor develop for each of the subspecialties a self-study module, that is, a package of learning aids about the topic. This package could include textbook chapters, a dozen journal articles on recent experiments, a set of exercises for applying the knowledge, and the names of one or more investigators—faculty members or advanced students— who can be consulted if necessary. With the help of this self-study guide, a bright and motivated student can dig out for himself most of what he needs to master that subtopic.

In his course, let the professor not try to cover all of the subtopics himself. Rather, during the first half of the semester, students should accept responsibility to learn a series of the self-study modules. The professor may give periodic background lectures. In the second half of the semester, he sets forth one or more complex problems, either applied or theoretical, the solving of which will require mastery of several subtopics. Small teams are encouraged to work together in tackling the problems. They may consult periodically with the professor or report to the entire class. Several principles are involved here. A major one is that the student takes initiative for his own learning. The motivation to learn is stimulated by seeing the relevance of the material to actual complex problems. There are multiple channels of decision making; the instructor, fellow students, and the individual all take part in the process.

The self-study modules are similar to the study units in the Keller plan, but the content of each is suggestive rather than fixed. The student would not necessarily master each module in a predetermined sequence; nor would each student necessarily cover the same sets. There might be fifteen or twenty modules of which he selects ten, and he might branch into relevant modules in a related course. The modules would be available not only to students in that course but to anyone who finds himself in need of that area of knowledge. The modules would be updated from year to year as new articles or textbooks appear. Advanced students could help in their preparation. In fact, developing one of the modules or coauthoring it with the professor could be a welcome challenge for an advanced student and could be a product in which he could take pride.

The traditional system of university education requires that each student go through a series of introductory courses, often rather dull, before he has a chance at some of the pioneering areas. Under a module system, a bright sophomore in a problem-focused course might undertake some rather advanced modules and be able to master them. Such a system could enhance the challenge of the undergraduate years and develop the flexibility the graduate will need for periodic adaptation to changing technologies in a changing society.

Curiosity. A professor of physics at a small college had a reputation for producing many students who went on to graduate work and later eminence. Asked what was his teaching secret, he replied: "I spend as much time talking about what physicists *don't* know, as what they do." Is this not the heart of arousing curiosity—to be confronted with something that defies understanding and to wonder whether one can solve the puzzle? What is implied is building instruction around problems. A mathematics professor at Wisconsin has written a book using problems in engineering to motivate the teaching of undergraduate mathematics to engineers (Noble, 1967). Many developments in basic mathematics have grown out of tackling specific problems. If these can be recreated for the student, he can be challenged to rediscover the solutions.

What I have in mind, however, is not the usual laboratory course with its standard experiments to which answers are already known. It is more challenging to let students wrestle with a real problem to which there is yet no solution. One hears, for example, of an engineering class at Dartmouth which is asked to help design the management of water resources in its area. An inorganic chemistry instructor at the University of Rochester, instead of handing out prepared water samples, has the students bring their own samples from the local river, the cafeteria coffee urns, the beer taps in the local tavern. A teacher might object that without a known answer, he cannot assess the accuracy of the student's analysis. One answer is to let two or more subgroups analyze the same samples, and compare results. Or let several teams each develop a transportation design. The element of friendly competition can lend zest.

The use of problems without known solutions has another educational payoff. Discovery doesn't happen the way textbooks are written. In actual research, the investigator may try nine things that fail before he finds a tenth that works. The effective researcher has realized this; he has learned to keep plugging despite failure. Students need a chance to comprehend this reality through their personal experience. In Kulik's survey of psychology departments (Kulik and others, 1973), many of the innovations reported were of this type; they allowed the student to grapple personally with a real research project, either as an individual or in a small team. As one chairman wrote: "In the experimental psychology course, our philosophy is that one complete individual research project provides greater generalizability than many standard replicated studies."

In an eastern city, the psychology department had been focusing its energies on inner-city concerns. But its graduates were giving its research methodology courses a very low rating in terms of interest level. Therefore in 1970 a significant restructuring was undertaken. In a one-year integrated course at the junior level, subgroups were formed around common interests, with the task during the first semester of designing a research project. Class hours were sometimes spent in subgroup planning and sometimes in lectures on research methods, with examples drawn from ongoing projects. By reversing the usual sequence of methods first and applications later, the student could learn statistics in the context of actual problems. The second semester was devoted to collecting data and to further lectures on methods, again illustrated with student projects. Evaluation in the course was based jointly on ratings of group projects, on peer ratings, and on self-grading. I regularly teach a course in survey research methods which is built around an actual problem for which a real client wants some answers. This is always intensely absorbing. The students work like beavers and learn, I think, tremendous amounts.

Let me cite another finding from our study of research laboratories which deals with what I call multiple channels of decision and evaluation (Pelz and Andrews, 1966b, chap. 2). Each scientist was asked how much weight was exerted by various people in deciding his technical assignments— how much weight by himself, his immediate superior, his colleagues, a client or sponsor, and so forth. To our surprise, we found that when several of these decision-making sources were involved, the scientist's level of performance increased. The most effective scientists were those whose technical tasks were established in consultation among four sources: themselves, their immediate chief, their colleagues, and higher executives or clients. As I interpret this finding, it does not mean that a committee makes the decision. Rather, the scientist confronts a diversity of viewpoints before deciding. This diversity, I believe, generates not only wiser decisions but also more interesting and challenging ones.

In traditional instruction, the professor alone is the sole decision maker. He assigns the learning tasks and he evaluates the student's success. In problem-centered instruction, however, there are usually several inputs. First, there may be a client with a stake in the outcome—a local firm, a government office, a service agency. Second, the student himself will have considerable voice in what part of the problem he tackles. Third, there is input from other students who serve as colleagues. A team can exchange ideas in mapping their attack; they may report to the rest of the class and get feedback. The fourth source, of course, is the professor or his teaching assistants, who suggest approaches and hear reports. This use of multiple inputs will help to stimulate curiosity and to generate involvement. It also tends to enhance self-confidence, for reasons which I shall now examine.

Self-Confidence. Another essential quality in a problem solver is faith in his own technical skills and reliance on his own judgment. In our study of research and development laboratories, trust in one's own ideas was consistently associated with high performance. This quality of intellectual independence or self-reliance is perhaps the central source of security. The traditional system of education does little to develop intellectual independence. In a traditional system the faculty sees its role as both to give instruction and to weed out the incompetent. Successive hurdles in the form of examinations are set, and students who fail to jump them are discarded. The professor is both mentor and judge. How can independence of thought be encouraged in such a system?

The world of research does not operate in this way. A man's reputation is built on his achievements and the composite evaluation of professional colleagues. It does not depend on the judgment of one superior. In our study of research and development organizations, we found that where a supervisor alone had the major voice in deciding the scientist's assignments, the scientist's performance was poor. But where the scientist shared decision making jointly with his chief or with his colleagues, his performance was substantially better. This is the same finding I described above on multiple channels of decision and evaluation.

What is the implication for university education? For one thing, this finding suggests that the student's grade in a course should not depend exclusively on the judgment of a single professor. There are several ways to avoid this. One way, of course, is to supplement the professor's judgment with inputs from teaching assistants or discussion leaders. Another device is to use an outside examiner. A third method is to use some form of team project, as in the example above of the methodology course in the eastern psychology department; with this method, grades depend partly on ratings of the group project and partly on peer ratings.

A fourth technique—a more radical one—is mastery grading. Here a series of study units is specified. When the student feels he has mastered a given unit he takes a short exam, and if he does not do well enough he may repeat the exam until he succeeds. In laboratory work he is allowed to rewrite his report as many times as needed until he has produced a high-caliber report. His grade, then, depends on the number of units he has mastered in a given time. If he has completed the number of units required for an A he gets that grade, no matter how many other students have also earned an A. Under this system the grade is largely under the control of the student himself—another example of a security factor.

More important than the method of grading, however, is the early opportunity to conduct projects with some degree of independence, either individually or in a small team. Various arrangements of this type were described in Kulik's survey. One chairman reported that "a program of individual study for seniors, culminating in open time for research during the month of January, provides opportunity for students to explore in depth an area of their own interest within their field of concentration." Another chairman described a two-semester sequence as follows: "A thorough examination of the work which has been done in the area of the student's interest is completed during the first semester and finalized in a research paper which reviews experiments and points up a problem area. Laboratory work in the second semester consists of an individual research project related to the discovered problem." The principle of course is simple: one learns how to be self-reliant through practice in being independent.

Another mechanism for strengthening self-reliance— perhaps the most potent one—is illustrated by the feedback loop in the lower right of Figure 1. The individual's achievement is reported in some public way to bring him recognition, and this in turn builds his prestige. In this regard, I would stress the value of early publication. Often this can be accomplished through a research internship on an ongoing research project, in which the student is given some piece of the total project to develop and write up. Let him enjoy early the pride of authorship. In the Kulik survey, one psychology chairman reported that students, by means of the apprenticeship method, began research projects as early as the sophomore year. Several had papers published in professional journals prior to graduation.

An additional interesting finding of the survey was that a number of psychology departments encourage involvement of undergraduates in the teaching process. Students participate by running courses, by acting as assistants in laboratory sections, or by becoming discussion-group leaders. Under mastery grading, student proctors assess the frequent quizzes. Course credit for such activities is often given, and these assistants have the additional benefit of gaining experience in independence and self-reliance.

Involvement. This fourth essential quality for creative problem solving is nourished by the personal characteristics of curiosity and self-confidence, but it depends also on specific tasks to which the student can whole-heartedly commit himself. How can the student be stimulated to fuller involvement in his educational experience? One finds many suggestions in the Kulik survey of psychology departments. Ten universities were selected for site visits. Several of them stressed opportunities for directed experience in field settings—mental hospitals, nursery schools, legal agencies, and other off-campus situations. In student interviews, much appreciation was expressed for the value of such experiences. As Kulik notes, experiences in applied settings can be important in conveying to students the nature of the problems confronting psychologists.

The term *involvement* is used in several senses, which are no doubt interrelated. We have, first, involvement in terms of commitment to a research activity, and many of the points I have made previously apply here as well. The student is more likely to become involved in those functions which require the tackling of actual problems. He will be more involved when he is given the opportunity for independent research and when he can achieve something which is publicly recognized. Another kind of involvement is participation in departmental activities such as course planning and policy making. From the Kulik survey of psychology departments, one finds many examples of student membership on the department's executive committee or on course-planning committees. A finding from our study of research organizations is also relevant here (Pelz and Andrews, 1966b, chap. 2). We found a factor related to scientific performance which has appeared in many studies of nontechnical performance as well. An effective scientist was likely to feel that he could influence the decisions of other people which affected him. I interpret the feeling of influence as another source of security.

The ability to exert influence on decisions that affect one as an individual has several payoffs. It enhances the sense of self-esteem. More directly, it permits the choice of activities which are seen to have greater relevance or interest, and hence it strengthens commitment. At the University of Michigan, a new course in clinical medicine illustrates the involvement of students in planning their own courses. A portion of the curriculum time is set aside to be used as specified by a student committee. The students have organized and are responsible for classes on society and medicine. The course was devised in order to give clinical relevance to the material being presented and to enable students to achieve the clinical perspective earlier than previously. The concepts of clinical relevance and clinical perspective imply the process of grappling with real problems.

Recent years have witnessed student unrest erupting on hundreds of campuses. This undoubtedly has many roots. One source may be dissatisfaction with the irrelevance of the college experience to the problems of today's society. Much of what is taught appears narrow and sterile—neither socially relevant nor intellectually demanding. Another source may be resentment of the facelessness of the "multiversity," with its sense of anonymity and powerlessness. Students are challenging the faculty's traditional power over their careers through control of curricula and grading. The movement toward greater student voice in departmental affairs is in part a response to these challenges. But in terms of my conceptual framework, this increase in student influence should also facilitate their growth in creative problem solving.

I would like to put forward one caution in this respect. Nowadays much stock is placed in student evaluations of instructors. It does not necessarily follow, however, that what students say they like in a teacher is what will help them to become effective problem solvers. A graduate school dean told me of a study he had done several years ago of students' preferences regarding teachers. One type of teacher was the "presenter"—the instructor who organizes clear, systematic lectures easily understood by his listeners. Another type was the "involver"—an instructor who is, no doubt, less systematic and orderly but who is caught up in his own work and is able to transmit this sense of excitement. The students, said the dean, clearly preferred the presenter.

Does this mean that the skillful presenter is the best teacher? That depends on the goal of the educational system. If the goal is the traditional one of imparting a fixed body of knowledge, then the presenter is more useful. But if the goal is the development of creative problem solvers, then the involver, I feel, can do more to build curiosity, self-reliance, and commitment.

It is sometimes said that an effective teacher is one who conveys enthusiasm. This is true, but I do not think a teacher can create enthusiasm in the manner of a football coach giving a pep talk. Rather, it arises from the instructor's own interest in solving problems and from his inviting students to share in this exciting activity. The work itself is the ultimate source of enthusiasm.

Implications for Faculty Development

Up to this point I have concentrated on the university's function in creative education of its students. It is also important to ask how the university can nurture the creative capacity of its professional staff—particularly the younger staff as they move from the role of student to that of faculty. Similar principles apply, I feel. To begin, let me stress again the importance of the feedback loop in the lower right of Figure 1. Early achievement is the key in this loop, and it is as important for faculty as it is for students. Successful solving of problems, if made visible through suitable reporting, results in the building of curiosity, self-confidence, and involvement in further research. For this reason, incidentally, I am in favor of pressing the doctoral student to complete his dissertation quickly. When a young Ph.D. joins the department staff, his chairman would be wise to keep up a benign pressure for early publication, in order to keep the vital cycle of reinforcement in motion.

How can early achievement in young faculty members be stimulated? Certain findings from our study of research laboratories are instructive. The best performance was found among men who spent about three quarters of their time on technical work (research or development) and one quarter of their time on either teaching or administration (Pelz and Andrews, 1966b, chap. 4). This fact suggests that the new instructor who is told to spend 75 percent of his time on teaching and 25 percent on research is not likely to achieve research output very soon. Perhaps, instead, he should be invited to spend most of a semester preparing a research project and then be given a semester or two off for full time on the research, with an expectation of producing a report at the end of this period.

Let me mention another result. In our research, effective scientists were found to interact with more colleagues both in their own section or department and in other groups elsewhere in the organization than did their less effective counterparts (Pelz and Andrews, 1966b, chap. 3). We also found that in loosely coordinated settings such as academic departments, excessive autonomy was dysfunctional. It was accompanied by overspecialization and insulation, and it was particularly in such amorphous settings that diversity of interests and communication with colleagues were essential to maintain significant performance (Pelz and Andrews, 1966b, chap. 3, 1966a). How, then, can colleague interaction and diversity of interests be encouraged? The mechanism of the doctoral committee is one useful device. The department chairman would be wise to make sure that each of his younger staff members has a chance to serve on a couple of dissertation committees each year, including projects outside his own specialty or discipline.

Inevitably the question arises as to the role of material rewards in stimulating research performance. How effective, for example, is the publish or perish policy as a means of motivating achievement? Some results from our study of scientific laboratories (Pelz and Andrews, 1966b, chap. 7) give a somewhat complex, but I think meaningful, answer. We found a distinct correlation between the individual's level of technical performance and his feeling that adequate salary and promotional opportunities were provided. Good performers, in short, felt that their achievements were recognized. On the other hand, when we asked how much importance the individual placed on material rewards, we found little correlation. Effective scientists were not motivated by the desire for material rewards. The results imply that if a university wants to promote good research, it must see that research achievement is properly appreciated by pay increases or promotion. It cannot, however, hope to stimulate such achievement by holding out the promise of higher pay. To put it another way: the absence of material rewards can undermine the motivation to achieve, but provision of such rewards cannot supply this incentive; it must come from challenge inherent in the work itself. In terms of my dual framework, pay and promotion can provide security, but they cannot provide challenge.

In summary, I have proposed that creative problem solving requires the presence of two somewhat contradictory conditions. One is security, some source of protection from demands of one's technical environment; the other is challenge, some source of exposure to demands of the environment.

If an educational system is to develop good researchers, it must strengthen personal sources of both security and challenge. An internal source of challenge is the quality of curiosity—meaning that the individual is intrigued by puzzles in his environment and enjoys trying to solve them. An internal source of security is the quality of self-confidence—intellectual independence and self-reliance. A third essential personal quality is competence—based on both ability and training. A fourth requisite for problem solving is involvement or enthusiasm.

Traditional systems of technical education concentrate on training competence and pay little attention to developing curiosity, self-confidence, or involvement. In fact, one might say that traditional education undermines the latter qualities instead of reinforcing them. Even in the area of competence it fails to develop flexibility.

In the present chapter I have offered a number of suggestions—many of them borrowed from current practices in undergraduate psychology programs—as to how curiosity, self-confidence, flexibility, and involvement might be encouraged. Among the most promising of the strategies suggested were problem-focused instruction, student initiative for learning, and multiple channels of decision and evaluation, which together illustrate the kinds of changes in student and faculty orientations that are needed if *higher* education is to signify education for creative problem solving.

16

Commentary: Person-Environment Interactions in Creative Performance

NORMAN FREDERIKSEN

Donald Pelz has presented many interesting suggestions for enhancing creativity in teaching and research management. In my discussion, however, I will concentrate on his model of creative performance and the methods by which such a model might be validated.

During the early years of behavioristic psychology, the S-R (stimulus-response) formula was the basic model employed. According to this conception, all individuals are essentially alike, and the task of psychology is to see how behavior varies as a function of changes in the environment. As time passed, the importance of individual differences came to be recognized, and the pendulum swung toward the notion that behavior is a function of the characteristics of the individual, such as ability and personality. This view is still very influential, especially in personnel psychology and in the selection of students for graduate school. The most

recent tendency is to study the joint effects of personal characteristics and situational variables. For example, the concept
of ATI, or aptitude-treatment interaction, has become a pop-
ular research topic in educational psychology (see Chapter
Eighteen).

Pelz has contributed to an area that has been neglected:
the influence of organizational climates on the performance
of scientists. The model he presents involves both individual
characteristics and organizational characteristics; it identifies
some important organizational variables, and it describes
interactions between the two classes of variables. It is highly
appropriate that we give serious consideration to the Pelz
model and other interaction models because of their potential contribution to understanding the joint effects of personal and situational characteristics on creative production.
A challenge to those who dare to undertake research on creativity is to develop more complete models of the processes
involved in creative production—models that not only take
account of the main effects of the traits of the scientists and
the main effects of the environmental conditions under which
they work, but that also make possible the discovery of how
these factors interact in influencing performance. Another
challenge is to devise suitable methods for testing the fit of
these models to empirical data.

At the risk of oversimplification, we can distinguish
three principal methods that have been used in studying creativity. One of these methods involves the identification of a
number of individuals who are acknowledged by their peers
to be the most outstanding members of a particular professional group (architects or mathematicians, for instance),
followed by a careful assessment of childhood treatment,
training, abilities, personality, and other influences that presumably have made these men and women the most outstanding people in their field (MacKinnon, 1962, 1963, 1967; Roe,
1953a, 1953b). Also assembled is a comparison group of
people in the same field who, also by common agreement,
have not achieved the same high degree of eminence. A comparison of the two groups is made in order to reveal fac-

tors that may be responsible for the differences in creative achievement.

It is usually easy to criticize research on creativity because it is an extraordinarily difficult field in which to work. The assessment of eminent people has been criticized as a method on several grounds. First, many of the assessment procedures are highly subjective, especially those involving interviews, ratings, and autobiographical reports by the subjects themselves. This subjectivity may lead not only to inaccuracies but, more important, to systematic error; it is possible that raters will tend to make judgments that are in accordance with their conceptions about the relationships involved. Second, reaching a position of eminence in a field may depend upon situational and personal variables other than those involving creativity. It is possible for example, that eminence is attributable in part to skills like those required in public relations and advertising. Finally, the method is retrospective; one would prefer a longitudinal method, in which prediction is possible.

Another method of studying creativity, perhaps the one most widely employed nowadays, is attributable to J. P. Guilford's insightful work on creativity, derived from his structure-of-intellect model. Guilford (1967) has developed and marshalled a great deal of evidence supporting the idea that intelligence can be described in terms of five operations (cognition, memory, convergent production, divergent production, and evaluation), four content areas (figural, symbolic, semantic, and behavioral), and six products (units, classes, relations, systems, transformations, and implications). The structure of intellect may be represented as a three-dimensional solid figure defined by the five operations, the four content areas, and the six kinds of products; thus 120 cells are generated, each corresponding to a particular intellectual ability (such as *memory* for *semantic classes*). Some of the cells correspond to abilities of the sort usually measured by a typical intelligence test. Other cells, those representing divergent production, include such creative-thinking abilities as fluency and flexibility. Guilford and his students have developed tests to represent many of the 120 hypothetical abilities (Guilford and Hoepfner, 1971), and the tests in the divergent production category have come to be used in much current research on creativity. One such test is the Consequences test, in which one is asked to think of possible consequences of certain bizarre conditions. (What would be the consequences of people no longer needing or wanting sleep?) Another is Brick Uses. (Think of as many unusual uses for a brick as you can.) Unfortunately, some of the tests used by Guilford to measure divergent thinking have come to be regarded as criterion measures of creativity rather than as abilities that may be involved in the whole process of creative production. Surely the ability to suggest a large number of uses for a brick is not sufficient to represent the domain of behaviors implied by the term creativity. I certainly do not quarrel with the use of these measures in research, even as dependent measures; I do quarrel with the equating of a score on the Brick Uses test with creativity.

The third method involves the study of creative performance of employees (for example, research scientists) in actual jobs in real organizations, the method that Pelz and Andrews used in their research. There is, of course, a great deal of appeal to the idea of using criteria based on real-life performance; what could be more valid than real life? Actually, real-life observations may not be very good sources of scientific data. On the contrary, the success of the scientific enterprise has been based on the idea of the laboratory, in which conditions can be rigorously controlled.

In the Pelz and Andrews study, data were obtained from 1,300 scientists and engineers. Many variables were based on judgments and ratings, although number of patents and number of publications were also used. The data included ratings of the personal characteristics of the scientists, the climate of the organization, and research productivity. I have already commented on the possibility that lay theories about organizational influences may actually produce the relationships that are later discovered in the data. The problem is magnified in a dynamic situation in which the dependent measures are to a degree public knowledge; everyone in the lab knows who the most successful scientists are because they get faster promotions, they are allowed to choose their research projects, and they get the research assistants they ask for. The result is that it becomes very difficult to differentiate between cause and effect. Pelz and Andrews have shown that self-confidence is a characteristic of the most successful scientists. Is the scientist successful because he is confident, or is he confident because he is successful? Similarly, the success of a scientist influences his environment, and it becomes difficult to tell whether the resources provided by the organization caused the success or the success influenced the organization to provide better resources. Pelz is, of course, very much aware of these relationships and has sensibly used them as feedback loops in his model. My point is merely that doing research in real-life situations has its difficulties.

I am not suggesting by this recital of criticisms that the methods are of no value and should not be used. On the contrary, all three methods are useful and should continue to be used. But it would be highly desirable to seek evidence for what Campbell and Stanley (1963) call external validity of the studies by attempting to replicate findings using different research methodologies.

Psychologists are often asked the question, What is the correlation between intelligence and creativity? Guilford says that the only correct way to answer is to ask another question: *What* intelligence, and *what* creativity? The work of L. L. Thurstone and his many followers has shown that intelligence is not one ability but many abilities, such as verbal ability, deductive reasoning, spatial ability, and perceptual speed. These abilities are usually moderately correlated, but by no means perfectly so. Similarly, creativity is not one but many abilities, some of which are ideational fluency, associational fluency, spontaneous flexibility, and adaptive flexibility. Both these lists can be placed in the same structure-of-intellect model. Both kinds of abilities, the divergent-production abilities and the abilities measured by the typical scholastic aptitude tests, are important in creative production.

Processes involved in creative production are no doubt influenced not only by cognitive abilities but also by many noncognitive traits and states, such as willingness to take risks, self-confidence, anxiety, security, perseveration, curiosity, and so forth. Clearly, the number of personal variables that might theoretically influence creative production is very great. We have no convenient source of information regarding the number and nature of organizational variables that might be involved, since a taxonomy of situational variables does not exist; but, no doubt, this number is also great (Frederiksen, 1972).

In contrast, the number of variables included in Pelz's model is small. He uses only four personal characteristics and four factors under institutional environment. One can easily think of a number of other organizational variables that could be included in a fine-grain theoretical model of person-situation interactions: tenure, closeness of supervision, size, profit-making status, and so on. In other words, a model of the processes of creative production in organizations could be constructed that would be far more complicated than the one presented by Pelz. The construction of such a model might have considerable heuristic value, even though it could not be empirically tested in its entirety.

How should one go about testing such a model, or parts of such a model? One approach involves the setting up of realistic situational tests intended to provide provisional criterion measures of creative performance. Frederiksen and Ward (1975), for example, have developed several tests that require graduate students to perform tasks like those performed by scientists, such as the Formulating Hypotheses test. If successful, these tests will require the demonstration of something approaching the real-world creativity that Kogan discusses in Chapter Six. We hope that these situational tests will bear enough resemblance to real-life tasks to possess a satisfactory degree of external validity as well as face validity, and that it will be possible to present the same tasks to subjects under controlled conditions. It may also be possible to simulate environmental variables, such as organizations with varying climates (Frederiksen, Jensen, and Beaton, 1972). Thus it may eventually be possible to carry out with some rigor experiments in which environmental factors will be made to vary experimentally. Then we can investigate the main effects and interactions of personal and environmental influences by use of test scores reflecting quantity, quality, and originality of performance on experimental tasks that realistically simulate the tasks of a scientist.

Pelz has provided many suggestions that should lead to improvement in graduate and undergraduate instruction. To me, however, the most intriguing contribution is his model of creative performance in organizations. It should stimulate a good deal of creative thinking about research on creative production.

17

Commentary: Interpersonal Climate of Creative Research Training

HAROLD M. PROSHANSKY

Donald Pelz has touched on some fundamental issues in graduate education in relation to scientific research that need not only continued analysis but repeated statement. I agreed with much of his analysis, but not all of it, and with most of his conclusions; in terms of the problem of how to train students and young researchers for productive and creative research performances, our basic orientations are the same.

During the past fifteen years my university teaching and research experiences have been confined almost exclusively to the graduate setting and to a large degree to working with doctoral students. As a graduate dean for several of these years, I was able to observe and compare my own experiences in teaching and research with those of my colleagues in psychology and to some extent with other research-oriented doctoral faculty in the behavioral and natural sciences. It was essentially from this vantage point that I read and pondered Pelz's chapter. I had been thinking for some time about some of the issues about graduate student research raised by him, and I finally put my thoughts together in a journal article (Proshansky, 1972). While my discussion was broader in scope and touched on other questions, part of the blueprint I sketched for graduate student training is provided with significant and very meaningful detail by Pelz's analysis.

Let me begin with a question of definition. Pelz refers to effective researchers, and, by implication, productive researchers. Creative or effective research, according to Pelz, depends on researchers or students who are competent, curious, and self-confident; and these characteristics in turn will only be fostered by carefully designed research environments. But what is creative or effective research? Do we mean well-designed and technically sound research which solves a specific problem, or do we mean something more than this? To me creative research implies innovation, not just in method, design, or measurement technique, but in theoretical construction as well. Creative theories about man, his society, and the natural world in which he lives may have to wait upon an equally creative methodology for testing and developing these conceptions. Research problems in any field vary in their complexity, significance, and degree of challenge. At what point on these continua are we willing to designate problem solution as the result of a creative research effort?

Given the difficulties in defining creativity generally, it would have been unfair to have expected Pelz to define creative research. By the same token, we have to have at least some criteria in mind if we believe that special research-training settings are required to foster competence, curiosity, and self-confidence in those being trained as researchers or those relatively new to the research enterprise. Oddly enough, even though it is hard to provide some general definition of creative research, we always seem to be able to recognize it, to appreciate that the researcher is showing talent in the way he formulates a problem, establishes a methodology to study it, and/or organizes, interprets, and integrates his findings. But we also have to remind ourselves that doing

research is a complex process involving not one but a con-
stellation of scientific talents. We may build curiosity, as Pelz
suggests, by confrontation with unsolved and important problems, and we may take steps to insure a research training
setting that instills self-confidence and technical research
competence, but the fact remains that with all the involvement, excitement, and enthusiasm generated in the researcher
by these essential attributes, he may be far more creative in
some aspects of the research process than in others. His potential to do creative research will most likely extend to some,
rather than all, of the dimensions of the research process.

Research settings, in other words, must also be sensitive to individual differences in the nature of the scientific
talents that exist among a cohort of graduate students or
young researchers. I have seen some brilliant research theoreticians whose capacities for research design and methodology before and after long research training and experience
were simply no match for their ability to generate and integrate theoretical ideas. And, of course, there are excellent
methodological innovators in research whose talents enable
them to make empirical breakthroughs in testing and elab-
orating the ideas and conceptions of others. I suspect that
even within each of these two types of research talent, other
differences in skill are evident. Given the scope and complexity of the problems now studied by means of scientific
research, it increasingly becomes evident that creative research will depend on the integration of the varying talents
of different investigators working together.

In this respect, it is important to note that in their study
of research laboratories, Pelz and his associates found that
the performance level of the researcher rose as several different sources shared in decision making. Exposed to a variety of viewpoints—clients, colleagues, supervisors—the
investigators apparently made more effective decisions in
their research and performed better as a result. In advocating problem-centered instruction as a means of developing
scientific curiosity, Pelz sees similar advantages for the student resulting from discussions with teachers, peers, or other

students, relevant agencies or clients, and from the process
of research teams reporting to each other. We take cogni-
zance of this recommendation and finding by Pelz because
it implies what we already have strongly suggested: no single
researcher, experienced or inexperienced, will be highly
talented in all of the basic capacities needed to produce a
high-level research performance. Consulting with diverse
groups is a critical method of compensating for this fact.

But what if a research setting, and particularly a graduate training program, is not sensitive to the fact of intraindividual differences in the required array of talents needed
for scientific research? What if it expects too much from its
students in terms of the breadth of abilities needed to do scientific research? Or—and I think this is probably even more
serious—what if the program's emphasis is on a type of research which demands one set of abilities but has no use for
other research abilities for which some students have the
greater talent? I think Pelz would agree that regardless of
what methods are used to build self-confidence in the graduate student as a researcher—doing research, working with
experienced mentors, sharing authorship—they will have
little effect unless genuine concern is given to the nature
and range of research talents in the student.

The Interdependence of Self-Confidence and Competence

Pelz's discussion of self-confidence as a factor underlying a
good research performance is both important and provocative. There is not one of us, however, who was unaware of
this, even when we ourselves were graduate students just
beginning to do research. But knowing about it and doing
something about it are two different things. The fact remains that insofar as the training of graduate students and
others to be effective researchers is concerned, little, if any,
systematic attention has been given to this problem. To me
it is quite incredible how faculty in psychology, sociology,
and anthropology who should know better have literally ignored this issue in the structure and substance of research

training settings established for graduate programs. Pelz deals with the matter directly and succinctly. He points out that faculty sees its role as teaching, examining, and weeding out the incompetent, and in all instances serving as both mentor and all-powerful judge. He is quite justified in questioning whether such a process can encourage independence of thought.

Furthermore—and this is a point Pelz does not stress sufficiently—if self-confidence or independence and initiative are not fostered, then curiosity and even competence are also liable to suffer. Intellectual or scientific curiosity presupposes intellectual or scientific security: security in one's ability to confront and to explore complex unsolved questions and in one's readiness to accept frustration in one approach and to find as yet undiscovered alternative approaches. I suspect that students and even faculty who continually depend on mentors for intellectual direction and support do not experience the kind of inner-directed curiosity required for creative scientific research. Indeed, it may well be that those who continue to travel the well-worn paths of theoretical conception and methodological approach in research are being impelled more by extrinsic considerations than intrinsic ones.

The failure to establish a sense of independence and self-reliance in graduate students has implications for their competence as researchers as well. Competence is ability plus knowledge, and in scientific fields, knowledge continues to grow and change. As Pelz indicates, no graduate curriculum can hope to provide the student with all the skills he may need for the future—even the near future. To overcome this problem he suggests a training program that is characterized by flexibility, in which self-study modules are used. As I see it, the key factor in this program is the student's having responsibility for his own learning and up-dating and, at root, for knowing when and how he must carry out this process. Pelz's recommendations that research competence should evolve from a flexible curricular and training structure in which self-initiative is the key element is clearly rooted in the assumption that the academic setting in which all of this is to occur also has built into it factors which will help to establish and maintain self-confidence and independence of thought and action in the student.

It should be obvious that I place great store in building self-confidence as the basis for training our creative researchers. Changing the traditional system of graduate education with this in mind is simple enough to recommend but far more difficult to achieve, even in terms of changing specific aspects of the system. I, too, have urged that the student have a chance to do research, that he be allowed to have a significant role in designing, carrying out, and writing up the research, and that he be given credit and recognition as a coauthor if it is published. In the graduate environmental psychology program at City University of New York, we have tried to put these principles into practice. From the moment the student is admitted to the program, he is involved in one of our ongoing research projects. As each year goes by, the nature and degree of freedom of his involvement increase. Long before they get to the thesis stage, our students have formulated, carried out, and written up systematic research studies. And, more important, they have worked in realistic research settings, have talked to practitioners, and even have had direct feedback on their efforts from those who wanted or accepted the research in the first place. The recently introduced National Science Foundation Student Research Support Program has been a critical adjunct to our efforts. We have urged our most advanced students to apply for such support, which has necessitated their functioning on their own and assuming complete responsibility for all the stages of the research.

Contributors to Self-Confidence and Curiosity

In my remaining comments, I would like to suggest two other factors that will build self-confidence and scientific curiosity in graduate students desiring a research career. Pelz tells us that involvement—excitement about a problem and motivation to solve it—is itself nourished by both curiosity and self-confidence. I would add that unless one experiences such involvement, the research is not likely to be very creative nor is the investigator likely to enjoy doing it. Research should be fun.

Except for brief references to the student in relation to his mentor and his peers, Pelz overlooks what I would call, for want of a better term, the "interpersonal element" as a factor in establishing self-confidence and curiosity in graduate students and young researchers. By this I mean both the attitudes and relationships between students and faculty in the academic setting; and I would place the greatest emphasis on how the faculty views, treats, and expects students to behave. To the extent that there emerges a colleague relationship between faculty member and student, in which the latter is encouraged to be independent, to think for himself, and to take the lead in designing and carrying out research, to that extent will self-confidence and curiosity develop. It is not enough to allow the student to participate in faculty research and to receive coauthorship in whatever papers are published. It is the quality of the student's participation in the research as determined by the faculty member's attitudes toward him that counts. Indeed, there should be equality of participation between faculty member and student; the student should not be viewed as a participant, assistant, or intern in the research project, but as a collaborator. The environmental psychology program I described above provides a good example of what I mean. Students are always involved in ongoing research, even while taking courses, and regardless of their level (first year, second, and so forth), they are given responsibility for some aspect of the project. They not only share in the responsibility but in the decision making and in the satisfactions that follow from systematic research. Obviously, this is much less true during the student's first year of graduate study; but by the third or fourth year, students and faculty have indeed become collaborators in research.

Faculty at all levels in our program are as likely to consult with students as are students with faculty, in the manner of Pelz's multiple channels of decision and evaluation. Indeed, we take the view that students, by virtue of their age, selected experiences, and role as student, are far more skilled in formulating and designing particular aspects of complex environmental research than are established faculty members. To take but one example: some of our students live and interact in ghetto areas, and these students are better prepared than are their faculty collaborators to deal with such issues as how to approach the community to do research, how to design the interview and observation schedules, and so on. But it goes even beyond this; these students have provided important input in conceptualizing the style of life of the ghetto residents they live and interact with.

Recently, Ittelson, Proshansky, Melzer, and Hayward formulated and designed a major research proposal on mental health in relation to the style of life associated with various types of housing and living conditions in New York City. Melzer and Hayward are students; Melzer is in sociology and Hayward in environmental psychology, although originally trained as an architect. Both students participated in the preliminary discussions, in formulating the problem and designing it, and in writing the proposal for submission to the National Institute of Mental Health. And they were expected to, and indeed did, carry their weight when a site visit team came to consider the proposal in more detail.

Creating this kind of training and research atmosphere for our students—one that seeks to instill self-confidence and scientific curiosity by making research a truly collaborative effort involving students and faculty—is made somewhat easier because we have environmental psychology students who are trained and experienced architects. Insofar as the conceptualization of the dimensions of the physical environment and other environmental design problems are concerned, they assume the mantle of authority and expertise. Our other students have the opportunity to observe that neither faculty nor students need necessarily run the research show.

As an environmental psychologist, I would like to point to one other omission in Pelz's presentation. What about the physical setting for research and training for research? I am not referring to equipment and supplies and other technical resources, but to questions of territoriality and place identity for the young researcher. I suppose the broader question concerns the kind of learning environment that induces self-confidence and curiosity, but at the moment the problem need not be that complex.

No single problem plagues the university more than providing space for its students and faculty. At the graduate and undergraduate levels, more is involved than just crowding, inconvenience, and frustration. We expect young faculty and graduate students to undertake research, but very often it is an expectation without a commitment on our part. We do not simply want research, we want creative research; but too often we fail to provide sufficient space and other facilities to make the achievement of this objective possible. To make matters worse, in much the same manner that course requirements and examinations thwart the development of independence of thought in research, so the bureaucracy and red tape of gaining access to and use of existing research facilities dampens, if it does not extinguish, scientific curiosity in students and young faculty. The bureaucratic problems—Where do you go? Who has to approve the purchase? How do you get permission?—may be there for senior, high-status researchers as well as for the younger ones; but the former, after long experience, know how to beat the system.

Perhaps nothing expresses a researcher's sense of autonomy and self-confidence more than his use of the phrase "my laboratory." Regardless of whether it is a room for interviewing people and analyzing data or a complicated microbiology setting, it identifies him as a researcher and gives him some control over his physical environment. In this way it increases the probability that he will do creative research. If, as I believe, individuals have a place identity, the laboratory must be the critical ingredient in this identity for the scientific researcher. To have this kind of identity unsatisfied means a weakening of both self-confidence and curiosity in doing research.

Paradoxically enough, those who need such satisfaction most, namely the young faculty member and the graduate student, are least likely to get it because the availability and quality of space and other resources usually correlate with faculty status and rank. We give the student a bullpen desk, sometimes a small office, and more often a place in the laboratory of his mentor. It comes as no surprise to me that the empirical research thesis becomes such a threat to graduate students that they will settle for just continuing a mentor's research or will be willing to settle on a routine and very "safe" problem. How can they be confident, curious, and challenged if even when there are resources available, they have little control over them.

In recent years we have been worried that Ph.D. training programs in most disciplines give almost exclusive attention to turning out researchers and ignore the need for inspired university teachers. I worry far less about this and far more about the fact that even after all the stress on research, we may be turning out uninspired and unimaginative investigators rather than highly effective or creative ones.

Part Seven

Differential Treatments for Differential Learning

Part Seven brings us to the pedagogical heart of the matter: to the possibility of tailoring instructional procedures and conditions to functional characteristics of students so as to optimize individual learning and creativity. In Chapter Eighteen, Richard Snow reviews several empirical examples of aptitude-treatment interactions, which reveal positive effects on learning for different types of students in different treatment conditions. These effects occur primarily in two major ways: first, when students receive instruction catering to their learning preferences (such as formal, structured teaching for students who achieve through conformance or self-directed procedures for students who achieve through independence) and, second, when students and teachers are matched on certain stylistic characteristics or ability patterns (such as high versus low divergent thinking or behavioristic versus humanistic orientation). These results tend to support the general strategy of tailoring instruction to capitalize on student strengths and preferences. However, Snow cautions against any uniform conclusion in this regard because the criterion or outcome measures used in much of the research on aptitude-treatment interactions have been relatively limited; they have embraced mainly subject matter achievement and specific behavioral skills and have paid scant attention to problem solving or creative behavior.

The need to broaden the range of outcome measures typical of much ATI research is further underscored by Winton Manning in Chapter Nineteen, with special reference to the area of higher education, where the objectives and hence the criteria of instruction are more diverse and more ambitious than at elementary and secondary levels. As important dimensions of instructional payoff in undergraduate and graduate education, Manning particularly emphasizes mathemagenic outcomes: those behaviors that engender and facilitate learning as a continuing process.

This concern with assessing instructional interactions in terms of a wide array of potential outcomes is akin to the concern with side effects in educational evaluation. Any instructional treatment produces multiple outcomes, and we should be alert to the possibility that treatments designed to optimize one outcome may have unintended adverse effects with respect to other outcomes. The routine use of multivariate criteria in ATI research would serve to monitor this possibility and help to assure us that a perverse form of Snow's Parkinsonian law of conservation of instructional effectiveness does not hold true for outcome variables. As recast for outcomes rather than individuals, this law would read: No matter how you try to make an instructional treatment better in regard to one outcome, you will make it worse in regard to some other outcome. Although such perverseness does not appear to be the rule, the intended moral is still important for prudent practice: we should evaluate differential instructional effects in terms of multiple dimensions of possible outcomes before formulating general strategies or specific prescriptions for individualizing instruction.

Nor are outcome dimensions the only variables of concern, as Brian Lewis points out in Chapter Twenty. Also at issue are the aptitude dimensions and associated treatment variables. Lewis warns that ATI research, like most research that impinges upon the realm of personality, is in danger of bogging down in a proliferation of findings with assorted superficial and faddish measures of individual differences. What is needed, he argues, is a relentless search for dimensions that are basic, that underlie and determine a whole range of observable surface differences, thereby providing a stable basis for differential instructional treatments of wide applicability.

18

Aptitude-Treatment Interactions and Individualized Alternatives in Higher Education

RICHARD E. SNOW

Individuals differ. For close to a century now, psychologists have been studying the ways in which individuals differ in personal and intellectual characteristics and the importance of these differences in various social contexts. There is, perhaps, no more important focus for such research than the problems of education, particularly those of higher education.

Beyond our natural interest in understanding human behavior for its own sake, there are three practical problems in higher education to which research on individual differences is applicable. One of these is the selection problem, in which institutions seek improved measures of aptitude for

A major portion of this paper was completed while the author was serving as Boerhaave Professor, Faculty of Medicine, University of Leyden, Netherlands. Some portions of the paper are condensed excerpts from a manuscript in preparation by L. J. Cronbach and R. E. Snow, "Aptitude and Instructional Methods: The Search for Interactions."

success in their particular curriculum and instructional settings. A second is the evaluation problem, in which improved measures of learning outcome are sought for assessing the qualities of alternative educational settings and of the individuals who pass through them. A third problem, less distinct and less well studied than the first two, has been variously called the classification, or individualization, or counseling problem. The purpose of this chapter is to explore, albeit sketchily, this third problem area and to suggest that in it lie some of the most interesting and important issues facing higher education today.

The history of research on selection is a long one, and the measurement technology relevant to this problem is highly developed. Research on evaluation is not nearly so old, however, and there are many new developments in this field today, one of which is to suggest that new measures of cognitive styles and creativity are needed for evaluation purposes. Yet the basic idea that alternative educational treatments can be evaluated by experimental comparisons to see which is best has remained the cornerstone conception of evaluation for decades. But educators are increasingly called upon to deal with the third type of problem, which, for the sake of brevity, I will call the individualization problem. We are no longer satisfied with a meritocracy concerned only with selecting the learners who best fit into existing educational environments; at least some of these environments, we think, can be redesigned to better fit the learners. And we are increasingly aware that the definition of the best educational environment depends heavily on the kinds of learners at hand; the old question, Which method is best? must be qualified by the question, Best for whom? In other words, the educator's responsibility today is to adapt instruction to the individual learner—to seek an optimal match between the individual's characteristics and the characteristics of alternative possible educational environments.

Some adaptations might be accomplished by building adaptive instrumentation, such as some forms of computerized instruction. Some adaptations involve classifying learners into different subgroups to receive instructional sequences specifically designed for them. Assigning students to the advisers or teachers who seem best suited to their special educational and psychological needs would be another example of such classification. At times, differential counseling or training might be used to prepare learners for alternative learning or study methods. Counseling of learners as to choice of field of specialization is a form of individualization, as is counseling on choice of institutional environment. Of course, some will say that educators have been adapting to individual differences all along; classroom teachers are constantly adapting on an intuitive basis. But such adaptation has rarely been adequate, and it has never been reproducible; for no one has known the principles governing the optimal match of person and environment. The task for research is to find these principles, which means finding interactions between person variables and environmental variables.

This is the task that Cronbach (1957) set for the unification of correlational and experimental psychology in his presidential address to the American Psychological Association nearly two decades ago. It is also consistent with Lewinian ideas and in its most general form amounts to the application of Darwinian thinking to the study of organism-environment relations in psychology. Research in this direction is expanding in several areas of psychology and educational research. In education, these interactions of person and environment can be called aptitude-instructional treatment interactions, or ATI for short.

The Problem of ATI Research

To state the problem of ATI research formally, let us assume that we have measures of individual differences at the start of some educational sequence and that we have some measures of learning outcome to represent evaluative criteria. The starting measures are here called aptitudes; this term should not be restricted to mean general intelligence or general scholastic ability; for I would argue that any aspect of an individual that predicts response to instruction, including prior achievement, special ability, personality, and stylistic characteristics, deserves to be regarded as a source of aptitude for learning. The old restrictive meaning of the term *aptitude* as applying only to ability tests is detrimental, in my view. The outcome criteria may be thought of as measures of attitude, or of achievement, or of problem-solving ability, or of creative production, or even of satisfaction with course of study or career choice. It is even likely that some measures may serve both as aptitude and as outcome, since, in a general sense, education's most important product is improved aptitude for future learning.

Assume further that each of these measures may be collected in each of several different educational treatments, and allow for the possibility that aptitude-outcome relations may or may not be similar across treatments. Treatment variables may be thought of as variations in instructional methods or media, variations in classroom or teacher characteristics, or even as differences in departmental or institutional environments.

The methodology of ATI research can be quite complicated; but to demonstrate some features of the approach without getting too involved in the statistics, a simple abstract example should suffice. Figure 1 shows some possible relationships between a single aptitude variable and a single learning outcome variable obtained under different instructional treatments. In each treatment, a separate regression line has been constructed to display the aptitude-outcome relationship. In Figure 1a, the two regression lines have distinctly different slopes and cross at a point within the aptitude distribution. This is an ATI. It suggests that different treatments are best for students in different parts of the aptitude distribution. Treatment A is best for students high on the aptitude continuum, while Treatment B is best for those low on the aptitude continuum. The interaction provides a decision rule for classifying students into different treatments, as shown. Figure 1b shows a case where the regression lines are differently sloped but do not cross within the aptitude distribution. This is also an ATI for theoretical purposes and might be useful for classification purposes as well if the two treatments differed substantially in cost or if some quota had to be imposed on assignment to Treatment A. If Treatment A involved use of computer time, for example, we might choose to use it only for students who would clearly benefit, placing others for whom the two treatments do not differ substantially into the cheaper treatment. Of course, cost factors might modify the use of the ATI in Figure 1a as well. Figure 1c shows the absence of interaction. Here the slopes are parallel, so Treatment A is best for everyone; no subdivision of students is worthwhile.

A traditional experimental approach seeking a best instructional method would have ignored aptitude variables and looked only at average outcome when comparing treatments, concluding that for the data of Figure 1a there was no important treatment difference—a false conclusion. The overall average comparison of treatments in Figure 1b would have produced the unlimited generalization that Treatment A was better than Treatment B for everyone—also false. Only data like those in Figure 1c fit this traditional mode of experimental evaluation. But the traditional correlational approach, seeking general predictors for use in selection, would have ignored treatment variations. The pooled regression lines for Figures 1a and 1b would be almost horizontal, suggesting that the aptitude measure has no predictive value and should be discarded—another false conclusion.

Note that ATI is studied with regression methods, not correlations, since the degree of interaction is influenced by differences in aptitude and outcome variation between treatments. When criterion measures have different variances in different treatments, ATI may appear even though correlations are identical. Also note that the statistical test for ATI is the same F test used to examine the assumption of regression homogeneity preceding analysis of covariance. In Figure 1c, the assumption is met, so the investigator can proceed to test mean differences with analysis of covariance, using the aptitude as covariate. Contrary to the view often

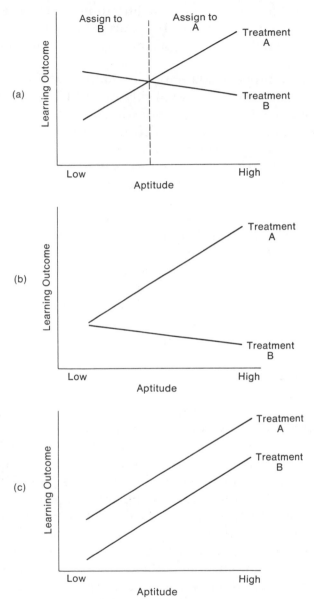

Figure 1. Regression lines showing three kinds of outcomes in ATI research. Figures 1a and 1b display disordinal and ordinal interactions, respectively. Figure 1c indicates the absence of interaction.

held by novice investigators, failure to meet this assumption is not a cause for dejection. It signals the presence of an ATI worthy of interpretation in its own right, as shown in Figure 1a and 1b.

All attempts at adaptation or individualization of education rest implicitly or explicitly on ATI hypotheses. Because of current interest in individualization, there has been a rapid expansion of research efforts in pursuit of ATI. Several people, including myself, have reviewed portions of this literature at various conferences. There have been several published reviews of the literature, including those by Bracht (1970), Berliner and Cahen (1973), Tyler (1972), and Glaser and Resnick (1972). Cronbach and I produced a report on the topic (Cronbach and Snow, 1969), a revised and enlarged version of which is now near completion. It is not necessary therefore to summarize the findings of this entire literature here. It need only be noted that for educational research generally, the possibilities for obtaining ATI results appear far brighter today than most critics, including the present author, predicted a few years ago.

Research Results

The present report presents only a few studies that demonstrate the kinds of ATI findings that have been, or might be, obtained in higher educational research when special ability, personality, or cognitive style variables are used as aptitudes and/or when creative and problem-solving behavior serves as outcome. The list of results appears as a patchwork, without showing much evidence of coherent or sustained attacks on well-formulated ATI hypotheses, because, frankly, that is the present state of the art. Past research has been a hodgepodge of oversimplified hypotheses investigated with research methods poorly designed for the purpose; hence progress has been slow, and significant findings are still quite scattered. Since ATI research requires the development of a new way of hypothesizing and a new research methodology, any kind of coherent theory about such phenomena is a long way off. Yet there are enough results to begin sketching improved hypotheses and methods for directing ATI research on instruction. A later section of this chapter will outline some of the approaches to ATI hypothesizing that appear helpful in thinking about instructional treatments aimed at fostering creativity. Ultimately, however, theory about ATI in higher education must overarch ideas as diverse as conceptions of vocational choice (Holland, 1966), the fit of personalities to occupational roles or college environments (Pace and Stern, 1958; Pervin, 1968), emphasis on grouping for the improvement of small-group teaching (Thelen, 1967), branching rules and strategies of computer-aided instruction, and even the matching of psychotherapist and client (Razin, 1971; Chartier, 1971).

Aptitude-Treatment Matching. One study by Salomon (1968) compared instructional treatments designed to promote either hypothesis generation (HG) or cue attendance (CA) behavior among first-year graduate students who were teachers-in-training at Stanford. In the HG treatment students were given practice in generating alternative explanations or hypotheses regarding the story shown in a film with randomly ordered scenes. In the CA treatment the same film was used, but students practiced noticing and reporting stimulus details, ignoring the underlying story theme. GRE Verbal scores served as aptitude. Later, a problem-solving test concerned with the development of English curriculum for Spanish-speaking schools was administered as a criterion. Students were required to list questions and information they would need resolved while working on the problem. A marked ATI was found, as shown in Figure 2. Students with GRE Verbal aptitude above a score of 550 asked more questions after the HG treatment than they did after the CA treatment; those with GRE Verbal aptitude scores below 550 produced more questions after the CA treatment. CA training seems to require one to lift restrictions on attention and report details without evaluating them. Perhaps this is better for lower aptitude students because it promotes attention to detail, but it may bore the more verbal students. HG, on the other hand, may require more verbal analytic and reasoning skill than CA, thus exceeding the ability of low students while challenging the high students. Such findings could indicate that HG and CA represent alternative problem-solving skills or strategies, but they might also result if skill in CA is a prerequisite to HG performance and both are dependent on general verbal ability. GRE Quantitative score was not investigated here, so we cannot know whether we are dealing with general ability or with verbal ability in particular. The information search criterion and the HG and CA training do seem similar to procedures used in some other studies of creative problem solving.

A study by Koran (1969) examined the development of analytic questioning skill among graduate student teachers-in-training, using a microteaching arrangement (see also Koran, Snow, and McDonald, 1971). Microteaching is a scaled-down teaching situation in which trainees teach a brief lesson to a few students, receive a videotaped playback of their own performance, replan the lesson, and try again with new students. The procedure is repeated for three or four trials. Koran's idea was to get teacher trainees to ask more penetrating questions when analyzing problems in class discussion. She used two treatments to provide trainees with a model of the skill. In the videomodeling treatment (VM), a videotape showed a master teacher performing the required skill. For the written modeling treatment (WM), the same master performance was presented as a typed transcript. A control treatment (NM) received no modeling. The criterion was the number of analytic questions each trainee asked in the subsequent ten-minute microteaching lessons. Aptitude was represented by a battery of cognitive ability tests.

The VM treatment was best on the average, but ATI was found for several ability measures. The interaction for Part 1 (the first half) of the Hidden Figures Test or Embedded Figures Test is shown in Figure 3. The WM treatment was best for those who scored high on Hidden Figures, while the VM treatment was best for low scorers. Hidden Figures

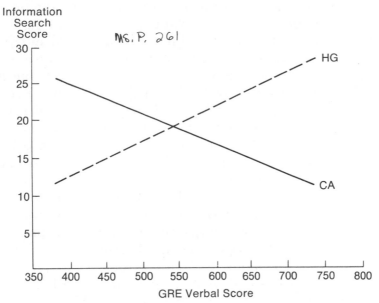

Figure 2. Interaction of GRE Verbal scores with hypothesis generation (HG) versus cue attendance (CA) training, using information search scores as criterion.

From Salomon (1968).

is constructed of the old Gottschaldt complex figures. It has been variously interpreted as an index of general ability, of Cattell's fluid ability, of Thurstone's flexibility-of-closure factor, of Guilford's convergent production of figural transformations, and of Witkin's field-independence style. But note that only the first part (perhaps the learning half) of the test provided ATI. A decision among these varying interpretations cannot be made with the Koran data; it requires more extensive study using a multitrait-multimethod approach (Campbell and Fiske, 1959).

It is worth adding here that the ATI and Campbell-Fiske approaches combine to provide the essential methodology for construct validation in psychology and education. To hazard a guess about the meaning of Koran's findings, one might suppose that in VM the key stimuli (certain types of questions) are clearly indicated to the learner in a standard, paced video presentation; in WM the learner must dig them out of a typed transcript for himself. Thus, field independence, or analytic ability, particularly as coupled with a rapid organizational style in test taking, is needed in WM but not in VM. The negative slope for VM suggests that interference or boredom is produced here for the more able learners.

Another test providing interaction in the Koran study was a measure of film memory, positively related to performance in VM but negatively related in WM. Apparently, effective use of video modeling required memory for filmed (or videotaped) live action, while for WM this variable represented an inaptitude for some reason. Combining results for the two aptitudes in a multiple-regression analysis produces the bivariate ATI shown in Figure 4. From this, one could conclude that VM should be used for trainees with good film memory and poor scores on Hidden Figures, Part 1. Trainees with the opposite attitude pattern should probably be placed in WM since it is less costly, even if not significantly superior to VM for these students. In Figure 3, the dashed vertical line indicates how the aptitude distribution can be partitioned into regions where treatments do and do not differ from one another, given some chosen significance level. In Figure 4, the solid line in the aptitude base plane shows the projection of the line where the two regression planes intersect. The curved dashed line again shows the partitioning of this aptitude base plane into regions of significance and nonsignificance. The statistical methodology for determining these regions is called the Johnson-Neyman technique, a helpful device for obtaining classification rules from ATI data. These particular analyses were completed by Aiken (1968), using Koran's data.

It is difficult to decide whether the combination of film memory and Hidden Figures, Part 1 to form a bivariate ATI is a step toward new conceptions of aptitude or simply an interesting demonstration built on chance. The finding has not been replicated; it rests on two measures with little or no prior substantiation as constructs. Film memory is one of a number of cine-psychometric devices developed to ex-

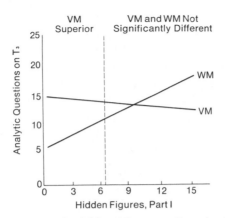

Figure 3. Interaction of Hidden Figures, Part 1 with videomodeling (VM) and written modeling (WM) treatments using number of analytic questions on microteaching trial 3 as criterion.

Reprinted from Koran, Snow, and McDonald (1971) by permission of American Psychological Association.

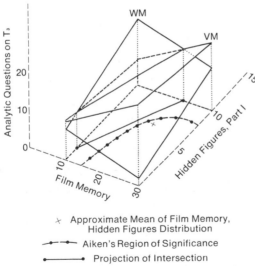

x Approximate Mean of Film Memory, Hidden Figures Distribution

Aiken's Region of Significance

Projection of Intersection

Figure 4. Multiple regression analysis for videomodeling (VM) and written modeling (WM) treatments with Hidden Figures, Part 1 and Film Memory Test scores as aptitudes.

Reprinted from Koran, Snow, and McDonald (1971), by permission of the American Psychological Association.

plore areas of cognitive ability not accessible to conventional printed media (Seibert and Snow, 1965; Seibert, Reid, and Snow, 1967). It is not an ordinary experience in test taking, even for college students. The content portrays complex human behavior, largely nonverbal, that is probably hard to encode completely in symbolic or verbal terms. As noted before, Hidden Figures, Part 1 is just the first half, perhaps the learning-trial half, of a test open to various interpretations; the second half of this test actually gave a nonsignificant interaction pattern with slopes in the opposite direction. But there are other instances of the first half of an ability test functioning differently from the second half in this way. This learning-half hypothesis deserves research as a side issue. Possibly, these measures represent information-processing characteristics in learning that are not clearly interpretable from past research on ability tests, which has usually relied solely on correlational methods. Certainly, much more ATI research on such measures will be needed before their interpretation is clarified. As with the Salomon study, however, the skill studied here seems quite relevant to creative problem-solving performance.

We turn now to two studies by Domino that show clear replication of an ATI result. He distinguished among study participants on the basis of the California Psychological Inventory scales Ai (achievement through independence) and Ac (achievement through conformity). The High Ai describes himself as mature, foresighted, demanding, and self-reliant. The High Ac describes himself as capable, efficient, organized, responsible, and sincere. Domino's question was whether students who exhibit one pattern or the other would reveal differences between their response to college instruction that is structured and demanding of conformity and their response to instruction that places weight on student initiative, interests, and independent thought. It is not obvious that a student high in independence should do better when allowed independence; if the result were to turn out in the opposite direction, one could rationalize by arguing that the student who cherishes independence has greater need for discipline imposed by a formal instructor.

The results of Domino's two studies are consistent: better work is produced when the instructor encourages the student's natural style. High Ac's do better with formal instruction, and High Ai's do better when allowed initiative and self-direction. The first study (1968) was nonexperimental; students were classified by personality, and a tally was made of those courses in which each student had done well. Domino then interviewed the instructor of every course each of his participants had taken, looking for emphasis on memorization, keeping of attendance records, objective examinations, and so on; this constraining style of teaching was hypothesized to require and reward student conformity. Instructional styles favorable to independent behavior were also noted. Some seventy-three courses were classified as encouraging conformity, and thirty-two as encouraging independence. The grades the student received were sorted according to the kind of course in which they had been earned. This gave the student two grade averages.

In the end, there were four groups of twenty-two Ss each, matched for sex and score on a nonverbal mental test. The four groups were chosen from the extreme corners of the Ac-Ai distribution. The grade averages were highest for the high-high pattern and lowest for the low-low pattern, so there was a substantial main effect. But there was also a clear hint of interaction: those students with the low independence-high conformity pattern earned a higher average in structured courses, while those with the high independence-low conformity pattern did better where they could perform more independently.

The second Domino study (1971) was an experiment designed to test the same relationship, again using extreme groups. From among sophomores enrolled for introductory psychology, Domino identified fifty with the high-Ai-low-Ac pattern, and fifty with the opposite pattern. These groups were divided in half, and twenty-five students with the same pattern were assigned to a section of the course, making four sections, two of each type. An instructor (who did not know the basis for assigning students) agreed to teach two sections in the style that encourages independence and two sections in the formal, structured style that requires conformity. Six outcome measures were used, representing multiple choice and rated quality of achievement, rated quality of original thinking, and student ratings of the course and teacher. While not all the differences between groups were large, there was a significant interaction on every variable except rated original thinking. High Ai's did best when the instructor's style favored independence; High Ac's, when he favored conformity. For the original-thinking measure, a significant main effect for personality dominated the results: the conforming students were unable to show good quality of original thinking, no matter how they were taught.

We skip now to a brief review of one study that examines the classroom effects of the sort of teaching skill studied by Koran (1969), and two other studies that extend the idea of matching teacher and student skills in ATI fashion. Although these studies were conducted in the public schools, they are suggestive for research at higher levels.

Hutchinson (1963) had high school social studies taught by two methods. In four classes, teachers tried to elicit independent thinking of an evaluative, convergent, or divergent sort. The same teachers taught control classes in a didactic mode, giving information and eliciting recall. For a unit on transportation and communication, pretest and posttest data were collected. The hypothesis was that conventional instruction was best for students with high IQ scores but that the experimental teaching style might be better suited for students with high scores on divergent-thinking tests. Mental age on the California Test of Mental Maturity (CTMM) and seven measures of divergent thinking served as aptitude pretests. The analysis, however, was not properly done, and the divergent-thinking data were not reported in usable form; only the regression of achievement on CTMM mental age can be examined here. Interaction occurred for two of the four teachers; their experimental teaching did have a shallower AT slope than did their conventional teaching. In other words, higher IQ students did better in conventional instruction than in experimental teaching; lower IQ students apparently were served as well or better with the experimental condition. For the other two teachers there was no difference in regression slope between the two methods. We would need observations of teachers and better representation of divergent-thinking abilities to evaluate this result properly, but the obtained interaction does appear to merit further study.

Student-Teacher Matching. Yamamoto (1963) used two of Torrance's creative-thinking tests to score nineteen fifth-grade teachers on divergent thinking. Teachers were categorized as above or below the median. In October and in March, reading and arithmetic subtests of the Iowa Test of Basic Skills and the California Test of Personality were administered. Lorge-Thorndike IQs were also obtained in October. The analysis was unnecessarily complex. To obtain a summary for our purposes the total of fluency, flexibility, originality, and elaboration scores can serve as a rough measure of divergent production.

There were marked ATIs for two dependent variables: arithmetic achievement and personal adjustment. Low-divergent students who had low-divergent teachers scored higher on arithmetic than similar students with high-divergent teachers. High-divergent students did better with high-divergent teachers but did not surpass lows who had high-divergent teachers. The ATI crossover for the personal adjustment outcome was quite distinct for boys: low-divergent boys were better off with low-divergent teachers, while high-divergent boys were better off with high-divergent teachers. Girls seemed better adjusted with low-divergent teachers, regardless of their own classification. The dependent measure of reading achievement gave no interaction. Teacher self-reports and observation data did not shed much light on the interactions. High-divergent teachers tended to score much higher on complexity and theoretical orientation. Perhaps this caused trouble for their low-divergent students.

It is possible that teachers differ in general styles of teaching and also vary within such categories in particular abilities, skills, and strategies. Profile-matching methods may

be needed to examine interactions and eventually to guide
the assignment of teachers to learners. Only one study has
attempted to examine this multivariate matching possibility.
Cleare (1966; see Kropp and others, 1967, pp. 88–97) administered seven cognitive tests to thirteen CHEM Study teachers
and their 917 high school students. Abilities tested were verbal comprehension, visualization, syllogistic reasoning, semantic redefinition, flexibility of closure, and induction.
A midterm examination was employed as a posttest. Students
were categorized by sex, by ability level (high or low), and
also by the similarity of the student's ability *pattern* to that
of his teacher (intraclass correlations having been categorized
as indicating high, medium, or low similarity). The results
were as predicted: a student having ability level or ability
pattern or sex similar to his teacher's tended to achieve more
than a student who was unlike his teacher in these respects.

Thus, it appears that teacher-student matching on ability
profile may be worthwhile. But caution should be exercised
in generalizing here. Profile similarity may not prove to be
the matching principle in many cases. Perhaps a teacher's
aptitude profile ought to complement the student's profile
in some respects, rather than to match it everywhere. Sophisticated statistical procedures will be needed to explore such
possibilities, particularly since multiple-outcome measures
will also be needed.

We come now to a study of a rather different sort, though
it also relates to teacher-student matching. Majasan (1972),
in a dissertation at Stanford, obtained rather dramatic results. Twelve college psychology teachers indicated their
views about the aims, content, and methods of work of scientific psychology on a questionnaire that allowed scoring of
each one's position on a behaviorist versus phenomenologist-
humanist scale. Their students in introductory psychology
also completed the questionnaire at the beginning and end of
the course. Ability measures were collected, but these, and
also the achievement measures, varied from class to class.
The classes ranged from about twenty to over sixty in size.
The residualized achievement score was plotted against the

student's belief. As he had predicted, Majasan often found a curvilinear regression with the peak achievement occurring among students whose initial view of psychology was similar to their instructor's. On either side of the instructor's scale position, achievement outcome decreased as the difference between students and instructor increased. In classes where the instructor's score was near the end of the class range (typically the behaviorist end) the regression was linear but in line with the prediction. In only one or two classes did the evidence seem not to support the prediction that a student achieves highest when his initial beliefs resemble those of his instructor, other things being equal. In Figure 5, the results for three representative classes are shown. For simplicity in this illustration, straight lines have been fitted to the data on either side of each instructor's position, rather than curves. Actually the linear fit works quite well. The results are not due to bias in marking, since most instructors used objective tests. The tests, however, were assembled by the instructor and could have been biased toward his preconceptions.

Now, what courses of action might be suggested by the results in Figure 5? We probably cannot change the teachers' tendencies regarding behaviorism, and we would be hesitant to recommend assigning students to those teachers most similar to them until this study was repeated with dependent measures other than achievement as criteria. It could be that average originality or independence of thinking would actually be reduced in each class by such an assignment policy. We might even find that each student should be matched with the most complementary rather than the most congruent teacher. One course of action is clear: the head of a psychology department with these results should hurry to hire a humanistic psychologist to cover the left end of the student spectrum.

Student-Environment Matching. While teacher variations may constitute an important class of treatment variables for ATI research in higher education, it is also appropriate to consider the possibility of interactions between student characteristics and those of college environments. Several studies

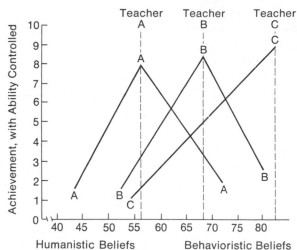

Figure 5. Linear regression lines fitted to students on each side of their teacher's position (shown by dashed vertical). From a study by Majasan, 1972.

in recent years have attempted to characterize the important dimensions along which college environments differ. As Astin (1970) pointed out, findings about the main effects of college environments are not of much use unless an existing institution can be drastically modified or a new one designed. But interactions are directly useful, even when major institutional change is unlikely. Interactions permit distribution of prospective students among existing institutions, facilitating mutual choice by student and college so that each student body is made up of the persons most likely to benefit from that college's instructional and community style. Indeed, the basic purpose of establishing schools of different types or independent colleges within a university campus is to provide options for students of different temperaments. Such person-situation matching ought to benefit personal growth.

One line of work in this area has been pursued by Linn, Rock, Centra, and others at Educational Testing Service. In one study, the possibility of differential regression of GRE posttests on SAT pretests in several colleges was examined. Centra, Linn, and Parry (1970) selected and matched seven white colleges with seven black colleges. Data from the senior class of each college ($N=733$) were used to compute a separate regression line for each college. The slopes were significantly heterogeneous; some colleges seemed better suited to lower ability students while others got better results from higher ability students. Slope seemed not to depend upon ethnicity. It is uncertain what other characteristics of the colleges might relate to the slope differences, but further work in this direction is certainly indicated.

Following a rather different approach, Pervin (1967) developed a semantic differential for examining student-college interaction. Students respond to the concepts college, self, students, faculty, administration, and ideal college on fifty-two bipolar scales. Discrepancy scores are computed for each pair of concepts for each student. In a study of twenty-one colleges ($N=3016$) these discrepancy scores were then correlated with the dissatisfaction the student reported about various aspects of his college. A substantial number of significant positive correlations were obtained. When the discrepancy scores for, say, self versus administration correlate highest with degree of dissatisfaction with the administration, Pervin interprets this as indicating validity for the instrument, though admittedly it is a correlation among two self-reports. A three-mode factor analysis, following Tucker's (1966) procedure, provided fourteen scale factors, three concept factors, and three college factors. These last factors distinguished first between public and private institutions and then divided the private schools into elite-conservative, elite-liberal, and less-conventional environments. As an example of the type of result obtained, it was demonstrated for two particular schools that "dissatisfied students at one school saw the college as more conservative, less equalitarian, and less scholarly, and the self as more liberal, more equalitarian, and more scholarly than did satisfied students. On each of these scales the relationship was reversed for dissatisfied students at the second school; that is, at the second school dissatisfied students saw the college as more liberal, more equalitarian, and more scholarly, and the self as less liberal, less equalitarian, and far less scholarly, than did satisfied students" (p. 299). Since data are not given in detail for all colleges, we cannot probe more deeply here. But it is clear that studies of college characteristics in interaction with student characteristics, using achievement, personal adjustment, and perhaps creative-production measures, might yield important clues about student-environment matching.

Some Implications for Future Research

I hope this brief review has provided a taste of ATI findings in several fields. It has not, unfortunately, provided good examples of really new forms of education having pronounced effects in developing creative thinking in students. There are two reasons for this. First, much research on so-called new forms of education has not considered individual differences among learners. Thus, comparisons of various kinds—filmed or televised instruction versus live instruction, lecture versus discussion methods, authoritarian versus democratic class organization, programed or computerized versus conventional instruction, varieties of text construction, and so forth—have often shown no average difference between methods. Even investigations of special laboratory settings or independent study arrangements or special "creativity" training programs often fail to consider that different conditions may be best for different learners. Second, much educational research, and particularly ATI research, has not yet concentrated on educational outcomes other than achievement. ATI studies concerned with original thinking or creative production or problem solving are very rare. Consequently, there is as yet no firm basis for hypothesizing about ATI in relation to creative-thinking criteria. But there are some implications that prompt speculation. In generating ATI hypotheses previously, it has sometimes proved worthwhile to use one or more heuristic devices. There are four such devices that may help in this new field.

First, one may start toward an ATI hypothesis by choosing a favorite aptitude and conceiving of treatment elements that might contribute to interaction, or by choosing a favorite treatment contrast and generating some list of aptitude attributes that could offer interaction, or by choosing a favorite criterion and working back through both treatment and aptitude variables. The third route characterizes the present task, since we are interested in any aptitude-treatment combinations that will promote creativity. One device for distinguishing classes of treatment variables, given a favorite criterion, can be called the functional uniqueness of instructional media. Each instructional medium has some communication functions it shares in common with other media and some that are unique to itself. The human being, as an instructional medium, is unique in his ability to recognize, encourage, and model creative behavior. Thus, as a class of treatment variables, teacher styles and characteristics may be far more important in fostering student creativity than the characteristics of alternative instructional technologies. The choice of studies for review in this paper reflected this view. Even the treatment variables examined by Salomon and by Koran are probably best thought of as teacher strategies rather than as packaged instructional programs.

Second, given a class of treatment variables on which to concentrate, we can distinguish between a capitalization and a compensatory mode of ATI hypothesizing. In the capitalization mode, we seek alternative treatments that would appear to capitalize on the strengths of particular kinds of learners, allowing each student to exercise his strongest, and perhaps also his most preferred, style of behavior. In the compensatory mode, the prosthetic qualities of treatments are emphasized. Treatments are fitted to the weaknesses of learners; each is designed to do for the learner what he cannot do for himself, just as an artificial limb serves as a prosthetic device for the amputee. The two modes of thinking often lead to opposite predictions about the outcome of a particular study. As noted earlier in the Domino study, we might have predicted that the independent students would do best with teachers who encourage independence—the capitalization or preferential view. Or we might have expected that independent students need some structure to compensate for their divergent tendencies—the prosthetic view. It appears, however, that our studies of teacher-learner interaction fit the first model; the findings of Yamamoto (1963), Cleare (1966), Majasan (1972), and Domino (1968, 1971) all can be understood as a match of preferred styles between teacher and student.

But it is important to note that achievement was the criterion in each case, not creative behavior. In the most important of these studies, the Domino research, conforming students did poorly on a measure of independent thinking no matter which kind of teacher they had. We may hypothesize then, following all of these studies, that the generally capable, independent, divergent thinking, analytic type of student will do best, in both achievement and creative performance if given his preferred style, namely, a teacher who encourages independent thinking and initiative. The conforming, nondivergent, field dependent, less capable student will also show his best achievement in his preferred treatment, a teacher who requires conformity. The promotion of creativity, however, in such a student requires modification of this treatment by adding some compensatory mechanisms without removing the structure that these learners find beneficial. Here is the crux of individualization by ATI. Treatments are tailored to fit the strengths and weaknesses of each type of student, and new mixes of instructional elements are created thereby. But we need a more detailed listing of possible elements available for the mix.

Thus, a third heuristic device is derived from Rothkopf's (1970) conception that some classes of behavioral events during instruction can be identified as mathemagenic (from the Greek root for "giving birth to learning"). These events give birth to learning by controlling some preceding information handling and attentional processes. We might also identify an opposing class of behavioral events that are *mathemathanic* (from the Greek term *thanatos*); they give death to learning. What, for example, do Majasan's (1972) teachers say or do that so destroys the achievement of students who are either more behavioristic or more humanistic than that teacher happens to be?

Both the positive and the negative events need to be identified. But the negative events may be particularly important in understanding the limits some treatments impose on creative production in some learners. Why in the Salomon study should CA training be so bad for students with high GRE Verbal scores? Perhaps this treatment makes students do something, or does something for them, that they can already do for themselves in their own way. Perhaps this produces interference, or boredom, or fatigue, or perhaps it triggers a decrease in motivation. Why in the Koran study was VM so bad for the field independent student? Does it impose an unwanted model of the desired act with an artificially slow pace, identifying stimuli that are already obvious to this learner? Again, interference, boredom, and fatigue may alienate the learner. Conversely, why are the Salomon HG treatment and the Koran WM treatment so bad for low scorers on the GRE, or for field dependent students? Do they force these learners into their weakest styles, producing interfering responses and debilitating anxiety?

Returning to the problem of Domino's structured or conforming treatment, what should we add to foster original thinking in the conforming students who are otherwise well suited to this treatment? Perhaps the Koran study suggests that teacher modeling of such factors as independent thought and question-asking skills would be a key ingredient. From the Salomon study, practice in attending to a variety of stimulus details might be another suggested addition. The conforming student may need to have self-imposed limits on his attention lifted by the teacher in a structured practice situation. There are some further ideas from other studies. A small experiment by Stephenson and Treadwell (1966) suggested that conforming students profited from a training program designed to improve Guilford fluency scores if such students were paired with one another. Perhaps guided small-group practice is especially well suited for them. Lemke and his coworkers (see Beane and Lemke, 1971) have also shown that lower ability college students do well in tasks involving concept-formation transfer when trained in homogeneous four-person groups, while higher ability students do their worst at these tasks in homogeneous groups. It is suggested that lower ability students benefit from homogeneous grouping when students can share information and cooperatively develop strategies. Students with high ability are thought to have their own strategies, which clash with other strategies in the group, so they are hindered by peers.

Admittedly, in reaching this hypothesis, we have glossed over distinctions between general ability, field independence, and the personality variable of independence versus conformity. But the hypothesis seems reasonable no matter which of these measures is used as aptitude. The proposed ATI study, then, should really include all three variables to determine which, if any, yield interaction. If the same ATI is found for two or three of these aptitudes, we might entertain the possibility that the same aptitude process underlies these variables and take steps to reach a more parsimonious construct. It is in this sense that new aptitude constructs as well as new kinds of treatment can be generated from ATI research.

The final point is more of a challenge than a heuristic device. The idea of mathemathanic behavior draws attention to the fact that ATI studies are turning up an increasing number of negative regression slopes—not just in studies using personality measures as aptitudes, but in those using ability and cognitive style constructs as well. We are not accustomed to negative relations among cognitive and learning measures. It may have been noted in earlier sections of this chapter that interpretation of such findings often falls back on concepts of interference or motivation. The negative slopes prompt the suggestion that there is a kind of conservation law for instructional effectiveness which, while Parkinsonian in flavor, can be taken seriously. Formally stated, it might be as follows: No matter how you try to make an instructional treatment better for someone, you will make it worse for someone else. If such a law actually holds, it implies that any treatment devised to promote creative thinking in some students will also interfere with creative thinking in some other students. Thus, it becomes imperative that we attend to the ways in which individual differences interact with treatments. There are likely to be new conceptions of aptitude and new kinds of instructional treatments derived from this emphasis. There will certainly be no one best method for promoting creativity in everyone.

19

Commentary: Consequences of Individual Differences for Higher Education

WINTON H. MANNING

I learned the other day that a movie has been made of Kurt Vonnegut's novel *Slaughterhouse Five*. This bit of information and the reading of Richard Snow's chapter brought back to my mind a passage from Vonnegut's book. Writing of himself, Vonnegut says: "I think about my education sometimes. I went to the University of Chicago for a while after the Second World War. I was a student in the Department of Anthropology. At that time, they were teaching that there was absolutely no difference between anybody. They may be teaching that still. . . . Another thing they taught was that nobody was ridiculous or bad or disgusting. Shortly before my father died he said to me, 'You know, you never wrote a story with a villain in it.' I told him that was one of the things I learned in college after the war" (Vonnegut, 1969, p. 7). It seems to me—with all due apologies to the University of Chicago—that Vonnegut is pointing out something that we

294

all know very well to be the case; namely, that it is comparatively easy for us to repress or avoid the existence of individual differences whenever it is convenient or economical or comfortable for us to do so. Society is littered with wreckage arising from our capacity to avoid troublesome facts, and education is no less subject to this judgment.

Snow is entirely correct then, it seems to me, in beginning his chapter with the blunt statement that individuals differ. Responding honestly and vigorously to this principle in education is really what he, Cronbach, and others have been doing so effectively in the past several years in their research on aptitude-treatment interactions. That such research is quite recent should not really surprise us: educators, especially in higher education—like Vonnegut's Trafalmadorians—have not hitherto accepted fully the consequences of the statement that individuals differ; and this avoidance has been reflected in their efforts to design educational programs. From these few remarks, it should be evident that I am in strong agreement with most of the perceptions and hypotheses offered by Snow.

In considering the reasons for the relatively late development of substantial research on aptitude-treatment interactions, Snow pointed out that there are three practical problems in education in which individual differences have historically played an important role. These are selection; evaluation; and classification or counseling, the problem of individualization. The representative questions these problems highlight are: Who is best for our program? Which program is best for our students? What is best for whom? The first two problems have a long and distinguished research history, but they tend to deal with only parts of the puzzle.

The third problem—that approached by ATI research—combines and adds to the earlier two problems by insisting that we deal more effectively and completely with the proposition that individuals differ. Cronbach stated the problem well in his APA presidential address (1957, pp. 680-681): "[We] should deal with treatments and persons simultaneously. Treatments are characterized by many dimensions; so are persons. The two sets of dimensions together determine a payoff surface. . . . We should design treatments, not to fit the average person, but to fit groups of students with particular aptitude patterns. Conversely, we should seek out aptitudes which correspond to (interact with) modifiable aspects of the treatment." Cronbach, Snow, and others engaged in aptitude-treatment interaction research have set themselves the task of amassing evidence and developing theory that will permit the effective classification of students so as to maximize payoff in terms of the outcomes of the educational process.

I would like to emphasize this last point—the outcome or payoff dimension—because it is, so to speak, the third leg of the aptitude-treatment interaction stool and it needs particular attention if the ATI enterprise is to support application in the classroom. My impression is that it is often not given the attention it deserves. It is a major component of the system, and it needs particular examination if we are ever to nurture creativity in higher education. Before turning to the question of outcomes or payoff dimensions, let me summarize briefly and very generally some other issues that are contained in Snow's chapter, or have been stimulated by it.

Issues in Individualization

The reasons for the pervasiveness of present measures of verbal and quantitative aptitude seem obvious. The emphasis up to now has been on devising practical means for selection of students for existing programs, rather than on creating alternative programs that reflect a broader array of aptitude variables and that require new methods of selection and classification of students. There has been too much reliance on the particular approaches to instruction that place great emphasis on language skills—reading and listening and formal symbolic manipulation—at the expense of alternatives embracing more diverse instructional strategies. Outcome variables also have been accepted primarily on the basis of administrative convenience rather than selected on the basis of planned evaluation in relation to objectives. Furthermore, it is also probably true that research on aptitude-treatment interactions has not yet brought us to the point where knowledgeable, informed revisions of existing practices can occur on a widespread scale.

There may be serious conceptual and practical issues in dealing with problems of designing diverse instructional situations; namely, that the nominal stimulus in an instructional situation may be quite different from the effective stimulus. Rothkopf (1968) refers to this problem as the principle of performance indeterminancy; that is, measured performance may be supported by different psychological states. To state this another way: the instructional situation is an extremely complex stimulus, in which it is typically very difficult to infer the psychological consequences of the stimulation on the basis of objective description of the instruction. As Rothkopf puts it: "The instructor does not determine effective stimulation. Realistically speaking, he can only see to it that instructionally desirable *effective stimuli are a possibility*. Whether this is a possibility depends critically on the actions of the student [emphasis added]" (1968, p. 113). Snow has strongly urged the need for constructs and theories of instruction that would rest upon multivariate descriptions (and measures) of instructional situations, and he would therefore attempt to contend empirically with the question of what are the effective stimuli in the instructional program.

From a strategic point of view, we can discern several different research strategies emerging from the growing body of ATI research. There are those who, in the traditional spirit of experimental research on learning, are undertaking studies on ever smaller instructional segments with increasingly specific aptitude measures. This line of development, though important to science, may lead to relatively sterile ends as far as educational practice is concerned. It is the familiar problem of those interested in research employing tightly designed experimental approaches, as contrasted with somewhat messier, more practical approaches within real-life instructional situations. It is significant that most of the research Snow has discussed falls more toward the latter end of the continuum than the former. I think this is good; I would personally regret the development of orientations within ATI research that would end in a parallel to the desolate wastelands of literature that sought to apply to the classroom the fruits of laboratory research of the 1930s and 1940s on distribution of practice, whole-part learning, reminiscence, and so forth.

The relationship between research on aptitude-treatment interactions and the studies of differential impacts of college environments is a direction that is an especially helpful one. Rather than moving in the direction of smaller, well-controlled studies of small groups of students, it would be useful to begin the attempt to design a macrosystem approach to the problem. Some years ago I proposed the establishment of an experimental consortium of undergraduate colleges, in sufficient numbers to embrace a wide range of environmental variation, with the commitment by each college to accept a significant portion, at least initially, of their freshman classes on the basis of random assignment from a defined pool of applicants. This would require a measure of commitment on the part of students as well as institutions. A corollary commitment would be the study of just the type of aptitude-treatment interactions that Snow has discussed. The aim would be to effect a more rational sorting of students to treatments. I think the promise that this line of research offers would be sufficient to merit the risk and the effort involved. We should note, however, that in attempting to develop a basis for a more effective and satisfying distribution of students, we come face to face with the problems Pelz referred to in discussing the concepts of security and challenge as they relate to creative problem solving (Chapter Fifteen). For graduate education, in particular, important aspects of the institutional environment depend on interpersonal stimulation of fellow students. Thus, it is difficult to know on which side of the equation of ATI interpersonal dimensions would fall. The system should not result in sending docile students to bucolic, pastoral environments; profile matching is probably not the answer.

Educational Outcomes Giving Birth
to Learning and Creativity

I would now like to return again to the question of outcomes, or payoff, to which I referred earlier. Much of the research on aptitude-treatment interactions has taken place within the context of elementary and secondary education, where outcome measures that reflect content mastery or achievement seem particularly relevant, though not, certainly, exclusively so. Snow has done a significant service in bringing together good examples of the admittedly scattered research at the higher education level. But it is just at this level that we presently need to bring about more thoughtful discussion concerning the objectives, and hence the criteria, of higher education. We are more uncertain, it seems, about the relevant payoff dimensions than we are about the assessment of aptitudes. When Rothkopf (1968) eloquently proposed some years ago that instructional research move away from its preoccupation with the calculus of practice—defining payoff in terms of measures of the efficiency of learning—and direct its attention to what he termed mathemagenic behavior—those behaviors which give birth to learning—he was certainly making a distinction that is applicable to all levels of education. But in a practical sense, the significance of the interactions of aptitudes with treatments, as defined in terms of mathemagenic outcomes may be particularly important. We may be discouraging many students from learning, particularly at the higher education level, by producing what Snow has provocatively labeled mathemathanic behavior, or activities that give death to learning. We can ill afford the losses of talent that this implies, particularly at the graduate level.

Following Snow's speculations on this point, it would seem desirable to define the payoff dimensions in ways that would measure more significant outcomes than conventional achievement. Nearly all students at the graduate level are probably capable of learning what needs to be learned. In most instances the aptitude-treatment interaction of greatest significance should be defined in terms of mathemagenic or mathemathanic behavior: Is the instructional process producing behaviors that give birth to learning or is it not? This immediately places the earlier problem of motivation or of curiosity, as Pelz described it in Chapter Fifteen, squarely in the setting of instructional research and converts the familiar question, How can we find (or select) motivated, intellectually curious students? into How can we devise educational programs that are motivating? Continuing along this line, we could also take up the question of defining outcome variables that are related to creative problem solving. What aptitudes interact with what treatments to produce activities that give birth to creativity? Self-confidence, curiosity, independence, and so forth have been mentioned. More research is needed along the lines of the Koran study (finding treatments that will increase analytic questioning) and the Majasan study (finding the mix of student and teacher that will promote the kinds of behavior that are critically important). If the verb in Greek meaning "to create" is *poieo* [poy-ee-oh], then I suppose what I am speaking of would be instructional strategies that produce poieogenic behavior, to follow the analogy given earlier.

Graduate education must give priority to systematic experimentation aimed at creating alternatives that accommodate better to the diversity of human aptitudes; at the same time it must maintain its commitment to outcomes of instruction that give birth to learning and to creativity. Snow and others engaged in research on aptitude-treatment interactions point the way toward systematic efforts to reach this dual goal.

20

Commentary: Avoidance of Aptitude-Treatment Trivialities

BRIAN N. LEWIS

Richard Snow has presented what seems to me to be an extremely lucid overview of the present state of ATI research. His account is also commendably modest in the claims that it makes for this comparatively new kind of inquiry. In the hands of researchers who are as capable as Cronbach and Snow, I have little doubt that ATI research could be developed into a highly worthwhile area of investigation. However, there is a very real possibility of the whole activity being trivialized—transformed into an easy bandwagon, in fact—unless certain pitfalls are avoided, and certain pedagogical issues faced.

A Bandwagon or a Search for Basics

Let me comment first on the bandwagon aspect. Below, I deliberately depict the ATI method at its very worst. As this

recipe shows, the simplest kind of ATI research is grounded
on nothing more than the commonsense insight that some
teaching methods are more suitable for some kinds of students than for others. Well, we always knew that much. What
worries me is the thought that this commonsense insight, if
pursued under the officially approved banner of "ATI Research," could lead to the production of literally thousands
of sterile doctorates and research programs.

Recipe for ATI Research

1. Think of a cognitive style (and its negation): for example,
   impulsive and/or reflective.
2. Think of a possibly related teaching style: for example,
   hurried and/or painstaking.
3. Think of a subject matter which, if taught in different
   ways, might establish a relationship between 1 and 2
   above.
4. Dream up success criteria which will increase the probability of establishing a relationship between 1 and 2 above
   (for example, recall of facts/explanations).
5. Devise some test items in same spirit as 4.
6. Select a promising "can't lose" design: for example, two
   styles and two student types.
7. Launch, analyze, and verify.
8. Publish!

All that the aspiring doctoral candidate has to do is to
pluck out of the air, or out of a standard thesaurus, some
word that describes a cognitive style or (more generally) a
character trait. Let us suppose that he sticks a pin into his
thesaurus and comes up with the word *aggressive*. He now
invents a teaching treatment which students with aggressive
natures are likely to enjoy. He then applies the treatment
to a heterogeneous group of students, some of whom will
inevitably be more aggressive than others. He discovers, of
course, that some students do better than others on his end-
of-treatment achievement test. To complete the ATI para-

digm, he therefore applies a little test of aggressiveness that he has devised. And he finds that students who score highly on his achievement test also tend to score highly on his test of aggressiveness. If, by any chance, he does not find this to be the case, he can represent his results as being even more newsworthy. An enviable "can't lose" situation for any researcher to be in.

By way of variety, our doctoral candidate might go on to use his aggressiveness scale as a device for preselecting students who are most likely to succeed under his teaching treatment in the future. He might even invent an aggression-enhancing counseling procedure for students who seem to be having difficulty with the treatment. As we have already indicated, he can also use his scale of aggressiveness to help explain, after the event, why some students performed better than others. These three approaches do in fact correspond to the three areas of applicability that Snow explicitly claims, early in his chapter, for ATI research.

This is clearly a game that anyone can play. There is no limit to the number of publications that can be generated in this way, simply because there is no limit to the number of specific ways in which the ATI research paradigm can be exemplified. To discourage this kind of endless repetition, the paradigm needs to be strengthened. But how? Well, instead of plucking words out of a thesaurus, our doctoral candidate might pluck them from the publications of acknowledged experts in the field of individual differences. He might, for example, think of the focusers and scanners of Bruner, Goodnow, and Austin (1956) and devise teaching treatments that are particularly favorable to one (or both) of these cognitive strategies. This approach is likely to appeal to the experts themselves because it is good for business, as well as being good for the ego, to see one's own distinctions—dichotomies, types, styles, dimensions, or whatever—taken up by other researchers. However, I do not personally regard this as a satisfactory solution. What is wanted, I suspect, is a moratorium on all ATI research until someone has done some hard and effective thinking on the kinds of individual differences that matter most.

When a new discipline or profession comes into existence, there is a tendency for its practitioners to "professionalize" their activities by concentrating on small manageable problems that can be solved, or at least tackled, in ways that are likely to impress outsiders. An illusion of promise and progress is created by addressing problems that are simple enough to be solved in seemingly elegant and rigorous ways. Skinner gave experimental psychology a professional boost when he invented the Skinner box for rats. Chomsky gave linguistics a similar boost when he invented generative grammar. The trick is to find problems that can be tackled in style, even if they are not the problems that really matter. A lot of research on individual differences is like this. Thousands of papers, for example, have been published on the introversion versus extraversion distinction, partly, I believe, because the distinction happens to lend itself rather well to empirical inquiry. There are other distinctions, such as the distinction between being able to do several things at a time and being able to do only one thing at a time, which are possibly much more basic and, for this very reason, more difficult to come to grips with via empirical investigation. However, as long as we restrict our attention to what is manageable, we are following an illusory route. We are doing the wrong thing well, rather than the right thing badly.

In my opinion, the right thing to do is to focus, and to focus mercilessly, on the search for individual differences that are basic, in the sense that they underlie (and, to that extent, *explain*) a whole range of more readily observable differences. For example, it seems to me that the ability to do several things at once, as opposed to being able to do only one thing at a time, might well underlie and explain the distinction between being a visualizer and being a verbalizer. If I happen to be right about this, then the visualizer versus verbalizer distinction would be explicable in terms of this more basic underlying distinction. Accordingly, a significant piece of ATI research would take the more basic distinction as being the one that it was most worthwhile to investigate in terms of differential teaching treatments.

At the present time, we have a situation in which different groups of researchers seem determined to pursue their own pet distinctions in cheerful disregard of one another. There is the focusing versus scanning distinction, which seems to indicate something about the way in which attention is distributed. There is the impulsive versus reflective distinction, which seems to indicate something about the tempo of learning. There is the field dependent versus field independent distinction, the serialists and the holists, and a lot more. In brief, there is no shortage of people doing active research on the subject of individual differences. But there seems to be an acute shortage of people who are trying to find out which kinds of individual differences are the most basic and thus most worth incorporating into individualized teaching programs of the kind that Snow is hoping to see one day.

Prospects for Research and Instruction

If I were asked to pass judgment on the various experiments that Snow describes in his chapter, I would be inclined to commend them all as being worthwhile pioneering efforts. There are at least three reasons for being grateful for these experiments: they establish the basic research paradigm and an appropriate statistical methodology to go with it: they remind us of some important truths that we tend, in our slacker moments, to forget; and they pose in a sharp and useful way a number of problems that still need to be taken seriously. My only reservation is that more experiments of the same kind are likely to be subject to the law of diminishing returns. They might well yield marginal improvements in the statistical methodology because statistical methodology is, by its very nature, capable of endless elaboration and refinement. Further experiments of the same kind might also alert us to a few more truths that we might otherwise forget and to a few more problems that deserve our consideration. But I doubt whether any truly dramatic changes will take place until the individual differences that are experimented with are grounded in a cogent and comprehensive theory about the ways in which human beings differ.

I do not want to underrate what *has* been achieved; however, I would like to comment briefly on the three positive aspects just mentioned. With regard to the first point, the basic paradigm and the associated statistical methodology seem to me to be impressively adequate. The only major improvement that I would like to see concerns the need to resample exceptional cases. Insofar as ATI correlations occur at a size less than 1.0, there must be some students (perhaps a very small minority) who go against the general trend. To take one of Snow's examples, this could mean that just a few students who are behaviorist-orientated actually learn better when taught by a phenomenologist teacher of psychology. It seems to me to be vitally important to reexamine these atypical cases to see why and how they arise. These atypical cases may, after all, be the intellectual giants of tomorrow.

With regard to the second point, Snow clearly indicates the way in which ATI research induces us to think twice about results which would be dismissed as statistically nonsignificant if pooled in an uncritical way. He also reiterates a fact that we sometimes forget: students generally seem to learn better from teachers who are most like themselves. We often say, for example, that people learn most from people who are different from themselves. This has a plausible feel to it until we remember that we usually reject such people and, in so doing, ensure that we learn nothing from them at all. In the face of escalating social and racial strife, there is once again an acute need to investigate the exceptional cases—to see, and see again, how it happens that some people can learn from people who are different from themselves.

With respect to the third point, I would like to single out just one problem that Snow touches on: the problem of deciding whether a teaching program should seek to develop a student's strengths or seek to eradicate his weaknesses. The two possibilities are not mutually exclusive, although it is clear that compensatory programs of education are predominantly orientated toward the latter. However, if we look around us, it does not take us very long to notice numerous cases in which a person's weaknesses hardly seem to matter at all. In modern technological society, we do not have to be good at very much in order to have a market value. Provided that a person is reasonably good at just one or two things, he can usually find some niche in life in which he can get by at a reasonably comfortable level. This is especially true of certain kinds of geniuses who are brilliant at one thing only— painting, perhaps—and almost hopeless at everything else.

In general, I am greatly in favor of helping students to develop their strengths. I have no time at all for the kind of educational system that sells people a load of guilts with respect to the things that they cannot do, while neglecting to cultivate, or even comment upon, any hidden potentialities that they may have. In fact, there are only two circumstances in which I would seriously worry about a student's weaknesses. The first circumstance would arise if I detected in the student a weakness that was holding back the development of a strength. The second circumstance arises in connection with weaknesses that are sufficiently grave to have some enduring social stigma attaching to them. I am thinking, in particular, of the inability to read and write. But, even here, I would pause to wonder whether time spent helping a backward reader to read might not be better spent by helping him in some other way.

The point is that ATI research, with its emphasis on matching the teaching method to the needs and interests and abilities of the student, poses a variety of pedagogical problems concerning the way in which the match should be made. As Snow points out, we could use the results of ATI research to give the student the kind of teaching experience he wants or to give him the kind of teaching experience that he does not want. My guess is that most students want to develop their strengths, unless they have been made to feel guilty and inadequate about their weaknesses. This is a conjecture that could, and ought to be, subjected to experimental test. But, even so, it is doubtful whether students should always be given the teaching experience that they prefer. Apart

from the fact that such an arrangement would hardly prepare them well for later life, it can be argued that "rounded"
citizens can be produced only by ensuring that they go through
the whole gamut of possible teaching experiences. For example, we might take the view that a student who likes a well-
structured teaching situation should, from time to time, be
plunged into an ill-structured teaching situation. And we
might take this view on the grounds that it would be good for
him. This kind of view is indeed frequently taken by business
consultants, by people who organize and pay for T-group
training. One of the more intriguing questions raised by Snow
and by ATI research in general is the question of determining the conditions under which this view is valid.

Part Eight

Epilogue: Creative Style in Higher Education

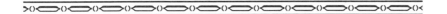

In the concluding section, Samuel Messick analyzes the concept of matching as an educational strategy and underscores the trade-offs between matching and mismatching as potential sources of both conflict and creativity in instructional design. He explores the problems and potentialities of various models of matching and mismatching and reviews several approaches to the development of mixed strategies. Complexities at the tactical level of educational prescription lead him to ask questions not only about what to prescribe and how to tailor the prescribed instruction, but also about who should decide among the alternatives. In attempting to resolve the issue of where the locus of choice should be, Messick examines the feasibility of self-matching as a general strategy and argues for informed student choice as the desirable route for higher education on developmental and pedagogical grounds. As a consequence of this choice, higher education is challenged to adopt a creative style that is flexible, open to provisional choice and change, and responsive to individual variation in student needs and preferences.

21

Personal Styles and Educational Options

SAMUEL MESSICK

Throughout this book evidence and testimony have been steadily mounting that individuals differ systematically in their patterns of ability, motivation, cognitive style, and mode of creative expression and that these differences have important consequences for the ways in which individuals learn and perform. In addition to consistent individual differences, there are also marked group differences related to sex, ethnicity, and cultural background. Individual differences have been long with us, but not until recently has the form of their interaction with instructional methods and conditions been examined extensively enough to offer some hope of accommodating them educationally through instructional design.

For decades educators, especially progressive educators, have held that individual differences among students must be recognized, but the educational responses to this credo have been primarily administrative and organizational rather than pedagogical (Cronbach, 1967; Lesser, 1971). Until recently educational systems, by and large, have adapted to individual differences through selection and classification in terms of type and level of achievement rather than through adjustments of instruction attuned to processes of learning. In Glaser's (1972) terms, education has operated in a selective mode rather than in an adaptive mode. The earliest and most persistent accommodation to individual differences, for example, was the sequential elimination of students who failed to achieve at each successive stage of the system. The opposite of this selecting-out policy is also frequently practiced; that is, instead of dropping or failing those students who do not keep pace, they are retained at a given level until key educational requirements have been mastered, as in the nongraded primary unit that can be completed in either two, three, or four years. Individual differences in rate of learning are thereby accommodated by gross differences in duration of schooling (Cronbach, 1967). This kind of adjustment in the time needed to attain established performance standards is one of the central precepts of the instructional approach known as mastery learning, although there the adjustments are frequently on a more refined and individualized basis.

Other common forms of educational accommodation to individual differences are primarily classificatory (Lesser, 1971). They involve such organizational mechanisms as differentiation by school type (separate colleges for specialization in science or art, schools for vocational or technical training, or schools for the retarded); differentiation by tracks or curricula within a school (academic and commercial curricula in high school or major and minor field requirements in college); differentiation by section within tracks (classes organized by general ability, specific ability, or achievement level in particular subjects; for example, honors and regular classes or elementary, intermediate, and advanced sections in language instruction); and differentiation within a class (ability grouping or remediation grouping).

Such administrative and organizational adaptations to individual differences are admittedly crude, and the desirability of more refined pedagogical adaptations is not in dispute; so the direction in which to move seems clear. The general strategy for movement also seems clear, although agreement on tactics is another story. As Snow has indicated in Chapter Eighteen, the preferred strategy at the present time involves the attempt to discover or construct aptitude-treatment interactions as grounds for tailoring specific instructional components and conditions to functional characteristics of learners. This ATI strategy confronts us squarely with the fundamental problem of the whole enterprise, namely, the problem of the match between individuality and instruction. On what basis should the match be made and to what end? Snow proposed two heuristic bases for matching instructional alternatives to learner characteristics, one as a means of compensating for learner weaknesses and the other as a means of capitalizing on learner strengths (see also Snow, 1970). Salomon (1972) elaborated these two principles and articulated a third, namely, matching in order to eliminate learner weaknesses through remediation. Let us next consider such heuristic bases for matching in more detail and then turn attention to tactical problems in the individualized prescription of instruction.

Models of Matching

The term *aptitude-treatment interaction* suggests that the main concern in matching is the linking of specific treatment components to functional characteristics of learners. This is indeed the case, but characteristics of teachers and of conditions or settings are also important and may interact with components of method and material to produce differential results. Treatment is usually intended to embrace all of these characteristics, but some writers prefer to make this more explicit by referring to person-environment interactions or person-treatment-setting interactions or person-teacher-treatment-setting interactions. In the definitions and descriptions of matching models that follow, *treatment* is used in the broadly inclusive sense.

Corrective Matches. In corrective matching, treatments are sought that rectify deficiencies in critical skills and knowledge that are jeopardizing further progress in learning. In this case, the interactive aptitudes—those traits that in one treatment facilitate learning but in alternative treatments are less facilitating or even debilitating—are usually trainable, task-specific capabilities that are important for later cumulative learning. Corrective, or what Salomon (1972) has called "remedial," treatments typically attempt to overcome deficiencies by exposing the student to more of the same instruction that was ineffective initially. The instruction proceeds more slowly, perhaps, and with more repetitions and specificity, but usually with no differences in method of presentation (such as changing from discovery to directive techniques), in content structure (such as breaking complex tasks into hierarchies of simpler tasks), or in modality (such as supplementing verbal formulations with visual models). When corrective treatments are applied to entire classes regardless of need, aptitude-treatment interactions arise because students who have already mastered the objectives and hence do not need remediation suffer interference from boredom and reduced motivation if unnecessarily exposed to it (Salomon, 1972).

Compensatory Matches. In compensatory matching, treatments are sought that offset learner deficiencies by providing the mediators, modalities, or organizing structures that the learner has difficulty providing for himself or by arranging conditions to neutralize the disabling effects of motivational disturbances, such as anxiety or defensiveness. In this case, the interactive traits are usually modes of information processing, motivational states or traits, or general abilities. Such characteristics are not easily modifiable nor is their modification in this instance a current instructional objective, even though changes in them may be highly correlated with learning outcomes. Compensatory treatments are designed to circumvent the debilitative effects of learner deficiencies or disturbances without trying to remove or improve them. As an example, highly anxious individuals have difficulty recalling the intermediate steps they take in problem solving and hence tend to repeat their errors; thus, an instructional program in problem solving that provides visual memory supports for anxious students would constitute a compensatory treatment (Sieber, 1969). Interactions arise in compensatory treatments because the compensating intervention introduces distracting and interfering redundancy for those learners who can provide the necessary mediators on their own (Salomon, 1972; Snow, 1970).

Capitalization Matches. In capitalization matching, or what Salomon (1972) has called "preferential matching," treatments are sought that draw on the strengths of particular learners, allowing them to exercise their strongest, which is usually also their most preferred, mode of functioning. Capitalization treatments exploit what the student is already capable of doing well and ignore learner deficiencies, attempting neither to correct them nor to compensate for them. An example of capitalization treatment is the use of mediational methods with students who have relatively high conceptual learning ability and the use of rote methods with students low in conceptual learning but relatively high in associative memory skills, without regard to possible associative weaknesses in the former group or, more importantly, probable conceptualizing deficiencies in the latter group (Jensen, 1969a, 1969b). In capitalization matches, the interacting traits are usually rather general personality characteristics, cognitive styles, or abilities indicative of well-developed or preferred modes of operating; their extension and enhancement, the adding of strength to strength, may also be a current or continuing educational objective. Interactions arise in capitalization treatments because each type of learner performs best in the treatment that calls upon his strong or preferred aptitudes or styles (Salomon, 1972; Snow, 1970).

Combination Matches. Since the three models just described are complementary and not conflicting, various combinations of matching principles can operate simultaneously.

As an instance, a treatment could compensate for a deficiency in a way that matched the learner's preferred style. In one of the studies summarized by Snow in Chapter Eighteen, for example, two interacting aptitudes were involved: perceptual analysis, or skill in disembedding items from their context, and film memory, or skill in remembering filmed live action. Teacher trainees who were deficient in perceptual disembedding but strong in film memory learned analytic question-asking skills better with a videotaped model than with a written model. Presumably the videotaped model compensated for deficiencies in perceptual analysis or disembedding by presenting stimulus elements concretely and explicitly, but this form of compensatory support was primarily effective for those students who also had good memory for sequential audiovisual material (Koran, Snow, and McDonald, 1971). Thus the treatment both compensated for a weakness and exploited a strength at the same time.

Challenge Matches. Challenge matches are really mismatches: A deliberate attempt is made to create conflict between treatment components and learner characteristics to challenge the learner to change, to become more flexible, to increase the variety of strategies and modes of functioning in his repertoire. Mismatching is particularly important where there are multiple educational objectives involving the learning of both content and process and where systematic and continuous matching serves to maximize one, usually content learning, and to limit the other, usually process learning. If students strong in associative memory, for example, are continuously taught by rote methods, they may never learn to conceptualize or discover anything in their entire school careers.

There are two basic types of mismatching: One is *substitutive mismatching*, where the aim is to replace suboptimal or maladaptive preferred strategies with alternative approaches that are more effective, although possibly less congenial. The other is *stimulative mismatching*, where the intent is to foster development, curiosity, or creativity. The notion of stimulative mismatching is supported by several conceptions in the psychological literature. One theory, for example, holds that conceptual conflict produces arousal and curiosity, which leads to directed thinking and facilitates creativity (Berlyne, 1960, 1965; Day and Berlyne, 1971). Other theories, especially those in the Piagetian orbit, hold that cognitive development depends on the equilibration of ordered discrepancies, on the coming to grips with problems or inconsistencies sufficiently beyond the individual's current level of mastery or competence to be challenging yet close enough to be manageable with some effort. This suggests a principle of optimal mismatching, whereby individuals are confronted with graded discrepancies or incongruities intended to stretch their existing capabilities (Flavell, 1963; J. McV. Hunt, 1961; Kohlberg, 1969; Rest, 1974; Rest, Turiel, and Kohlberg, 1969; Turiel, 1966). Thus, instead of matching the treatment or environment to the learner's present mode of functioning (contemporaneous matching), the environmental conditions are shaped to stimulate the conceptual work required for growth (developmental matching); see D. E. Hunt (1975).

Mixtures of Matches and Mismatches. Underlying the concept of matching is the assumption that different instructional treatments interacting with learner characteristics will produce the same learning outcomes, that different methods will achieve the same fixed goals. But with differential instruction, even though the specific informational content taught may be the same, the intellectual processes or operations imparted may be quite different. "The achievement of fixed, common goals may be attained, if this is true, only at the cost of *differential* achievement of other goals" (Carroll, 1967, p. 43). Perhaps this is one of the reasons, aside from benign accretion, that long-range educational treatments tend to be complex and eclectic, utilizing both matching and mismatching in various combinations. Mixtures of matches and mismatches are important because they are so widespread, even if often by default. Some of the major ways that such mixtures may come about are described below.

Supplemental mixes involve a main strategy, either matching or mismatching, employed most of the time but supported by the alternate strategy in the same lesson or lesson sequence. As an example, traditional verbal teaching methods represent a mismatch for Eskimo students, who have exceptionally strong figural skills; but the prevalent verbal approach might be supplemented by figural methods to clarify difficult learning tasks, as in using Venn diagrams to teach superordinate and subordinate class relationships (Kleinfeld, 1973).

Sporadic mixes also involve a main strategy, either matching or mismatching, employed most of the time, but here occasional sessions are based upon the alternate approach. In supplemental mixes the alternate approach is applied to the teaching of the same topic or subject matter in the same session as the main approach. In sporadic mixes both the main and the alternate approaches are applied to the teaching of the same subject matter, but in different sessions.

Sequential mixes also employ matching and mismatching at different times but with relative balance in their application; neither would be considered the main approach. One type of sequential mix, which might be called switching, starts with matching, usually in terms of some very general bipolar learner characteristic (such as cognitive style) that would provide a common basis for matching in all subject areas. Then the treatments are systematically switched to mismatching in an effort to facilitate flexibility and bicognitive functioning, the systematic development of the adaptive features of both poles of the cognitive style (Ramirez and Castaneda, 1974).

Split mixes utilize matching and mismatching simultaneously—at the same time, in the same session, with the same subject matter—but with different treatment components being matched and mismatched. For example, students and teachers might be matched in terms of cognitive style in order to capitalize on mutuality of esteem and congeniality of communication modes (see Witkin, Chapter Three), but instructional methods might be mismatched in order to stimulate flexibility in thinking.

Stratified mixes employ matching to support and optimize the learning of educational objectives considered most important, with mismatching being used at other times and in

318

Individuality in Learning

other areas to forestall rigidity of functioning. Instructional goals must first be stratified in terms of importance or centrality; then matching or mismatching is employed, depending upon the status of the goal. As Cronbach (1967) has put it: "We probably want to arrange strongly supporting conditions for the schoolwork we take most seriously. But . . . we have two coordinate problems: capitalizing on the existing aptitude pattern and modifying that pattern. The school need not deal with both at the same moment, but neither should be neglected" (p. 36).

Student mixes entail matching and mismatching simultaneously—in the same session, with the same treatment components, and the same subject matter—but with different students being matched and mismatched. This type of mix is characteristic of most traditional classrooms, where a teacher using any particular teaching method will happen to match some of the students and mismatch others. In the long run, it might be argued, with enough successive differences in teachers and preferred teaching methods, each student would be matched some of the time and mismatched some of the time, and the benefits of both strategies would accrue. If the preceding stratified mix were considered a status mix, then the present approach might be called a status quo mix.

The Problem of Prescription

This rich variety of bases for matching, mismatching, or mixing instructional treatments and learner characteristics attests to the complexity of accommodating individual differences within educational programs. This complexity is heightened by the realization that the relative desirability of matching or mismatching varies as a function of many things, among which are the following:

The developmental level of the learner. At the lower levels of education, where abilities and styles are still relatively malleable and responsive to stimulation, mismatching (or, more likely, mixtures of matching and mismatching) might predominate. At higher levels of education, where abilities and styles may have become crystallized, matching might prove to be a more widely functional strategy.

The subject matter to be learned. A consideration of subject matter includes the degree of structure entailed and the stylistic requirements for effective performance. The learning of highly structured subjects having specific stylistic and skill demands, such as mathematics or physics, may benefit more from matching, especially capitalization matching, than from other strategies; whereas learning in fields more diversified in their stylistic and skill requirements, such as the humanities and social sciences, may be quite responsive to a variety of individualization strategies.

The surrounding context. This comprises both the psychological context of the learner's ability patterns and personality and the environmental context of social and situational influences. For instance, rigidities of personality (a psychological factor) might make mismatching debilitative; the availability of audiovisual and computer-based technology (an environmental factor) might facilitate certain compensatory treatments, whereas its unavailability would preclude such treatments.

The goals of education. These include institutional or societal goals as well as personal goals, universal or common goals as well as particular goals. Fixed institutional field requirements would make corrective matches critical in instances of substandard achievement. In contrast, intense individual interests, whether in physics, poetry, or any other area, might justify intense emphasis on capitalization matches, even at the risk of uneven development in other areas.

This last point, the moderating role of goals, is extremely important, for in choosing among the multiplicity of ways of matching instruction to individual differences, one must have a clear idea of desired outcomes in order to proceed. The choice of matching variables, for example, and indeed the choice of strategies for matching or mismatching, varies depending on whether one emphasizes a content goal, such as increasing arithmetic skills; a process goal, such as fostering creative thinking; an affective goal, such as enhancing self-confidence; or any two of these—or even all three in combination (Bissell, White, and Zivin, 1971).

Complex as the situation seems at the level of strategy, the picture is even more complicated at the tactical level of instructional design. Consider some possibilities. In tailoring instructional treatments to learner characteristics, one can vary content, level of difficulty, form of presentation, scope, sequence, schedule of repetitions, quantity, pace, and mathemagenic information (Merrill and Boutwell, 1973). Or one could vary the techniques of instruction, using discovery versus expository methods or Socratic versus recitation methods; the content structure of instruction, setting complex versus simple or fixed versus flexible task requirements; the goal structure of instruction, setting cooperative, competitive, or individualistic goal-attainment conditions (Johnson and Johnson, 1974); the reinforcement of instruction, using extrinsic versus intrinsic reward systems or personal versus task feedback; the modality of instruction, using visual versus oral methods or manipulation versus verbalization methods; the distribution of instruction, using short-term intensive workshops and classes versus traditional long-term concurrent courses; and the setting of instruction, requiring students to work alone or in groups (Lesser, 1971).

If one is to tailor instructional treatments to individual differences using this vast array of potentially interactive variables, one will very likely have to turn to computer-managed procedures and computer-assisted techniques, as Holtzman implied in Chapter Two. Only computers appear to have the capabilities required. On the face of it, we need to be able to integrate large sets of interacting variables to converge upon individually prescribed treatments, which, with computers, can also readily be self-paced with immediate feedback and reinforcement of behavior. But even if we were to succeed in this effort, such finely individualized, computer-based prescriptions are likely to be insufficient if they constitute fixed treatments derived from aptitude-treatment interactions of questionable generalizability. The stark realities of ATI research reveal recurrent inconsistencies that are apt to be indicative of higher-order interactions: thus a particular ATI result may not represent a general conclusion but instead might itself be moderated by other variables (Cronbach, 1975). A particular aptitude-treatment interaction may hold only under certain conditions or for certain kinds of individuals. Under these circumstances, we need techniques that are more tentative and dynamic, that are response sensitive in the sense of monitoring responses to the treatment in order to adjust it to local or specific influences (Atkinson and Paulson, 1972; Groen and Atkinson, 1966). We would thereby attempt to adapt the treatment to current learner responses rather than to prescribe a fixed treatment on the basis of a generalization—even an ATI generalization—derived from prior experience with other persons or other settings (Cronbach, 1975).

Because of their interactive capabilities, computers appear to be ideal vehicles for such responsively tailored instruction, but there are other alternatives. The key requirements are flexibility and feedback, a willingness and facility to permit short-run changes in treatment on the basis of responses to initially prescribed instruction. Aptitude-treatment interactions, then, would not determine irreversible assignments, but rather would constitute hypotheses to be confirmed or modified on the basis of early reactions to treatment (Cronbach, 1975).

Without computers, finely branching treatments are difficult to manage, to be sure, but such microadaptations to individual differences, although highly responsive, are not necessarily superior. Each microdecision must be made with considerable uncertainty on the basis of little information. As Cronbach (1967) notes: "Microdecisions keep such a multiplicity of treatments in play that it becomes impossible to evaluate every branching rule with care. Macrotreatments, being fewer, can be designed on the basis of theory and can be empirically validated" (p. 28). To forego computers, then, we need flexible choice from a generous array of macrotreatments or program alternatives, such as the options of contract learning and programed learning described by Chickering (Chapter Five); but these options must be sufficiently varied and well-grounded in validated theory to avoid the kind of misalignments between program and personal style that Chickering deplored. Building blocks for such an array of program alternatives already exist in the sense that a variety of contents can be presented in a variety of modes in various combinations. For example, in addition to formal and open classrooms, small group discussions, tutorials, independent study, and supervised laboratory and clinical practice, we also now see increasing recourse to work-study arrangements and experiential learning in real-life settings. In addition to textbooks, films, videotapes, cassettes, programed texts, educational television, and instructional radio, most of which have been with us for some time, we also now have access to computer-based technology. Within each of these modes are numerous options for content and form of instruction. The PLATO system described in Chapter Two, for example, is one of several computer-based instructional resources containing rich sets of computer-interactive lessons in a number of subject areas; these lessons can be sequenced selectively at the instructor's (or student's) discretion and combined with text, classroom, laboratory, or other experiences to form a course curriculum.

An enormous variety of program alternatives is thus currently feasible, but as yet only a few models have been specifically formulated in detail. Some examples illustrative of the range of possibilities have appeared throughout this volume: the TICCIT system described by Holtzman (Chapter Two), for instance, the contract learning and programed learning alternatives described by Chickering (Chapter Five), Wallach's apprenticeship model (Chapter Twelve) and Proshansky's collegial model for graduate training (Chapter Seventeen), Pelz's security-challenge model for fostering creative problem solving (Chapter Fifteen), and several specific instructional alternatives described by Snow in the aptitude-treatment interaction paradigm (Chapter Eighteen). In addition to an extensive array of program alternatives, however, the options must also be organized within an educational system that readily permits tentative enrollments or tryouts, a system that tolerates, or even encourages, switches in programs on the basis of short-run experience. With this kind of flexibility and responsiveness, whether with computers or without, the consequences of mistakes in prescription are rarely devastating, and thus the possibility of *student* choice among options comes to the fore.

The Challenge of Choice

The issue of student choice is important not only as a humanistic antidote to dispel the mechanistic overtones of concepts like matching and prescription, but also for developmental and pedagogical reasons. According to theorists on cognitive development and proponents of progressive and open education (Dewey, 1938; Kohlberg and Mayer, 1972; Nyquist and Hawes, 1972), for example, conditions should be arranged throughout all levels of education to facilitate what Erikson (1950) has called the "process of mutual regulation," in this case a progressive shift in relative balance from teacher regulation of education to student regulation of education as a means of fostering independence and ultimate competence (Nardine, 1971). It follows, then, that student self-management and choice should especially flower in higher education, with individuals assuming increasing responsibility for their own learning and for selecting which of a variety of educational treatments and environments they will experience.

This brings us to the notion of *self-matching*, which has considerable potential as a groundwork for adult real-world functioning but which also entails inherent difficulties in implementation. The major difficulty is in self-assessment, particularly in the student's being able to distinguish between the treatments or environments he needs and those he prefers. This is a classical problem in educational guidance and is typically handled in the humanistic tradition by providing the student with sufficient information and experience for him to make an informed judgment. A straightforward approach to that end would be to develop a system in which the student can directly sample various learning options or instructional modes so that he can base relatively long-term commitments upon short-term experiences. This approach has been variously called an "open stack" or "browsing" model (Glaser, 1973), using the metaphor of a library, or an "environmental cafeteria" model (D. E. Hunt, 1975), using the metaphor of a restaurant. This latter metaphor is also relevant to a more restrictive approach that may be most appropriate when there is a marked tension between student needs and student preferences. This approach employs a combination of prescribed requirements and elective treatments and might be called a "blue-plate special," a single, fixed entree with free choice of appetizer and dessert.

Implementing the browsing, or cafeteria, model of self-matching in higher education requires ingenuity and creativity on the part of faculty and administrators and flexibility and tolerance of ambiguity on the part of all concerned, especially the students. The students must be able to avoid premature closure, and the institution must be able to tolerate an initial period of uncertainty when dabbling and course tryouts are encouraged. The development of mechanisms to facilitate instructional browsing is a challenge that has not yet been vigorously addressed, but a handful of possibilities have been seriously entertained. For example, students might sample several different modes of instruction (such as lecture, discussion, discovery, and computer interaction) for a period or two before deciding which was most congenial. Or the institution might organize "course fairs" at the beginning of the year, exposing students to the content and orientation of a number of fields with which they are unfamiliar. A series of freshman seminars might be offered for the same purpose. Institutions relying even partially upon educational television might broadcast representative segments from several courses during the opening weeks as a means of familiarizing students with the range of possibilities. Or something akin to open admissions might apply on a course basis during the first week or so; at the least, permission to add and drop courses might be greatly liberalized.

Critical to the success of self-matching is the flexibility afforded by provisional choice—by viewing choices as starting points, not end points, as hypotheses to be explored, not obligations to be deplored. Also critical is the willingness of the institution to vest in the student the major responsibility for determining means as well as ends. D. E. Hunt (1975) has summarized it well: "Educational arrangements in which the student is entirely responsible for matching himself to an educational environment raise basic questions about the nature of student needs and who is to define them. Whatever one's stance on this issue, it seems clear that more attention should be paid to the question of how students can learn to make more appropriate choices. The issue is not so much whether a student at any age knows what is best for himself, but rather how he can become more self-responsible through experiencing the consequences of his actions without being overwhelmed by irreversibly negative consequences" (pp. 224–225).

The Primacy of Personal Style

We have now come full circle. The prospect of self-matching and student choice leads naturally to questions of the determinants of that choice. And as Witkin has anticipated in Chapter Three, the roots of educational and vocational preferences lie in cognitive style and personality. As they crystallize in development, cognitive styles influence not only preferences for major fields but preferences for modes of functioning, whether interpersonal or impersonal, as well as preferences for modes of learning and instruction. Cognitive styles thus influence the choice not only of program content but also of program process, whenever options as to orientation or method are available. Cognitive styles are also likely to influence the amount and type of information the student seeks in informing his judgment and the manner and degree to which he uses that information.

The challenge for higher education is to create an array of program alternatives attuned to the diversity of personal styles and a system of guidance and advisement facilitative of informed student decision making about needs and preferences. To meet this challenge we should increase the number and variety of courses or packaged programs, to be sure, thereby increasing the number of macrotreatments. But we should also develop a set of program components or modules that could be orchestrated in various ways to meet individual needs. As indicated in an earlier section, a number of these building blocks already exist, but more in principle than in practice. What we seek is a "keyboard of possibilities," to use Solzhenitsyn's (1975) resonant phrase. In this way—as we reprise the musical metaphor with which this book began— we can create a higher education capable of playing not only major themes but endless variations.

References

Adorno, T. W., Frenkel-Brunswik, E., Levinson, D. J., and Sanford, R. N. *The Authoritarian Personality.* New York: Harper & Row, 1950.

Aiken, L. R. *Interactions Among Group Regressions: An Old Method in a New Setting.* R&D Memorandum No. 42. Stanford, Calif.: Stanford Center for Research and Development in Teaching, 1968.

Albert, R. S. "Toward a Behavioral Definition of Genius." *American Psychologist,* 1975, *30,* 140–151.

Allard, M., and Carlson, E. R. "The Generality of Cognitive Complexity." *Journal of Social Psychology,* 1963, *59,* 73–75.

Anastasi, A. *Differential Psychology.* (3rd ed.) New York: Macmillan, 1958.

Arbuthnot, J., and Gruenfeld, L. "Field Independence and Educational-Vocational Interests." *Journal of Consulting and Clinical Psychology,* 1969, *33,* 631.

Astin, A. W. "The Methodology of Research on College Input, Part One." *Sociology of Education,* 1970, *43,* 223–254.

Astin, A. W., and Panos, R. J. *Educational and Vocational Development of College Students.* Washington, D.C.: American Council on Education, 1969.

Atkinson, R. C., and Paulson, J. A. "An Approach to the Psychology of Instruction." *Psychological Bulletin,* 1972, *78,* 49–61.

Austin, M. "Dream Recall and the Bias of Intellectual Ability." *Nature,* 1971, *231,* p. 59.

Backman, M. E. "Patterns of Mental Abilities: Ethnic, Socioeconomic, and Sex Differences." *American Educational Research Journal,* 1972, *9,* 1–12.

Bakan, D. *The Duality of Human Existence.* Chicago: Rand McNally, 1966.

Bandura, A. "Behavioral Modification Through Modeling Procedures." In L. Krasner and L. P. Ullmann (Eds.), *Research in Behavior Modification.* New York: Holt, Rinehart and Winston, 1965.

Bandura, A. *Principles of Behavior Modification.* New York: Holt, Rinehart and Winston, 1969.

Barrett, G. V., and Thornton, C. L. "Cognitive Style Differences Between Engineers and College Students." *Perceptual and Motor Skills,* 1967, *25,* 789–793.

Barron, F. *Creativity and Psychological Health.* New York: D. Van Nostrand, 1963.

Bartlett, F. C. *Remembering.* Cambridge, England: Cambridge University Press, 1932.

Barzun, J. *The American University.* New York: Harper & Row, 1968.

Bauman, G. "Stability of Individual's Mode of Perception and of Perception-Personality Relationships." Unpublished doctoral dissertation. New York University, 1951.

Bayley, N. "Development of Mental Abilities." In P. H. Mussen (Ed.), *Carmichael's Handbook of Child Psychology.* Vol. 1. New York: Wiley, 1970.

Beane, W. E., and Lemke, E. A. "Group Variables Influencing the Transfer of Conceptual Behavior." *Journal of Educational Psychology,* 1971, *62,* 215–218.

Bell, D. R. "The Relationship Between Reward and Punishment-Avoidance Orientations and Selected Perceptual Variables." Unpublished doctoral dissertation. University of Oregon, 1964.

Beller, E. K. "Methods of Language Training and Cognitive Styles in Lower-Class Children." Paper presented at the annual meeting of the American Educational Research Association. New York, Feb. 1967.

Bem, S. L. "The Measurement of Psychological Androgyny." *Journal of Consulting and Clinical Psychology,* 1974, *42,* 155–162.

Benfari, R. "The Scanning Control Principle and Its Relationship to Affect Manipulation." *Perceptual and Motor Skills,* 1966, *22,* 203–216.

Berelson, B. *Graduate Education in the United States.* New York: McGraw-Hill, 1960.

Berg, I. "Education and Performance: Some Problems." *Journal of Higher Education,* 1972, *43,* 192–202.

Berliner, D. C., and Cahen, L. S. "Trait-Treatment Interactions in Learning." In F. N. Kerlinger (Ed.), *Review of Research in Education.* Itasca, Ill.: Peacock, 1973.

Berlyne, D. E. *Conflict, Arousal, and Curiosity.* New York: McGraw-Hill, 1960.

Berlyne, D. E. *Structure and Direction in Thinking.* New York: Wiley, 1965.

Bernard, J. *Academic Women.* University Park, Pa.: Pennsylvania State University Press, 1964.

Berry, J. W. "Temne and Eskimo Perceptual Skills." *Interactional Journal of Psychology,* 1966, *1,* 207–229.

Bettelheim, B. "The Commitment Required of a Woman Entering a Scientific Profession in Present-Day American Society." In J. A. Mattfeld, and C. G. Van Aken (Eds.), *Women and the Scientific Professions.* Cambridge, Mass.: MIT Press, 1965.

Bieri, J. "Parental Identification, Acceptance of Authority, and Within-Sex Differences in Cognitive Behavior." *Journal of Abnormal and Social Psychology,* 1960, *60,* 76–79.

Bieri, J. "Complexity-Simplicity as a Personality Variable in Cognitive and Preferential Behavior." In D. W. Fiske and S. R. Maddi (Eds.), *Functions of Varied Experience.* Homewood, Ill.: Dorsey Press, 1961.

Bieri, J., Atkins, A. L., Briar, J. S., Leaman, R. L., Miller, H., and Tripodi, T. *Clinical and Social Judgment: The*

Discrimination of Behavioral Information. New York: Wiley, 1966.

Bieri, J., Bradburn, W. M., and Galinsky, M. D. "Sex Differences in Perceptual Behavior." *Journal of Personality,* 1958, *26,* 1–12.

Birch, H. G., and Lefford, A. "Intersensory Development in Children." *Monographs of the Society for Research in Child Development,* 1963, *28* (5, Serial No. 89).

Birch, H. G., and Lefford, A. "Visual Differentiation, Intersensory Integration, and Voluntary Motor Control." *Monographs of the Society for Research in Child Development,* 1967, *32*(2, Serial No. 110).

Bissell, J., White, S., and Zivin, G. "Sensory Modalities in Children's Learning." In G. S. Lesser (Ed.), *Psychology and Educational Practice.* Glenview, Ill.: Scott, Foresman, 1971.

Bitzer, D., and Skaperdas, D. "The Economics of a Large-Scale Computer-Based Education System: PLATO IV." In W. H. Holtzman (Ed.), *Computer-Assisted Instruction, Testing, and Guidance.* New York: Harper & Row, 1970.

Block, J. H. "Conceptions of Sex Role: Some Cross-cultural and Longitudinal Perspectives." *American Psychologist,* 1973, *28,* 512–526.

Block, J., Block, J. H., and Harrington, D. M. "Some Misgivings About the Matching Familiar Figures Test as a Measure of Reflection-Impulsivity." *Developmental Psychology,* 1974, *10,* 611–632.

Bloom, B. S. "Report on Creativity Research by the Examiner's Office of the University of Chicago." In C. W. Taylor and F. Barron (Eds.), *Scientific Creativity: Its Recognition and Development.* New York: Wiley, 1963.

Boas, F. *The Mind of Primitive Man.* New York: Macmillan, 1938.

Bracht, G. H. *The Relationship of Treatment Tasks, Personological Variables and Dependent Variables to Aptitude-Treatment Interaction.* Boulder: University of Colorado, Laboratory of Educational Research, 1969.

Bracht, G. H. "Experimental Factors Related to Aptitude-Treatment Interactions." *Review of Educational Research,* 1970, *40,* 627–645.

Bracht, G. H., and Glass, G. V. "The External Validity of Experiments." *American Educational Research Journal,* 1968, *5,* 437–474.

Broverman, D. M. "Cognitive Style and Intra-Individual Variation in Abilities." *Journal of Personality,* 1960a, *28,* 240–256.

Broverman, D. M. "Dimensions of Cognitive Style." *Journal of Personality,* 1960b, *28,* 167–185.

Broverman, D. M. "Generality and Behavioral Correlates of Cognitive Styles." *Journal of Consulting Psychology,* 1964, *28,* 487–500.

Broverman, D. M., Broverman, I. K., Vogel, W., Palmer, R. D., and Klaiber, E. L. "The Automatization Cognitive Style and Physical Development." *Child Development,* 1964, *35,* 1343–1359.

Broverman, D. M., Klaiber, E. L., Kobayashi, Y., and Vogel, W. "Roles of Activation and Inhibition in Sex Differences in Cognitive Abilities." *Psychological Review,* 1968, *75,* 23–50.

Broverman, D. M., and Lazarus, R. S. "Individual Differences in Task Performance Under Conditions of Cognitive Interference." *Journal of Personality,* 1958, *26,* 94–105.

Brubacher, J. S. *A History of the Problems of Education.* New York: McGraw-Hill, 1947.

Bruininks, R. H. "Auditory and Visual Perceptual Skills Related to the Reading Performance of Disadvantaged Boys." *Perceptual and Motor Skills,* 1969, *29,* 179–186.

Bruner, J. S., Goodnow, J. J., and Austin, G. A. *A Study of Thinking.* New York: Wiley, 1956.

Bruner, J. S., Olver, R. R., and Greenfield, P. M. *Studies in Cognitive Growth.* New York: Wiley, 1966.

Bruner, J. S., and Tajfel, H. "Cognitive Risk and Environmental Change." *Journal of Abnormal and Social Psychology,* 1961, *62,* 231–241.

Buffery, A. W. H., and Gray, J. A. "Sex Differences in the Development of Spatial and Linguistic Skills." In F. Ounsted, and D. C. Taylor (Eds.), *Gender Differences: Their Ontogeny and Significance*. London: Churchill, 1972.

Bunderson, C. V. "The Computer and Instructional Design." In W. H. Holtzman (Ed.), *Computer-Assisted Instruction, Testing, and Guidance*. New York: Harper & Row, 1970.

Busch, J. C. *Conformity in Preschool Disadvantaged Children as Related to Field Dependence, Sex, and Verbal Reinforcement*. Doctoral dissertation. University of Tennessee, 1970. Ann Arbor, Mich.: University Microfilms, 1971, No. 71-334.

Butts, R. F. *A Cultural History of Education*. New York: McGraw-Hill, 1947.

Campbell, D. P. "Admissions Policies: Side Effects and Their Implications." *American Psychologist*, 1971, *26*, 636–647.

Campbell, D. T., and Fiske, D. W. "Convergent and Discriminant Validation by the Multitrait-Multimethod Matrix." *Psychological Bulletin*, 1959, *56*, 81–105.

Campbell, D. T., and Stanley, J. C. "Experimental and Quasi-experimental Designs for Research on Teaching." In N. L. Gage (Ed.), *Handbook of Research on Teaching*. Chicago: Rand McNally, 1963.

Carlson, R. "Understanding Women: Implications for Personality Theory and Research." In M. S. Mednick and S. S. Tangri (Eds.), New Perspectives on Women. *Journal of Social Issues*, 1972, *28*, 17–32.

Carnegie Commission on Higher Education. *New Students and New Places*. New York: McGraw-Hill, 1971.

Carnegie Commission on Higher Education. *The Fourth Revolution*. New York: McGraw-Hill, 1972a.

Carnegie Commission on Higher Education. *The More Effective Use of Resources*. New York: McGraw-Hill, 1972b.

Carnegie Commission on Higher Education. *Reform on Campus*. New York: McGraw-Hill, 1972c.

Carnegie Foundation for the Advancement of Teaching, The. *The Graduate Record Examination: A Memorandum on the General Character and Purpose of the Examination In-*

cluding a Summary of Initial Studies of Its Validity. New York, 1941.

Carroll, J. B. "Instructional Methods and Individual Differences." In R. M. Gagné (Ed.), *Learning and Individual Differences.* Columbus, Ohio: Merrill, 1967.

Cartwright, L. K. "Personality Differences in Male and Female Medical Students." *Psychiatry and Medicine,* 1972, *3,* 213–218.

Centra, J. A., Linn, R. L., and Parry, M. E. "Academic Growth in Predominantly White Colleges." *American Educational Research Journal,* 1970, *7,* 83–98.

Chartier, G. M. "A-B Therapist Variable: Real or Imagined?" *Psychological Bulletin,* 1971, *75,* 22–33.

Chase, J. L. *Graduate Teaching Assistants in American Universities: A Review of Recent Trends and Recommendations.* Washington, D. C.: U. S. Government Printing Office, 1970.

Chickering, A. W. *Education and Identity.* San Francisco: Jossey-Bass, 1969.

Chomsky, N. *Cartesian Linguistics.* New York: Harper & Row, 1966.

Chung, W-S. *Relationships Among Measures of Cognitive Style, Vocational Preferences, and Vocational Identification.* Doctoral dissertation, George Peabody College for Teachers, 1966. Ann Arbor, Mich.: University Microfilms, 1967, No. 67-3611.

Clar, P. N. *The Relationship of Psychological Differentiation to Client Behavior in Vocational Choice Counseling.* Doctoral dissertation, University of Michigan, 1971. Ann Arbor, Mich.: University Microfilms, 1971, No. 71-23, 723.

Clayton, M. G., and Jackson, D. N. "Equivalence Range, Acquiescence, and Overgeneralization." *Educational and Psychological Measurement,* 1961, *21,* 371–382.

Cleare, B. E. "An Investigation of the Interaction Between Student-Teacher Cognitive Ability Patterns Using Achievement in Chemical Education Material Study Course as the Criterion Variable." Unpublished doctoral dissertation. Florida State University, 1966.

Cohen, J. "The Factorial Structure of the W.A.I.S. Between Early Adulthood and Old Age." *Journal of Consulting Psychology*, 1957, *21*, 283–290.

Cohen, J. "The Factorial Structure of the W.I.S.C. at Ages 7-6, 10-6, and 13-6." *Journal of Consulting Psychology*, 1959, *23*, 8–59.

Cole, J. R., and Cole, S. *Social Stratification in Science.* Chicago: University of Chicago Press, 1973.

Cole, M., and Bruner, J. S. "Cultural Differences and Inferences about Psychological Processes." *American Psychologist*, 1971, *26*, 867–876.

Cole, M., Gay, J., Glick, J. A., and Sharp, D. W. *The Cultural Context of Learning and Thinking.* New York: Basic Books, 1971.

Coleman, J. S., Campbell, E. Q., Hobson, C. J., McPartland, J., Mood, A. M., Weinfeld, F. D., and York, R. L. *Equality of Educational Opportunity.* U.S. Department of Health, Education, and Welfare, Office of Education. Washington, D. C.: U.S. Government Printing Office, 1966.

Coop, R. H., and Brown, L. D. "The Effects of Teaching Method and Cognitive Style on Categories of Achievement." *Journal of Educational Psychology*, 1970, *61*, 400–405.

Corah, N. L. "Differentiation in Children and Their Parents." *Journal of Personality*, 1965, *33*, 300–308.

Cronbach, L. J. "The Two Disciplines of Scientific Psychology." *American Psychologist*, 1957, *12*, 671–684.

Cronbach, L. J. "How Can Instruction Be Adapted to Individual Differences?" In R. M. Gagné (Ed.), *Learning and Individual Differences.* Columbus, Ohio: Merrill, 1967.

Cronbach, L. J. "Intelligence? Creativity? A Parsimonious Reinterpretation of the Wallach-Kogan Data." *American Educational Research Journal*, 1968, *5*, 491–511.

Cronbach, L. J. "Beyond the Two Disciplines of Scientific Psychology." *American Psychologist*, 1975, *30*, 116–127.

Cronbach, L. J., and Snow, R. E. *"Individual Differences in Learning Ability as a Function of Instructional Variables."* Stanford, Calif.: Stanford University, 1969.

Cross, P. "The Woman Student." In *Women in Higher Education.* Washington, D. C.: American Council on Education, 1972.

Crutchfield, R. S., Woodworth, D. G., and Albrecht, R. E. *Perceptual Performance and the Effective Person.* Report No. WADC-TN-58-60. ASTIA Document No. AD 151 039. Wright Air Development Center, Texas, 1958.

Dahlstrom, E. (Ed.) *The Changing Roles of Men and Women.* Boston: Beacon Press, 1971.

Davis, J. A. *Great Aspirations.* Chicago: Aldine, 1964.

Dawson, J. L. M. "Cultural and Physiological Influence upon Spatial-Perceptual Processes in West Africa—Part I." *International Journal of Psychology,* 1967a, *2*(2), 115–128.

Dawson, J. L. M. "Cultural and Physiological Influence upon Spatial-Perceptual Processes in West Africa—Part II." *International Journal of Psychology,* 1967b, *2*(3), 171–185.

Dawson, J. L. M. "Theoretical and Research Bases of Bio-social Psychology: An Inaugural Lecture from the Chair of Psychology, University of Hong Kong." *Supplement to the Gazette,* 1969, *16*(3), 1–10.

Dawson, J. L. M. "Theory and Research in Cross-cultural Psychology." *Bulletin of the British Psychological Society,* 1971, *24*(85), 291–306.

Day, H. I., and Berlyne, D. E. "Intrinsic Motivation." In G. S. Lesser (Ed.), *Psychology and Educational Practice.* Glenview, Ill.: Scott Foresman, 1971.

Deever, S. G. *Ratings of Task-Oriented Expectancy for Success as a Function of Internal Control and Field Independence.* Doctoral dissertation, University of Florida, 1967. Ann Arbor, Mich.: University Microfilms, 1968, No. 68-9470.

DeHaan, R. F., and Havighurst, R. J. *Educating Gifted Children.* Chicago: University of Chicago Press, 1957.

De Hirsch, K., Jansky, J., and Langford, W. S. *Predicting Reading Failure.* New York: Harper & Row, 1966.

Dellas, M., and Gaier, E. L. "Identification of Creativity: The Individual." *Psychological Bulletin,* 1970, *73*, 55–73.

DeRussy, E. A., and Futch, E., "Field Dependence-Independence as Related to College Curricula." *Perceptual and Motor Skills,* 1971, *33*, 1235–1237.

Dewey, J. *Experience and Education.* New York: Macmillan, 1938.

DiStefano, J. J. "Interpersonal Perceptions of Field-Independent and Field-Dependent Teachers and Students." Unpublished doctoral dissertation. Cornell University, 1969.

Domino, G. "Differential Predictions of Academic Achievement in Conforming and Independent Settings." *Journal of Educational Psychology,* 1968, *59,* 256–260.

Domino, G. "Interactive Effects of Achievement Orientation and Teaching Style on Academic Achievement." *Journal of Educational Psychology,* 1971, *62,* 427–431.

Doob, L. W. "Behavior and Grammatical Style." *Journal of Abnormal and Social Psychology,* 1958, *56,* 398–400.

Doob, L. W. *Becoming More Civilized.* New Haven: Yale University Press, 1960.

Durkheim, E., and Mauss, M. *Primitive Classification.* Chicago: University of Chicago Press, 1963.

Dye, N., and Very, P. S. "Growth Changes in Factorial Structure by Age and Sex." *Genetic Psychology Monographs,* 1968, *78*(1), 55–58.

Dyk, R. B. "An Exploratory Study of Mother-Child Interaction in Infancy as Related to the Development of Differentiation." *Journal of the Academy of Child Psychiatry,* 1969, *8,* 657–691.

Dyk, R. B., and Witkin, H. A. "Family Experiences Related to the Development of Differentiation in Children." *Child Development,* 1965, *30,* 21–55.

Eagle, M., Fitzgibbons, D., and Goldberger, L. "Field Dependence and Memory for Relevant and Irrelevant Incidental Stimuli." *Perceptual and Motor Skills,* 1966, *23,* 1035–1038.

Eagle, M., Goldberger, L., and Breitman, M. "Field Dependence and Memory for Social vs. Neutral and Relevant vs. Irrelevant Incidental Stimuli." *Perceptual and Motor Skills,* 1969, *29,* 903–910.

Eby, F., and Arrowood, C. F. *The History and Philosophy of Education: Ancient and Medieval.* Englewood Cliffs, N. J.: Prentice-Hall, 1940.

Erickson, E. H. *Childhood and Society.* New York: Norton, 1950.

Evans-Prichard, E. "Sanza: A Characteristic Feature of Zande Language and Thought." *Essays in Social Anthropology.* New York: Free Press, 1963.

Farnham-Diggory, S. "Cognitive Synthesis in Negro and White Children." *Monographs of the Society for Research in Child Development,* 1970, *35* (2, Serial No. 135).

Feldman, S. *Escape from the Doll's House: Women in Graduate and Professional School Education.* New York: McGraw-Hill, 1973.

Ferrel, J. G. *The Differential Performance of Lower Class Preschool Negro Children as a Function of E, Sex of S, Reinforcement Condition and Level of Field Dependence.* Doctoral dissertation, University of Southern Mississippi, 1970. Ann Arbor, Mich.: University Microfilms, 1971, No. 71-28, 831.

Fillenbaum, S. "Some Stylistic Aspects of Categorizing Behavior." *Journal of Personality,* 1959, *27,* 187–195.

Fink, D. "Sex Differences in Perceptual Tasks in Relation to Selected Personality Variables." Unpublished doctoral dissertation. Rutgers University, 1959.

Fitz, R. J. *The Differential Effects of Praise and Censure on Serial Learning as Dependent on Locus of Control and Field Dependency.* Doctoral dissertation, Catholic University of America, 1970. Ann Arbor, Mich.: University Microfilms, 1971, No. 71-1457.

Fitzgibbons, D., and Goldberger, L. "Task and Social Orientation: A Study of Field Dependence, 'Arousal,' and Memory for Incidental Material." *Perceptual and Motor Skills,* 1971, *32,* 167–174.

Fitzgibbons, D., Goldberger, L., and Eagle, M. "Field Dependence and Memory for Incidental Material." *Perceptual and Motor Skills,* 1965, *21,* 743–749.

Fitzsimmons, S. J., Cheever, J., Leonard, E., and Mancunovich, D. "School Failures." *Developmental Psychology,* 1969, *1,* 134–146.

Flaugher, R. *Patterns of Test Performance by High School Students of Four Ethnic Identities.* RB-71-25. Princeton, N.J.: Educational Testing Service, 1971.

Flavell, J. H. *The Developmental Psychology of Jean Piaget*. New York: D. Van Nostrand, 1963.

Frederiksen, C. H. "Abilities, Transfer, and Information Retrieval in Verbal Learning." *Multiple Behavioral Research Monographs*, 1969, No. 69-2.

Frederiksen, N. "Toward a Taxonomy of Situations." *American Psychologist*, 1972, *27*, 114–123.

Frederiksen, N., Jensen, D., and Beaton, A.E. *Prediction of Organizational Behavior*. New York: Pergamon Press, 1972.

Frederiksen, N., and Ward, W. *Development of Measures for the Study of Creativity*. RB-75-18. Princeton, N.J.: Educational Testing Service, May 1975.

Freedman, N., O'Hanlon, J., Oltman, P., and Witkin, H. "The Imprint of Psychological Differentiation on Kinetic Behavior in Varying Communicative Contexts." *Journal of Abnormal Psychology*, 1972, *79*, 239–258.

Frehner, V. L. *"Cognitive Style as a Determinant of Educational Achievement Among Sixth Grade Elementary School Students."* Unpublished doctoral dissertation. Utah State University, 1971.

Gardner, R. W. "Cognitive Styles in Categorizing Behavior." *Journal of Personality*, 1953, *22*, 214–233.

Gardner, R. W., Holzman, P. S., Klein, G. S., Linton, H. B., and Spence, D. "Cognitive Control: A Study of Individual Consistencies in Cognitive Behavior." *Psychological Issues*, 1959, *1*, Monograph 4.

Gardner, R. W., Jackson, D. N., and Messick, S. "Personality Organization in Cognitive Controls and Intellectual Abilities." *Psychological Issues*, 1960, *2*, Monograph 8.

Gardner, R. W., Lohrenz, L. S., and Schoen, R. A. "Cognitive Control of Differentiation in the Perception of Persons and Objects." *Perceptual and Motor Skills*, 1968, *26*, 311–330.

Gardner, R. W., and Long, R. I. "Cognitive Controls of Attention and Inhibition: A Study of Individual Consistencies." *British Journal of Psychology*, 1962a, *53*, 381–388.

Gardner, R. W., and Long, R. I. "Control Defense and Centration Effect: A Study of Scanning Behavior." *British Journal of Psychology*, 1962b, *53*, 129–140.

Gardner, R. W., and Moriarty, A. E. *Personality Development at Preadolescence.* Seattle: University of Washington Press, 1968.

Gardner, R. W., and Schoen, R. A. "Differentiation and Abstraction in Concept Formation." *Psychological Monographs*, 1962, *76*, No. 41 (Whole No. 560).

Garron, D. C. "Sex-Linked, Recessive Inheritance of Spatial and Numerical Abilities, and Turner's Syndrome." *Psychological Review*, 1970, *77*, 147–152.

Getzels, J. W., and Jackson, P. W. *Creativity and Intelligence: Explorations with Gifted Children.* New York: Wiley, 1962.

Glaser, R. "Individuals and Learning: The New Aptitudes." *Educational Researcher*, June 1972, pp. 5–13.

Glaser, R. "Educational Psychology and Education." *American Psychologist*, 1973, *28*, 557–566.

Glaser, R., and Resnick, L. B. "Instructional Psychology." *Annual Review of Psychology*, 1972, *23*, 207–276.

Glatt, C. J. W. *The Relationship of Level of Differentiation, Acceptance of Authority and Locus of Control to Readiness for Vocational Planning in Eighth Grade Boys.* Doctoral dissertation, New York University, 1969. Ann Arbor, Mich.: University Microfilms, 1970, No. 70-21, 132.

Glixman, A. F. "Categorizing Behavior as a Function of Meaning Domain." *Journal of Personality and Social Psychology*, 1965, *2*, 370–377.

Golann, S. E. "Psychological Study of Creativity." *Psychological Bulletin*, 1963, *60*, 548–565.

Goldberger, L., and Bendich, S. "Field Dependence and Social Responsiveness as Determinants of Spontaneously Produced Words." *Perceptual and Motor Skills*, 1972, *34*, 883–886.

Goldstein, A. G., and Chance, J. E. "Effects of Practice on Sex-Related Differences in Performance on Embedded Figures." *Psychonomic Science*, 1965, *3*, 361–362.

Good, H. G. *A History of Western Education.* (2nd ed.) New York: Macmillan, 1960.

Goodenough, D. R. "The Role of Individual Differences in Field Dependence as a Factor in Learning and Memory." *Psychological Bulletin,* 1976, *83,* 675–694.

Goodenough, D. R., and Karp, S. A. "Field Dependence and Intellectual Functioning." *Journal of Abnormal and Social Psychology,* 1961, *63,* 241–246.

Gough, H. G., and Woodworth, D. G. "Stylistic Variations Among Professional Research Scientists." *Journal of Psychology,* 1960, *49,* 87–98.

Gray, J. A., and Drewett, R. F. "The Genetics and Development of Sex Differences." In R. B. Cattell and R. M. Dreger (Eds.), *Handbook of Modern Personality Theory.* New York: Appleton-Century-Crofts, 1973.

Greenberg, J. *Universals of Language.* Cambridge, Mass.: MIT Press, 1963.

Greene, M. A. "Client Perception of the Relationship as a Function of Worker-Client Cognitive Styles." Unpublished doctoral dissertation. Columbia University, School of Social Work, 1972.

Greenfield, P. M., and Bruner, J. S. "Culture and Cognitive Growth." In D. Goslin (Ed.), *Handbook of Socialization Theory and Research.* Chicago: Rand McNally, 1969.

Greenwald, E. R. *Perceptual Style in Relation to Role Choices and Motivational Variables.* Doctoral dissertation, Yeshiva University, 1968. Ann Arbor, Mich.: University Microfilms, 1968, No. 68-17, 167.

Grieve, T. D., and Davis, J. K. "The Relationship of Cognitive Style and Method of Instruction to Performance in Ninth Grade Geography." *Journal of Educational Research,* 1971, *65,* 137–141.

Grigg, C. M. *Graduate Education.* New York: Center for Applied Research in Education, 1965.

Groen, G. J., and Atkinson, R. L. "Models for Optimizing the Learning Process." *Psychological Bulletin,* 1966, *66,* 309–320.

Guilford, J. P. *The Nature of Human Intelligence.* New York: McGraw-Hill, 1967.

Guilford, J. P., and Hoepfner, R. *The Analysis of Intelligence.* New York: McGraw-Hill, 1971.

Guilford, J. P., Merrifield, P. R., and Cox, A. B. *Creative Thinking in Children at the Junior High School Level.* Report from the Psychology Laboratory. University of Southern California, 1961.

Gutmann, D. "Female Ego Styles and Generational Conflict." In J. M. Bardwick, E. Douvan, M. S. Horner, and D. Gutmann (Eds.), *Feminine Personality and Conflict.* Monterey, Calif.: Books/Cole, 1970.

Hammond, A. L. "Computer-Assisted Instruction: Two Major Demonstrations." *Science,* 1972, *176,* 1110–1112.

Harmon, L. R. "The Development of a Criterion of Scientific Competence." In C. W. Taylor and F. Barron (Eds.), *Scientific Creativity: Its Recognition and Development.* New York: Wiley, 1963.

Hartlage, L. C. "Sex-Linked Inheritance of Spatial Ability." *Perceptual and Motor Skills,* 1970, *31,* 610.

Harvey, O. J., Hunt, D. E., and Schroder, H. M. *Conceptual Systems and Personality Organization.* New York: Wiley, 1961.

Heiss, A. M. *Challenges to Graduate Schools: The Ph.D. Program in Ten Universities.* San Francisco: Jossey-Bass, 1970.

Heist, P., and Yonge, G. *Omnibus Personality Inventory, Form F Manual.* New York: Psychological Corporation, 1968.

Helson, R. "Sex Differences in Creative Style." *Journal of Personality,* 1967, *35,* 214–233.

Helson, R. "Generality of Sex Differences in Creative Style." *Journal of Personality,* 1968, *36,* 33–48.

Helson, R. "Sex-Specific Patterns in Creative Literary Fantasy." *Journal of Personality,* 1970, *38,* 344–363.

Helson, R. "Women Mathematicians and the Creative Personality." *Journal of Consulting and Clinical Psychology,* 1971, *36,* 210–220.

Helson, R. "The Heroic, the Comic, and the Tender: Patterns of Literary Fantasy and Their Authors." *Journal of Personality,* 1973, *41,* 163–184.

Helson, R. "Creativity in Women." In J. Sherman and F. Denmark (Eds.), *The Futures of Women: Issues in Psychology.* New York: Psychological Perspectives, 1976.

Helson, R., and Crutchfield, R. S. "Mathematicians: The Creative Researcher and the Average Ph.D." *Journal of Consulting and Clinical Psychology,* 1970, *34,* 250–257.

Herskovits, M. J. *Man and His Works.* New York: Knopf, 1948.

Holland, J. L. "Creative and Academic Performance among Talented Adolescents." *Journal of Educational Psychology,* 1961, *52,* 136–147.

Holland, J. L. "The Selection of Students for Special Scholarships." *Journal of Higher Education,* 1964, *35,* 32–37.

Holland, J. L. *The Psychology of Vocational Choice.* Waltham, Mass.: Blaisdell, 1966.

Holland, J. L., and Nichols, R. C. "Prediction of Academic and Extra-curricular Achievement in College." *Journal of Educational Psychology,* 1964, *55,* 55–65.

Holland, J. L., and Richards, J. M., Jr. "Academic and Nonacademic Accomplishment: Correlated or Uncorrelated?" *Journal of Educational Psychology,* 1965, *56,* 165–174.

Holland, J. L., and Richards, J. M., Jr. *Academic and Nonacademic Accomplishment in a Representative Sample Taken from a Population of 612,000.* ACT Research Report, No. 12. Iowa City, Iowa: American College Testing Program, 1966.

Holland, J. L., and Richards, J. M., Jr. "The Many Faces of Talent: A Reply to Werts." *Journal of Educational Psychology,* 1967, *58,* 205–209.

Hollis, E. V. *Toward Improving Ph.D. Programs.* Washington, D. C.: American Council on Education, 1945.

Holmes, M. "Cognitive Style, Repression and Dream Recall." Research paper, Research Unit on Intellectual Development. University of Edinburgh, 1972.

Holtzman, W. H., Swartz, J. D., and Thorpe, J. S. "Artists, Architects and Engineers—Three Contrasting Modes of Visual Experience and Their Psychological Correlates." *Journal of Personality,* 1971, *39,* 432–499.

Holzman, P. S. "The Relation of Assimilation Tendencies in Visual, Auditory, and Kinesthetic Time-Error to Cognitive Attitudes of Leveling and Sharpening." *Journal of Personality,* 1954, *22,* 375–394.

Holzman, P. S. "Scanning: A Principle of Reality Contact." *Perceptual and Motor Skills,* 1966, *23,* 835–844.

Holzman, P. S. "Cognitive Control Principles: An Addendum." *Perceptual and Motor Skills,* 1971, *33,* 949–950.

Holzman, P. S., and Gardner, R. W. "Leveling and Repression." *Journal of Abnormal and Social Psychology,* 1959, *59,* 151–155.

Holzman, P. S., and Gardner, R.W. "Leveling-Sharpening and Memory Organization." *Journal of Abnormal and Social Psychology,* 1960, *61,* 176–180.

Holzman, P. S., and Klein, G. S. "Cognitive System Principles of Leveling and Sharpening: Individual Differences in Assimilation Effects in Visual Time-Error." *Journal of Psychology,* 1954, *37,* 105–122.

Holzman, P. S., and Rousey, C. "Disinhibition of Communicated Thought: Generality and Role of Cognitive Style." *Journal of Abnormal Psychology,* 1971, *77,* 263–274.

Hoyt, D. P. *The Relationship Between College Grades and Adult Achievement: A Review of the Literature.* ACT Research Report, No. 7. Iowa City, American College Testing Program, 1965.

Hoyt, D. P. "College Grades and Adult Accomplishment: A Review of Research." *Educational Record,* 1966, *47,* 70–75.

Hudson, L. "Degree Class and Attainment in Scientific Research." *British Journal of Psychology,* 1960, *51,* 67–73.

Hudson, L. "Arts/Science Specialization." Unpublished doctoral dissertation. University of Cambridge, 1961.

Hudson, L. "Academic Sheep and Research Goats." *New Society,* 1964, *108,*9.

Hudson, L. *Contrary Imaginations: A Psychological Study of the Young Student.* New York: Schocken Books, 1966.

Hudson, L. *Frames of Mind: Ability, Perception and Self-perception in the Arts and Sciences.* New York: Norton, 1968.

Hudson, L. "Odd Fish in the Academic Grove." Paper presented at the 7th annual conference of the Society for Research into Higher Education. Edinburgh, United Kingdom, 1972.

Hudson, L. *The Cult of the Fact: A Psychologist's Autobiographical Critique of His Discipline.* New York: Harper & Row, 1973a.

Hudson, L. "Fertility in the Arts and Sciences." *Science Studies,* 1973b, *3,* 305–318.

Hudson, L. *Originality.* London: Oxford University Press, 1973c.

Hudson, L., and Fulton, O. "The Ivory Tower." Occasional paper, Centre for Research in the Educational Sciences. University of Edinburgh, 1973.

Hudson, L., and Jacot, B. "Education and Eminence in British Medicine." *British Medical Journal,* 1971a, *4,* 162–163.

Hudson, L., and Jacot, B. "Marriage and Fertility in Academic Life." *Nature,* 1971b, *229,* 531–532.

Hudson, L., Jacot, B., and Johnson, J. "Perception and Communication in Academic Life." Occasional paper, Centre for Research in the Educational Sciences. University of Edinburgh, 1972.

Hunt, D. E. *Matching Models in Education.* Monograph Series No. 10. Ontario Institute for Studies in Education, 1971.

Hunt, D. E. "Person-Environment Interaction: A Challenge Found Wanting Before It Was Tried." *Review of Educational Research,* 1975, *45,* 209–230.

Hunt, J. McV. *Intelligence and Experience.* New York: Ronald Press, 1961.

Husen, T. (Ed.) *International Study of Achievement in Mathematics.* Vol. 2. New York: Wiley, 1967.

Hutchinson, W. L. "Creative and Productive Thinking in the Classroom." Unpublished doctoral dissertation. University of Utah, 1963.

Israel, N. "Leveling-Sharpening and Anticipatory Cardiac Response." *Psychosomatic Medicine,* 1969, *31,* 499–509.

Jacklin, C. N., and Maccoby, E. E. "Sex Differences in Intellectual Abilities: A Reassessment and a Look at Some New Explanations." Paper presented at the annual meeting of the American Educational Research Association. Chicago, April 1972.

Jackson, P. W., and Messick, S. "The Person, the Product, and the Response: Conceptual Problems in the Assessment of Creativity." *Journal of Personality*, 1965, *33*, 309–329.

Jackson, P. W., and Messick, S. "Creativity." In P. London and D. L. Rosenhan (Eds.), *Foundations of Abnormal Psychology*. New York: Holt, Rinehart and Winston, 1968.

Jencks, C., and Riesman, D. *The Academic Revolution*. Garden City, N.Y.: Doubleday, 1968.

Jennings, B. S. *Some Cognitive Control Variables and Psycholinguistic Dimensions*. Doctoral dissertation, University of Florida, 1967. Ann Arbor, Mich.: University Microfilms, 1968, No. 68-13, 011.

Jensen, A. R. "How Much Can We Boost IQ and Scholastic Achievement?" *Harvard Educational Review*, 1969a, *39*, 1–123.

Jensen, A. R. "Reducing the Heredity-Environment Uncertainty: A Reply." *Harvard Educational Review*, 1969b, *39*, 449–484.

Jensen, A. R. "The Role of Verbal Mediation in Mental Development." *Journal of Genetic Psychology*, 1971, *118*, 39–70.

Jensen, A. R., and Rohwer, W. D. "The Stroop Color-Word Test: A Review." *Acta Psychologica*, 1966, *25*, 36–93.

Johnson, D. W., and Johnson, R. T. "Instructional Goal Structure: Cooperative, Competitive, or Individualistic." *Review of Educational Research*, 1974, *44*, 213–240.

Jung, C. G. *The Collected Works of C. G. Jung*. Vol. 14. Bollingen Series 20. New York: Pantheon Books, 1963.

Justice, M. T. *Field Dependency, Intimacy of Topic and Interperson Distance*. Doctoral dissertation, University of Florida, 1969. Ann Arbor, Mich.: University Microfilms, 1970. No. 70-12, 243.

Kagan, J., and Kogan, N. "Individual Variation in Cognitive Processes." In P. H. Mussen (Ed.), *Carmichael's Manual of Child Psychology*. Vol. 1. New York: Wiley, 1970.

Kagan, J., and Messer, S. G. A reply to "Some Misgivings About the Matching Familiar Figures Test as a Measure of Reflection-Impulsivity." *Developmental Psychology,* 1975, *11,* 244–248.

Kagan, J., Moss, H. A., and Sigel, I. E. "Conceptual Style and the Use of Affect Labels." *Merrill-Palmer Quarterly,* 1960, *6,* 261–278.

Kagan, J., Moss, H.A., and Sigel, I. E. "Psychological Significance of Styles of Conceptualization." *Monographs of the Society for Research in Child Development,* 1963, *28*(2, Serial No. 86), 73–112.

Kagan, J., Rosman, B. L., Day, D., Albert, J., and Phillips, W. "Information Processing in the Child: Significance of Analytic and Reflective Attitudes." *Psychological Monographs: General and Applied,* 1964, *78*(1, Whole No. 578).

Karp, S. A. Personal communication. 1957.

Karp, S. A. "Field Dependence and Overcoming Embeddedness." *Journal of Consulting Psychology,* 1963, *27,* 294–302.

Karp, S. A., Kissin, B., and Hustmyer, F. E. "Field Dependence as a Predictor of Alcoholic Therapy Dropouts." *Journal of Nervous and Mental Disease,* 1970, *150,* 77–83.

Keller, F. S. "Goodby, Teacher. . . ." *Journal of Applied Behavior Analysis,* 1968, *1,* 79–89.

Kelly, G. A. *The Psychology of Personal Constructs.* Vol. 1. New York: Norton, 1955.

Keogh, B. K., and Donlon, G. McG. "Field Dependence, Impulsivity, and Learning Disabilities." *Journal of Learning Disabilities,* 1972, *5,* 16–21.

Kinsbourne, M. "The Contrary Imaginations of Arts and Science Students: A Critical Discussion." *Developmental Medicine and Child Neurology,* 1968, *10,* 461–464.

Klein, G. S. "Need and Regulation." In M. R. Jones (Ed.), *Nebraska Symposium on Motivation.* Lincoln: University of Nebraska Press, 1954.

Klein, G. S. "Cognitive Control and Motivation." In G. Lindzey (Ed.), *Assessment of Human Motives.* New York: Holt, Rinehart and Winston, 1958.

Klein, G. S. *Perception, Motives and Personality.* New York: Knopf, 1970.

Klein, G. S., Gardner, R. W., and Schlesinger, H. J. "Tolerance for Unrealistic Experiences: A Study of the Generality of a Cognitive Control." *British Journal of Psychology,* 1962, *53,* 41–55.

Klein, G. S., and Schlesinger, H. J. "Perceptual Attitudes Toward Instability: I. Prediction of Apparent Movement Experiences from Rorschach Responses." *Journal of Personality,* 1951, *19,* 289–302.

Kleinfeld, J. S. "Intellectual Strengths in Culturally Different Groups: An Eskimo Illustration." *Review of Educational Research,* 1973, *43,* 341–359.

Knox, C., and Kimura, D. "Cerebral Processing of Nonverbal Sounds in Boys and Girls." *Neuropsychologia,* 1970, *8,* 227–237.

Kogan, N. "Educational Implications of Cognitive Styles." In G. S. Lesser (Ed.), *Psychology and Educational Practice.* Glenview, Ill.: Scott Foresman, 1971.

Kogan, N. "Creativity and Cognitive Style: A Life-Span Perspective." In P. B. Baltes and K. W. Schaie (Eds.), *Life-Span Developmental Psychology: Personality and Socialization.* New York: Academic Press, 1973.

Kogan, N., and Morgan, F. T. "Task and Motivational Influences on the Assessment of Creative and Intellectual Ability in Children." *Genetic Psychology Monographs,* 1969, *80,* 92–127.

Kogan, N., and Pankove, E. "Creative Ability over a Five-Year Span." *Child Development,* 1972, *43,* 427–442.

Kogan, N., and Wallach, M. A. *Risk Taking: A Study in Cognition and Personality.* New York: Holt, Rinehart and Winston, 1964.

Kogan, N., and Wallach, M. A. "Risk Taking as a Function of the Situation, the Person, and the Group." *New Directions in Psychology III.* New York: Holt, Rinehart and Winston, 1967.

Kohlberg, L. "Stage and Sequence: The Cognitive-Developmental Approach to Socialization." In D. A. Goslin (Ed.),

Handbook of Socialization Theory and Research. Chicago: Rand McNally, 1969.

Kohlberg, L., and Mayer, R. "Development as the Aim of Education." *Harvard Educational Review,* 1972, *42,* 449–496.

Konstadt, N., and Forman, E. "Field Dependence and External Directedness." *Journal of Personality and Social Psychology,* 1965, *1,* 490–493.

Koran, M. L. "The Effect of Individual Differences on Observational Learning in the Acquisition of a Teaching Skill." Unpublished doctoral dissertation. Stanford University, 1969.

Koran, M. L., Snow, R. E., and McDonald, F. J. "Teacher Aptitude and Observational Learning of a Teaching Skill." *Journal of Educational Psychology,* 1971, *63,* 219–228.

Kozol, J. *Free Schools.* New York: Bantam Books, 1972.

Krienke, J. W. *Cognitive Differentiation and Occupational-Profile Differentiation on the Strong Vocational Interest Blank.* Doctoral dissertation, University of Florida, 1969. Ann Arbor, Mich.: University Microfilms, 1970, No. 70-20 599.

Kroeber, A. L. *Anthropology.* New York: Harcourt Brace Jovanovich, 1948.

Kropp, R. P., Nelson, W. H., and King, F. J. *Identification and Definition of Subject-Matter Content Variables Related to Human Aptitudes.* Unpublished report, Cooperative Research Project, No. 2914. Tallahassee, Florida: Florida State University, 1967. (ERIC Document Reproduction No., Vol. 1 ED 010 627; Vol. 2 ED 001 628)

Kulik, J. A. "Keller-Based Plans for Teaching and Learning: A Review of Research." Ann Arbor, Mich.: Center for Research on Learning and Teaching, University of Michigan, 1972.

Kulik, J. A., Brown, R. E. Vestewig, D. R., and Wright, J. *Undergraduate Education in Psychology.* Washington, D.C.: American Psychological Association, 1973.

Kulik, J. A., Kulik, C., and Carmichael, K. "The Keller Plan in Science Teaching." *Science,* 1974, *183,* 379–383.

Labov, W. "The Logic of Non-standard English." In F. Williams (Ed.), *Language and Poverty.* Chicago: Markham, 1970.

Langley, C. W. "Differentiation and Integration of Systems of Personal Constructs." *Journal of Personality,* 1971, *39,* 10–25.

Lerner, I. M. *Heredity, Evolution, and Society.* San Francisco: W. H. Freeman, 1968.

Lesser, G. S. "Matching Instruction to Student Characteristics." In G. S. Lesser (Ed.), *Psychology and Educational Practice.* Glenview, Ill.: Scott, Foresman, 1971.

Lesser, G. S., Fifer, G., and Clark, D. H. "Mental Abilities of Children from Different Social-Class and Cultural Groups." *Monographs of the Society for Research in Child Development,* 1965, *30* (4, Serial No. 102).

Levi, E. H. *Point of View: Talks on Education.* Chicago: University of Chicago Press, 1969.

Levi-Strauss, C. *The Savage Mind.* Chicago: University of Chicago Press, 1966.

Linton, H. "Relations Between Mode of Perception and the Tendency to Conform." Unpublished doctoral dissertation. Yale University, 1952.

Linton, H., and Graham, F. "Personality Correlates of Persuasibility." In C. I. Hovland and I. L. Janis (Eds.), *Personality and Persuasibility.* New Haven: Yale University Press, 1959.

Luborsky, P. Personal communication. 1969.

Maccoby, E. E. "Sex Differences in Intellectual Functioning." In E. E. Maccoby (Ed.), *The Development of Sex Differences.* Stanford, Calif.: Stanford University Press, 1966.

Maccoby, E. E. "Sex Differences in Intellectual Functioning." Paper presented at the ETS Invitational Conference on Testing Problems. New York, October 1972.

Maccoby, E. E., and Jacklin, C. N. *The Psychology of Sex Differences.* Stanford, Calif.: Stanford University Press, 1974.

Mackinnon, D. W. "The Personality Correlates of Creativity: A Study of American Architects." In G. S. Nielsen (Ed.),

Proceedings of the XIV International Congress of Applied Psychology. Copenhagen, 1961. Vol. II. Copenhagen: Munksgaard, 1962.

MacKinnon, D. W. "Creativity and Images of the Self." In R. W. White (Ed.), *The Study of Lives.* New York: Atherton Press, 1963.

MacKinnon, D. W. "The Study of Creative Persons: A Method and Some Results." In J. Kagan (Ed.), *Creativity and Learning.* Boston: Houghton Mifflin, 1967.

MacKinnon, D. W. "Selecting Students with Creative Potential." In P. Heist (Ed.), *The Creative College Student: An Unmet Challenge.* San Francisco: Jossey-Bass, 1968.

MacKinnon, D. W. "Creativity: A Multi-faceted Phenomenon." In J. D. Roslansky (Ed.), *Creativity.* London: North-Holland, 1970.

Maddi, S. R. "Motivational Aspects of Creativity." *Journal of Personality,* 1965, *33,* 330–347.

Majasan, J. K. "College Students' Achievement as a Function of the Congruence Between Their Beliefs and Their Instructor's Beliefs." Unpublished doctoral dissertation. Stanford University, 1972.

Marcus, E. S. "The Relationship of Psychological Differentiation to the Congruence of Temporal Patterns of Speech." Unpublished doctoral dissertation. New York University, 1970.

Marjoribanks, K. "Ethnicity and Learning Patterns: A Replication and an Explanation." *Sociology,* 1972, *6,* 417–431.

Marston, A. R. "It Is Time to Reconsider the Graduate Record Examination." *American Psychologist,* 1971, *26,* 653–655.

Maxey, E. J., and Ormsby, V. J. "The Accuracy of Self-Report Information Collected on the ACT Test Battery: High School Grades and Items of Nonacademic Achievement." ACT Research Report, No. 45. Iowa City, Iowa: American College Testing Program, 1971.

Mayhew, L. B. *Graduate and Professional Education, 1980: A Survey of Institutional Plans.* New York: McGraw-Hill, 1970.

Mayhew, L. B. "Higher Education, Work, and the Professions: An Introduction." *Journal of Higher Education,* 1972, *43,* 169–178.

McClelland, D. C. "Issues in the Identification of Talent." In D. C. McClelland, A. L. Baldwin, U. Bronfenbrenner, and F. L. Strodtbeck (Eds.), *Talent and Society: New Perspectives in the Identification of Talent.* New York: D. Van Nostrand, 1958.

McKeachie, W. J. "Motivation, Teaching Methods, and College Teaching." In M. R. Jones (Ed.), *Nebraska Symposium on Motivation.* Lincoln: University of Nebraska Press, 1961.

McNemar, Q. "Lost: Our Intelligence? Why?" *American Psychologist,* 1964, *19,* 871–882.

Mead, M. "Research on Primitive Children." In L. Carmichael (Ed.), *Manual of Child Psychology.* New York: Wiley, 1946.

Mebane, D., and Johnson, D. L. "A Comparison of the Performance of Mexican Boys and Girls on Witkin's Cognitive Tasks." *Interamerican Journal of Psychology,* 1970, *4,* 3–4.

Mednick, M. T. "Research Creativity in Psychology Graduate Students." *Journal of Consulting Psychology,* 1963, *27,* 265–266.

Menges, R. J. *Academic Ability, Nonacademic Accomplishments and Ideational Productivity in High Risk and Regularly Admitted College Students.* Final Report, Project O-E-121, Grant No. OEG-5-70-0040 (509). Washington, D.C.: Office of Education, U.S. Department of Health, Education and Welfare, 1972.

Merrill, M. D., and Boutwell, R. C. "Instructional Development: Methodology and Research." In F. N. Kerlinger (Ed.), *Review of Research in Education I.* Itasca, Ill.: Peacock, 1973.

Messick, S. "The Criterion Problem in the Evaluation of Instruction: Assessing Possible, Not Just Intended, Outcomes." In M. C. Wittrock and D. W. Wiley (Eds.), *The*

Evaluation of Instruction: Issues and Problems. New York: Holt, Rinehart and Winston, 1970.

Messick, S. "Beyond Structure: In Search of Functional Models of Psychological Process." *Psychometrika,* 1972, *37,* 357–375.

Messick, S. "Multivariate Models of Cognition and Personality: The Need for Both Process and Structure in Psychological Theory and Measurement." In J. R. Royce (Ed.), *Multivariate Analysis and Psychological Theory.* New York: Academic Press, 1973.

Messick, S., and Damarin, F. "Cognitive Styles and Memory for Faces." *Journal of Abnormal and Social Psychology,* 1964, *69,* 313–318.

Messick, S., and Fritzky, F. J. "Dimensions of Analytic Attitude in Cognition and Personality." *Journal of Personality,* 1963, *31,* 346–370.

Messick, S., and Kogan, N. "Differentiation and Compartmentalization in Object-Sorting Measures of Categorizing Style." *Perceptual and Motor Skills,* 1963, *16,* 47–51.

Messick, S., and Kogan, N. "Category Width and Quantitative Aptitude." *Perceptual and Motor Skills,* 1965, *20,* 493–497.

Messick, S., and Kogan, N. "Personality Consistencies in Judgment: Dimensions of Role Constructs." *Multivariate Behavioral Research,* 1966, *1,* 165–175.

Miller, A. "Investigation of Some Hypothetical Relationships of Rigidity and Strength and Speed of Perceptual Closure." Unpublished doctoral dissertation. University of California, 1953.

Miller, C. and Parlett, M. R. *Up to the Mark.* London: Society for Research in Higher Education, 1974.

Milton, G. A. *Five Studies of the Relationship Between Sex-Role Identification and Achievement in Problem-Solving.* Technical Report 3, Contract Norm 609 (20). New Haven, Conn.: Department of Industrial Administration and Department of Psychology, Yale University, 1958.

Mischel, W. *Personality and Assessment.* New York: Wiley, 1968.

Mischel, W. "Sex-Typing and Socialization." In P. H. Mussen (Ed.), *Carmichael's Manual of Child Psychology.* Vol. 2. New York: Wiley, 1970.

Mischel, W. "Direct Versus Indirect Personality Assessment: Evidence and Implications." *Journal of Consulting and Clinical Psychology,* 1972, *38,* 319–324.

Mitchell, J. V. "Education's Challenge to Psychology: Person × Environment Interactions." *Review of Educational Research,* 1969, *39,* 695–721.

Morrison, J. "The Comparative Effectiveness of Intellective and Nonintellective Measures in the Prediction of the Completion of a Major in Theater Arts." *Educational and Psychological Measurement,* 1963, *23,* 827–830.

Mos, L., Wardell, D., and Royce, J. R. "A Factor Analysis of Some Measures of Cognitive Style." *Multivariate Behavioral Research,* 1974, *9,* 47–57.

Myers, E. D. *Education in the Perspective of History.* New York: Harper & Row, 1960.

Nagle, R. M. *Personality Differences Between Graduate Students in Clinical and Experimental Psychology at Varying Experience Levels.* Doctoral dissertation, Michigan State University, 1967. Ann Arbor, Mich.: University Microfilms, 1968, No. 68-11, 081.

Nardine, F. E. "The Development of Competence." In G. S. Lesser (Ed.), *Psychology and Educational Practice.* Glenview, Ill.: Scott, Foresman, 1971.

National Science Board, U. S. National Science Foundation. *Graduate Education: Parameters for Public Policy.* Washington, D. C.: U. S. Government Printing Office, 1969.

Neumann, E. *The Origins and History of Consciousness.* New York: Bollingen Foundation, 1954.

Nevill, D. D. *Expected Manipulation of Dependency Motivation and Its Effect on Eye Contact and Measures of Field Dependency.* Doctoral dissertation, University of Florida, 1971. Ann Arbor, Mich.: University Microfilms, 1971, No. 72-16, 639.

Newman, F. (Task Force Chm.) *Report on Higher Education.* Washington, D. C.: U.S. Office of Education, 1971.

Nicholls, J. G. "Creativity in the Person Who Will Never Produce Anything Original and Useful: The Concept of Creativity as a Normally Distributed Trait." *American Psychologist,* 1972, *27,* 717–727.

Nichols, R. C. "Non-intellective Predictors of Achievement in College." *Educational and Psychological Measurement,* 1966, *26,* 899–915.

Nichols, R. C., and Holland, J. L. "The Selection of High Aptitude High School Graduates for Maximum Achievement in College." *Personnel and Guidance Journal,* 1964, *43,* 33–40.

Noble, B. *Application of Undergraduate Mathematics in Engineering.* New York: Macmillan, 1967.

Nowlis, V., Clark, K. E., and Rock, M. *The Graduate Student as Teacher.* Washington, D. C.: American Council on Education, 1968.

Nussbaum, H. *Systems and Nonsystems Engineers: An Exploratory Study of Discriminating Characteristics.* Doctoral Dissertation, Wayne State University, 1963. Ann Arbor, Mich.: University Microfilms, 1965, No. 65-1842.

Nyquist, E. B., and Hawes, G. R. *Open Education: A Sourcebook for Parents and Teachers.* New York: Bantam Books, 1972.

Ohnmacht, F. W. *Relationships Among Field Independence, Dogmatism, Teacher Characteristics and Teaching Behavior of Preservice Teachers.* Paper presented at the annual meeting of the American Educational Research Association. New York, February 1967a.

Ohnmacht, F. W. "Teacher Characteristics and Their Relationship to Some Cognitive Styles." *Journal of Educational Research,* 1967b, *60,* 201–204.

Ohnmacht, F. W. "Factorial Invariance of the Teacher Characteristics Schedule and Measures of Two Cognitive Styles." *Journal of Psychology,* 1968, *69,* 193–199.

Oltman, P. K. "A Portable Rod-and-Frame Apparatus." *Perceptual and Motor Skills,* 1968, *26,* 503–506.

Oltman, P. K., Goodenough, D. R., Witkin, H.A., Freedman, N., and Friedman, F. "Psychological Differentiation as a Factor in Conflict Resolution." *Journal of Personality and Social Psychology,* 1975, *32,* 730–736.

O'Neill, J. *Productivity Trends in Higher Education.* Conference on Education as an Industry. Chicago: National Bureau of Economic Research, 1971.

Osipow, S. H. "Cognitive Styles and Educational-Vocational Preferences and Selection." *Journal of Counseling Psychology*, 1969, *16*, 534–546.

Pace, C. R., and Stern, G. G. "An Approach to the Measurement of Physiological Characteristics of College Environments." *Journal of Educational Psychology*, 1958, *49*, 269–277.

Paclisanu, M. I. *Interacting Effects of Stimulus Deprivation, Field Dependence and Two Types of Reinforcement upon Problem-Solving in Elementary School Children*. Doctoral dissertation, Temple University, 1969. Ann Arbor, Mich.: University Microfilms, 1970, No. 70-19, 763.

Parlett, M. R. "Evaluating Innovations in Teaching." In H. J. Butcher and E. Rudd (Eds.), *Contemporary Problems in Higher Education*. New York: McGraw-Hill, 1972.

Parlett, M. R., and Hamilton, D. "Evaluation as Illumination." Occasional paper, Centre for Research in the Educational Sciences. University of Edinburgh, 1972.

Parloff, M. B., Datta, L., Kleman, M., and Handlon, J. H. "Personality Characteristics Which Differentiate Creative Male Adolescents and Adults." *Journal of Personality*, 1968, *36*, 528–552.

Parsons, T., and Platt, G. M. "Higher Education and Changing Socialization." In M. W. Riley, M. Johnson, and A. Foner (Eds.), *Aging and Society, Vol. 3: A Sociology of Age Stratification*. New York: Russell Sage Foundation, 1972.

Pelz, D. C. "Creative Tensions in the Research and Development Climate." *Science*, 1967, *157*, 160–165.

Pelz, D. C. Memorandum to a dean of graduate studies, on climate for research. June 1, 1970a.

Pelz, D. C. "What It Takes to Make a Problem Solver Productive." *Innovation*, Jan. 1970b, *9*, 2–13.

Pelz, D. C., and Andrews, F. M. "Autonomy, Coordination, and Stimulation in Relation to Scientific Achievement." *Behavioral Science*, 1966a, *11*(2), 89–97.

Pelz, D. C., and Andrews, F. M. *Scientists in Organizations: Productive Climates for Research and Development*. New York: Wiley, 1966b.

Perney, L. R. *The Relationship of Field Dependence-Field Independence with Academic Achievement.* Doctoral dissertation, Case Western Reserve University, 1971. Ann Arbor, Mich.: University Microfilms, 1971, No. 71-22, 834.

Pervin, L. A. "A Twenty-College Study of Student × College Interaction Using TAPE (Transactional Analysis of Personality and Environment): Rationale, Reliability, and Validity." *Journal of Educational Psychology,* 1967, *58,* 290–302.

Pervin, L. A. "Performance and Satisfaction as a Function of Individual Environment Fit." *Psychological Bulletin,* 1968, *69,* 56–68.

Pettigrew, T. F. "The Measurement and Correlates of Category Width as a Cognitive Variable." *Journal of Personality,* 1958, *26,* 532–544.

Pierson, J. S. *Cognitive Styles and Measured Vocational Interests of College Men.* Doctoral dissertation, University of Texas, 1965. Ann Arbor, Mich.: University Microfilms, 1965, No. 65-8082.

Podell, J. E., and Phillips, L. "A Developmental Analysis of Cognition as Observed in Dimensions of Rorschach and Objective Test Performance." *Journal of Personality,* 1959, *27,* 439–463.

Pollack, I. W., and Kiev, A. "Spatial Orientation and Psychotherapy: An Experimental Study of Perception." *Journal of Nervous and Mental Disease,* 1963, *137,* 93–97.

Pounds, R. L. *The Development of Education in Western Culture.* New York: Appleton-Century-Crofts, 1968.

Price, D. J. deS., and Beaver, D. "Collaboration in an Invisible College." *American Psychologist,* 1966, *21,* 1011–1018.

Price-Williams, D. R. "A Study Concerning Concepts of Conservation of Quantities Among Primitive Children." *Acta Psychologica,* 1961, *18,* 297–305.

Price-Williams, D. R. (Ed.) *Cross-cultural Studies.* Harmondsworth, Middlesex, England: Penguin, 1969.

Proshansky, H. M. "For What Are We Training Our Graduate Students?" *American Psychologist,* 1972, *27,* 205–212.

Quinlan, D. M., and Blatt, S. J. "Field Articulation and Performance under Stress: Differential Prediction in Surgical and Psychiatric Nursing Training." *Journal of Consulting and Clinical Psychology*, 1973, *39*, 517.

Radcliffe Committee on Graduate Education for Women. *Graduate Education for Women.* Cambridge, Mass.: Harvard University Press, 1956.

Ramirez, M., and Castaneda, A. *Cultural Democracy, Bicognitive Development, and Education.* New York: Academic Press, 1974.

Randolph, L. C. *A Study of the Effects of Praise, Criticism and Failure on the Problem Solving Performance of Field-Dependent and Field-Independent Individuals.* Doctoral dissertation, New York University, 1971. Ann Arbor, Mich.: University Microfilms, 1971, No. 71-28, 555.

Razin, A. M. "A-B Variable in Psychotherapy: A Critical Review." *Psychological Bulletin*, 1971, *75*, 1–21.

Rennels, M. R. "The Effects of Instructional Methodology in Art Education upon Achievement on Spatial Tasks by Disadvantaged Negro Youths." *Journal of Negro Education*, 1970, *39*, 116–123.

Rest, J. "Developmental Psychology as a Guide to Value Education: A Review of Kohlbergian Programs." *Review of Educational Research*, 1974, *44*, 241–259.

Rest, J., Turiel, E., and Kohlberg, L. "Level of Moral Development as a Determinant of Preference and Comprehension of Moral Judgments Made by Others." *Journal of Personality*, 1969, *37*, 225–252.

Richards, J. M., Jr., Holland, J. L., and Lutz, S. W. "The Assessment of Student Accomplishment in College." ACT Research Report, No. 11. Iowa City, Iowa: American College Testing Program, 1966.

Richards, J. M., Holland, J. L., and Lutz, S. W. "Prediction of Student Accomplishment in College." *Journal of Educational Psychology*, 1967, *58*, 343–355.

Rivers, W. H. R. "Introduction and Vision." In A. C. Haddon (Ed.), *Reports of the Cambridge Anthropological Expedition to the Torres Straits.* Cambridge, England: Cambridge University Press, 1901.

Rivers, W. H. R. "Observations on the Senses of the Todas." *British Journal of Psychology,* 1905, *1,* 321–396.

Robbins, H. "Field Articulation: Its Relationship to Reading Disability and Social Class." Unpublished doctoral dissertation. New York University, 1962.

Roe, A. "A Study of Imagery in Research Scientists." *Journal of Personality,* 1951, *19,* 459–470.

Roe, A. *The Making of a Scientist.* New York: Dodd, Mead, 1953a.

Roe, A. "A Psychological Study of Eminent Psychologists and Anthropologists, and a Comparison with Biological and Physical Scientists." *Psychological Monographs,* 1953b, *67,* (Whole No. 2).

Rokeach, M. *The Open and Closed Mind.* New York: Basic Books, 1960.

Rosenfeld, I. J. "Mathematical Ability as a Function of Perceptual Field-Dependence and Certain Personality Variables." Unpublished doctoral dissertation. University of Oklahoma, 1958.

Rosenthal, R. *Experimenter Effects in Behavioral Research.* New York: Appleton-Century-Crofts, 1966.

Rosett, H. L., Nackerson, B. L., Robbins, H., and Sapirstein, M. R. "Personality and Cognitive Characteristics of Engineering Students: Implications for the Occupational Psychiatrist." *American Journal of Psychiatry,* 1966, *122,* 1147–1152.

Rossi, A. "Barriers to the Career Choice of Engineering, Medicine or Science Among American Women." In J. A. Mattfeld and C. G. Van Aken (Eds.), *Women and the Scientific Professions.* Cambridge, Mass.: MIT Press, 1965.

Rossi, N., and Cole, T. (Trans.) *Letters to a Teacher by the Schoolboys of Barbiana.* New York: Random House, 1970.

Rossmann, J. E., and Kirk, B. "Factors Relating to Persistence and Withdrawal in University Students." *Journal of Counseling Psychology,* 1970, *17,* 56–62.

Rothkopf, E. Z. "Two Scientific Approaches to the Management of Instruction." In R. M. Gagne and W. J. Gephart (Eds.), *Learning Research and School Subjects.* Itasca, Ill.: F. E. Peacock, 1968.

Rothkopf, E. Z. "The Concept of Mathemagenic Activities." *Review of Educational Research,* 1970, *40,* 325–336.

Royce, J. R. "The Conceptual Framework for a Multi-factor Theory of Individuality." In J. R. Royce (Ed.), *Multivariate Analysis and Psychological Theory.* New York: Academic Press, 1973.

Ruble, D. N., and Nakamura, C. Y. "Task Orientation Versus Social Orientation in Young Children and Their Attention to Relevant Social Cues." *Child Development,* 1972, *43,* 471–480.

Salomon, G. "Interaction of Communication-Medium and Two Procedures of Training for Subjective Response Uncertainty of Teachers." Unpublished doctoral dissertation. Stanford University, 1968.

Salomon, G. "Heuristic Models for the Generation of Aptitude-Treatment Interaction Hypotheses." *Review of Educational Research,* 1972, *42,* 327–343.

Sanford, N. *Graduate Education and the Androgynous Society.* Paper presented at the Radcliffe Symposium on Women. Cambridge, Mass., May 1972.

Santostefano, S. G. "A Developmental Study of the Cognitive Control Leveling-Sharpening." *Merrill-Palmer Quarterly,* 1964, *10,* 343–360.

Santostefano, S. G., and Paley, E. "Development of Cognitive Controls in Children." *Child Development,* 1964, *35,* 939–949.

Sapir, E. *Language: An Introduction to the Study of Speech.* New York: Harcourt Brace Jovanovich, 1921.

Schachtel, E. *Metamorphosis.* New York: Basic Books, 1959.

Schlesinger, H. J. "Cognitive Attitudes in Relation to Susceptibility to Interference." *Journal of Personality,* 1954, *22,* 354–374.

Schroder, H. M., Driver, M. J, and Streufert, S. *Human Information Processing.* New York: Holt, Rinehart and Winston, 1967.

Schudson, M. S. "Organizing the 'Meritocracy': A History of the College Entrance Examination Board." *Harvard Educational Review,* 1972, *42,* 34–69.

Scott, W. A. "Cognitive Complexity and Cognitive Flexibility." *Sociometry,* 1962, *25,* 405–414.

Scott, W. A. "Conceptualizing and Measuring Structural Properties of Cognition." In O. J. Harvey (Ed.), *Motivation and Social Interaction.* New York: Ronald Press, 1963.

Scott, W. A. "Varieties of Cognitive Integration." *Journal of Personality and Social Psychology,* 1974, *42,* 563–578.

Sears, R. R. "Graduate Education and the Creative Process." In A. B. Friedman (Ed.), *Creativity in Graduate Education.* Claremont, Calif.: Claremont Graduate School and University Center, 1964.

Seder, J. A. "The Origin of Difference in Extent of Independence in Children: Developmental Factors in Perceptual Field Dependence. Unpublished B.A. thesis, Radcliffe College, 1957.

Segall, M. H., Campbell, D. T., and Herskovits, M. J. *The Influence of Culture on Visual Perception.* Indianapolis, Ind.: Bobbs-Merrill, 1966.

Seibert, W. F., and Snow, R. E. *Studies in Cine-Psychometry I: Preliminary Factor Analysis of Visual Cognition and Memory.* Final Report, U. S. Office of Education, Grant No. 7-24-0280-257. Lafayette, Ind.: Purdue University Audio Visual Center, 1965.

Seibert, W. F., Reid, J. C., and Snow, R. E. *Studies in Cine-Psychometry II: Continued Factoring of Audio and Visual Cognition and Memory.* Final Report, U. S. Office of Education, Grant No. 7-24-0280-247. Lafayette, Ind.: Purdue University Audio Visual Center, 1967.

Severson, R. A. *Some Nonreading Correlates of Reading Retardation.* Doctoral dissertation, State University of Iowa, 1962. Ann Arbor, Mich.: University Microfilms, 1963, No. 63-966.

Shapiro, D. *Neurotic Styles.* New York: Basic Books, 1965.

Shapson, S. M. "Influence of Field Independence-Field Dependence and Sex on the Effectiveness of Verbal Reinforcement Combinations." Unpublished M.A. thesis, York University, Toronto, Canada, 1969.

Sheldrake, P., and Berry, S. *Looking at Innovation.* Slough, Berks, England: National Foundation for Educational Research, 1975.

Sherman, J. A. "Problem of Sex Differences in Space Perception and Aspects of Intellectual Functioning." *Psychological Review,* 1967, *74,* 290–299.

Shouksmith, G. *Intelligence, Creativity and Cognitive Style.* New York: Wiley-Interscience, 1970.

Shows, W. D. "Psychological Differentiation and the A-B Dimension: A Dyadic Interaction Hypothesis." Unpublished doctoral dissertation. Duke University, 1967.

Sieben, G. A. *Cognitive Style and Children's Performance on Measures of Elementary Science Competencies.* Unpublished M.A. thesis. University of British Columbia, 1971.

Sieber, J. E. "A Paradigm of Experimental Modification of the Effects of Test Anxiety on Cognitive Processes." *American Educational Research Journal,* 1969, *6,* 46–62.

Signell, K. A. "Cognitive Complexity in Person Perception and Nation Perception: A Developmental Approach." *Journal of Personality,* 1966, *34,* 517–537.

Silverman, J. "Scanning-Control Mechanism and Cognitive Filtering in Paranoid and Nonparanoid Schizophrenia." *Journal of Consulting Psychology,* 1964, *28,* 385–393.

Silverman, J. "Attentional Styles and the Study of Sex Differences." In D. I. Mostofsky (Ed.), *Attention: Contemporary Theory and Analysis.* New York: Appleton-Century-Crofts, 1970.

Simon, R. J., Clark, S. M., and Galway, K. "The Woman Ph.D." *Social Problems,* 1967, *15,* 221–236.

Sloane, H. N., Gorlow, L., and Jackson, D. N. "Cognitive Styles in Equivalence Range." *Perceptual and Motor Skills,* 1963, *16,* 389–404.

Slovic, P. "Convergent Validation of Risk-Taking Measures." *Journal of Abnormal and Social Psychology,* 1962, *65,* 68–71.

Smith, I. M. *Spatial Ability.* San Diego, Calif.: Knapp, 1964.

Snow, R. E. "Aptitude-Instructional Treatment Interactions: Selected Findings and Hypotheses." Paper presented at the annual meeting of the American Educational Research Association. Los Angeles, 1968.

Snow, R. E. "Research on Media and Aptitudes." *Bulletin of the Indiana University of Education,* 1970, *46,* 63–91.

Solzhenitsyn, A. I. "Schlesinger and Kissinger." *New York Times,* December 1, 1975.

Sperry, L. "Counsellors and Learning Styles." *Personnel and Guidance Journal,* 1973, *51,* 478–483.

Spitler, G. *An Investigation of Various Cognitive Styles and the Implications for Mathematics Education.* Doctoral dissertation, Wayne State University, 1970. Ann Arbor, Mich.: University Microfilms, 1971, No. 71-17, 317.

Stafford, R. E. "Sex Differences in Spatial Visualization as Evidence of Sex-Linked Inheritance." *Perceptual and Motor Skills,* 1961, *13,* 428.

Stark, R., Parker, A., and Iverson, M. "Field Dependency and Response to Ego Orientation." Paper presented at the annual meeting of the Eastern Psychological Association. Atlantic City, N.J., April 1959.

Stein, F. *Consistency of Cognitive, Interest, and Personality Variables with Academic Mastery: A Study of Field-Dependence-Independence, Verbal Comprehension, Self-Perception, and Vocational Interest in Relation to Academic Performance Among Male Juniors Attending an Urban University.* Doctoral dissertation, New York University, 1967. Ann Arbor, Mich.: University Microfilms, 1968, No. 68-11, 809.

Stephenson, R. W., and Treadwell, Y. "Personality Variables Related to the Effectiveness of a Creativity Training Program." *The Journal of Experimental Education,* 1966, *35,* 64–75.

Stodolsky, S. S., and Lesser, G. S. "Learning Patterns in the Disadvantaged." *Harvard Educational Review,* 1967, *37,* 546–593.

Strothmann, F. W. *The Graduate School Today and Tomorrow: Reflections for the Profession's Consideration.* New York: Fund for the Advancement of Education, 1955.

Stuart, I. R. "Perceptual Style and Reading Ability: Implications for an Instructional Approach." *Perceptual and Motor Skills,* 1967, *24,* 135–138.

Taylor, C. W. (Ed.) *The 1957 University of Utah Research Conference on the Identification of Creative Scientific Talent.* Salt Lake City: University of Utah Press, 1958.

Taylor, C. W. (Ed.) *The 1959 University of Utah Research Conference on the Identification of Creative Scientific Talent.* Salt Lake City: University of Utah Press, 1959.

Taylor, C. W. (Ed.) *Creativity: Progress and Potential.* New York: McGraw-Hill, 1964.

Taylor, D. W. "Variables Related to Creativity and Productivity Among Men in Two Research Laboratories." In C. W. Taylor (Ed.), *The 1957 University of Utah Research Conference on the Identification of Creative Scientific Talent.* Salt Lake City: University of Utah Press, 1958.

Taylor, D. W., Garner, W. R, and Hunt, H. F. "Education for Research in Psychology." *American Psychologist,* 1959, *14,* 167–179.

Taylor, S. P., and Epstein, S. "Aggression as a Function of the Interaction of the Aggressor and the Sex of the Victim." *Journal of Personality,* 1967, *35,* 474–486.

Thelen, H. A. *Classroom Grouping for Teachability.* New York: Wiley, 1967.

Thomas, S. A. W. *The Role of Cognitive Style Variables in Mediating the Influence of Aggressive Television upon Elementary School Children.* Doctoral dissertation, University of California, 1971. Ann Arbor, Mich.: University Microfilms, 1972, No. 72-16, 351.

Thurstone, L. L. "Primary Mental Abilities." *Psychometric Monographs,* 1938, No. 1.

Toomey, T. C. "Alteration of a Perceptual Mode Correlate Through a Televised Model." *Journal of Experimental Research in Personality,* 1972, *6,* 52–59.

Torrance, E. P. "Factors Affecting Creative Thinking in Children: An Interim Research Report." *Merrill-Palmer Quarterly,* 1961, *7,* 171–180.

Tripodi, T., and Bieri, J. "Information Transmission in Clinical Judgments as a Function of Stimulus Dimensionality and Cognitive Complexity." *Journal of Personality,* 1964, *32,* 119–137.

Tripodi, T., and Bieri, J. "Cognitive Complexity, Perceived Conflict, and Certainty." *Journal of Personality,* 1966, *34,* 144–153.

Trow, M. *Preliminary Findings from National Surveys of Higher Education.* Berkeley, Calif.: Carnegie Commission on Higher Education, 1971.

Tucker, L. R. "Some Mathematical Notes on Three-Mode Factor Analysis." *Psychometrika,* 1966, *31,* 279–311.

Turiel, E. "An Experimental Test of the Sequentiality of Developmental Stages in the Child's Moral Judgment." *Journal of Personality and Social Psychology,* 1966, *3,* 611–618.

Tyler, L. E. *The Psychology of Human Differences.* New York: Appleton-Century-Crofts, 1965.

Tyler, L. E. "Human Abilities." *Annual Review of Psychology,* 1972, *23,* 177–206.

Tyler, L. E., and Sundberg, N. D. "Factors Affecting Career Choices of Adolescents." Cooperative Research Project No. 2455, Cooperative Research Program, United States Office of Education. Eugene, Ore. University of Oregon, 1964.

Ulyatt, K., and Ulyatt, F. M. "Field and Training Performance of a Group of Women Doctors." *Medical Officer,* 1970, *124,* 33–34.

Ulyatt, K., and Ulyatt, F. M. "Some Attitudes of a Group of Women Doctors Related to Their Field Performance." *British Journal of Medical Education,* 1971, *5,* 242–245.

Vannoy, J. S. "Generality of Cognitive Complexity-Simplicity as a Personality Construct." *Journal of Personality and Social Psychology,* 1965, *2,* 385–396.

Vernon, P. E. "Psychological Studies of Creativity." *Journal of Child Psychology and Psychiatry,* 1967, *8,* 153–174.

Vernon, P. E. "The Distinctiveness of Field Independence." *Journal of Personality,* 1972, *40,* 366–391.

Vernon, P. E. "Multivariate Approaches to the Study of Cognitive Styles." In J. R. Royce (Ed.), *Multivariate Analysis and Psychological Theory.* New York: Academic Press, 1973.

Vonnegut, K. *Slaughterhouse-Five, or The Children's Crusade.* New York: Delta Publishing, 1969.

Wachtel, P. L. "Conceptions of Broad and Narrow Attention." *Psychological Bulletin,* 1967, *68,* 417–429.

Wachtel, P. L. "Style and Capacity in Analytic Functioning." *Journal of Personality,* 1968, *36,* 202–212.

Wade, E. B. *Field Independence, Authoritarianism, and Verbal Reinforcement in Anagram Solution.* Doctoral dissertation, Columbia University, 1971. Ann Arbor, Mich.: University Microfilms, 1972, No. 72-1397.

Wallach, M. A. "Active-Analytical vs. Passive-Global Cognitive Functioning." In S. Messick and J. Ross (Eds.), *Measurement in Personality and Cognition.* New York: Wiley, 1962.

Wallach, M. A. "Creativity." In P. H. Mussen (Ed.), *Carmichael's Manual of Child Psychology.* Vol. 1. New York: Wiley, 1970.

Wallach, M. A. *The Intelligence/Creativity Distinction.* New York and Morristown, N. J.: General Learning Press, 1971a.

Wallach, M. A. "Intelligence Tests, Academic Achievement and Creativity." *Impact of Science on Society,* 1971b, *21,* 333–345b.

Wallach, M. A., and Caron, A. J. "Attribute Criteriality and Sex-Linked Conservatism as Determinants of Psychological Similarity." *Journal of Abnormal and Social Psychology,* 1959, *59,* 43–50.

Wallach, M. A., and Kogan, N. *Modes of Thinking in Young Children.* New York: Holt, Rinehart and Winston, 1965.

Wallach, M. A., Kogan, N., and Burt, R. B. "Group Risk Taking and Field Dependence-Independence of Group Members." *Sociometry,* 1967, *30,* 323–338.

Wallach, M. A., and Wing, C. W., Jr. *The Talented Student: A Validation of the Creativity-Intelligence Distinction.* New York: Holt, Rinehart and Winston, 1969.

Wallach, M. A., and Leggett, M. I. "Testing the Hypothesis that a Person Will Be Consistent: Stylistic Consistency Versus Situational Specificity in Size of Children's Drawings." *Journal of Personality,* 1972, *40,* 309–330.

Wapner, S., Kaplan, B., and Cohen, S. "An Organismic-Developmental Perspective for Understanding Transactions of Men in Environments." *Environment and Behavior,* 1973, *5,* 255–289.

Weisstein, N. "Psychology Constructs the Female." In V. Gornick, and B. K. Moran (Eds.), *Women in Sexist Society.* New York: Basic Books, 1971.

Weitzman, R. A. "It Is Time to Reconsider the GRE: A Reply to Marston." *American Psychologist,* 1972, *27,* 236–238.

Werner, H. "Process and Achievement." *Harvard Educational Review,* 1937, *7,* 353–368.

Werner, H. *Comparative Psychology of Mental Development.* Chicago: Follett, 1948.

Werts, C. E. "The Many Faces of Intelligence." *Journal of Educational Psychology,* 1967, *58,* 198–204.

White, B. O., and Kernaleguen, A. P. "Comparison of Selected Perceptual and Personality Variables Among College Women Deviant and Nondeviant in Their Appearance." *Perceptual and Motor Skills,* 1971, *32,* 87–92.

Whorf, B. L. *Language, Thought and Reality: Selected Writings of Benjamin Whorf."* Edited by J. B. Carroll. New York: Wiley, 1956.

Wickes, F. *The Inner World of Choice.* New York: Harper & Row, 1963.

Wing, C. W., Jr., and Wallach, M. A. *College Admissions and the Psychology of Talent.* New York: Holt, Rinehart and Winston, 1971.

Wisdom, J. *The Unconscious Origin of Berkeley's Philosophy.* London: Hogarth, 1953.

Witkin, H. A. "Perception of the Upright When the Direction of the Force Acting on the Body Is Changed." *Journal of Experimental Psychology,* 1950, *40,* 93–106.

Witkin, H. A. "Further Studies of Perception of the Upright When the Force Acting on the Body Is Changed." *Journal of Experimental Psychology*, 1952, *43*, 9–20.

Witkin, H. A. "Psychological Differentiation and Forms of Pathology." *Journal of Abnormal Psychology*, 1965, *70*, 317–336.

Witkin, H. A. "A Cognitive-Style Approach to Cross-Cultural Research." *International Journal of Psychology*, 1967, *2*, 233–250.

Witkin, H. A. "Social Influences in the Development of Cognitive Style." In D. Goslin (Ed.), *Handbook of Socialization Theory and Research*. Chicago: Rand McNally, 1969a.

Witkin, H. A. "Some Implications of Research on Cognitive Style for Problems of Education." In M. Gottsegen and G. Gottsegen (Eds.), *Professional School Psychology*. Vol. III. New York: Grune & Stratton, 1969b.

Witkin, H. A. "A Cognitive-Style Perspective on Evaluation and Guidance." *Proceedings of the 1973 Invitational Conference on Testing Problems—Measurement for Self-Understanding and Personal Development*. Princeton, N.J.: Educational Testing Service, 1974.

Witkin, H. A., Dyk, R. B., Faterson, H. F., Goodenough, D. R., and Karp, S. A. *Psychological Differentiation*. New York: Wiley, 1962.

Witkin, H. A., Faterson, H. F., Goodenough, D. R., and Birnbaum, J. "Cognitive Patterning in Mildly Retarded Boys." *Child Development*, 1966, *37*, 301–316.

Witkin, H. A., Goodenough, D. R., and Karp, S. A. "Stability of Cognitive Style from Childhood to Young Adulthood." *Journal of Personality and Social Psychology*, 1967, *7*, 291–300.

Witkin, H. A., Lewis, H. G., Hertzman, M., Machover, K., Meissner, P. B., and Wapner, S. *Personality Through Perception*. New York: Harper & Row, 1954.

Witkin, H. A., Lewis, H. B., and Weil, E. "Affective Reactions and Patient-Therapist Interactions Among More Differentiated and Less Differentiated Patients Early in Therapy." *Journal of Nervous and Mental Disease*, 1968, *146*, 193–208.

Witkin, H. A., Oltman, P. K., Cox, P. W., Erlichman, E., Hamm, R. M., and Ringler, R. W. *Field-Dependence-Independence and Psychological Differentiation: A Bibliography Through 1972 with Index*. ETS RB 73-62. Princeton, N. J.: Educational Testing Service, 1973.

Witkin, H. A., Price-Williams, D., Bertini, M., Christiansen, B., Oltman, P. K., Ramirez, M., and Van Meel, J. "Social Conformity and Psychological Differentiation." *International Journal of Psychology*, 1974, *9*, 11–29.

Woodworth, R. S. "Racial Differences in Mental Traits." *Science*, 1910, *31*, 171–186.

Wu, J. J. *Cognitive Style and Task Performance—A Study of Student Teachers*. Doctoral dissertation, University of Minnesota, 1967. Ann Arbor, Mich.: University Microfilms, 1968, No. 68-7408.

Wyer, R. S. "Assessment and Correlates of Cognitive Differentiation and Integration." *Journal of Personality*, 1964, *32*, 394–409.

Yamamoto, K. "Relationships Between Creative Thinking Abilities of Teachers and Achievement and Adjustment of Pupils." *Journal of Experimental Education*, 1963, *32*, 3–25.

Yando, R. M., and Kagan, J. "The Effect of Teacher Tempo on the Child." *Child Development*, 1968, *39*, 27–34.

Zimring, F. M. "Cognitive Simplicity-Complexity: Evidence for Discrete Processes." *Journal of Personality*, 1971, *39*, 1–9.

Zuckerman, H., and Cole, J. R. "Women in American Science." *Minerva*, 1975, *13*, 82–102.

Zytowski, D. G., Mills, D. H., and Paepe, C. "Psychological Differentiation and the Strong Vocational Interest Blank." *Journal of Counseling Psychology*, 1969, *16*, 41–44.

Index

YANDO, R., 19, 81
YONGE, G., 128

Z

ZIMRING, F., 18
ZUCKERMAN, H., 123
ZUCKERMAN, H.,, 123
ZYTOWSKI, D., 50